In Defence of Organization Theory

This book provides a concise, clear survey and defence of organization theory. That theory and its associated research have in recent years become subject to strong criticism.

Rival perspectives on organizations have been put forward. One of these stresses that organizations need to be understood as made up of individual people. Another asserts the need to see organizations as part of the conflicts and radical struggles in society. These alternative views have led to a host of critiques of conventional organization theory. It is attacked as being tautological, philosophically naive, ideological, managerially biased and flawed in methods.

To date there has been no substantial reply to these criticisms by a protagonist of organization theory. This volume uniquely fills that gap.

In part one the author examines and rebuts each of the major lines of criticism. In part two the rival approaches suggested by the critics are themselves subjected to an analysis of their limitations. The book concludes with a new model of organizational design which provides a synthesis of previous research.

Management and Industrial Relations Series

Editors:

DOROTHY WEDDERBURN
Principal of Bedford College, London

ANTHONY HOPWOOD and PAUL WILLMAN
London Business School

and

DOUGLAS BROOKS
Director, Walker Brooks and Partners

Social science research has much to contribute to the better understanding and solution of problems in the field of management and industrial relations. The difficulty, however, is that there is frequently a gap between the researcher and the practitioner who wants to use the research results. This new series is designed to make available to practitioners in the relevant fields the results of the best research which the Economic and Social Research Council (ESRC) has supported in the fields of management and industrial relations. The subjects covered and the style adopted will appeal to managers, trade unionists and administrators because there will be an emphasis upon the practical implications of research findings. But the volumes will also serve as a useful introduction to particular areas for students and teachers of management and industrial relations.

The series is published by Cambridge University Press in collaboration with the Economic and Social Research Council.

Other books in the series

In Defence of Organization Theory

A reply to the critics

LEX DONALDSON

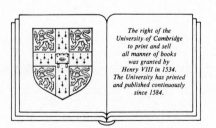

The right of the
University of Cambridge
to print and sell
all manner of books
was granted by
Henry VIII in 1534.
The University has printed
and published continuously
since 1584.

CAMBRIDGE UNIVERSITY PRESS

Cambridge
London   New York   New Rochelle
Melbourne   Sydney

Published by the Press Syndicate of the University of Cambridge
The Pitt Building, Trumpington Street, Cambridge CB2 1RP
32 East 57th Street, New York, NY 10022, USA
10 Stamford Road, Oakleigh, Melbourne 3166, Australia

First published 1985

Printed in Great Britain at the University Press, Cambridge

Library of Congress catalogue card number: 85–4220

British Library Cataloguing in Publication Data
Donaldson, Lex
In defence of organization theory: a reply
to the critics.
1. Organization
I. Title
302.3'5   HD31

ISBN 0 521 26869 9 hard covers
ISBN 0 521 31539 5 paperback

To June

Contents

Figures and tables

Figures

Tables

Preface

The study of organizations has expanded considerably as an academic specialty over the past three decades. This has been based upon a concern to understand the differing forms or structures which organizations have, and their effects on effectiveness, on the satisfaction of their members, and so on. Since the situation or circumstance, such as size and market position, seems to influence which structure will produce the best performance, students of organization have sought to identify these contingency factors. Modern organization studies has developed an interest in more precisely specifying the relationship between the three classes of variables: contingency, structure and performance. There is equally an interest in how to bring about change in organizations. Organization design and its implementation are twin related themes around which much enquiry is focused.

Theoretical starting points are provided by sociological theories, such as those of bureaucracy, which yield models of structure and hypotheses about their antecedents and their performance. By refining and testing such notions, a body of empirically based knowledge has gradually come into being. This is of value, in its own right, and also provides a useful input to sociologists involved in constructing explanations of societal structure, functioning and change, who can draw upon findings about organizations as sub-units of the whole.

The task of research is to build knowledge through the use of scientific method by more exactly specifying the relationship between contingencies, structure, performance and other variables. This involves empirical study and theoretical development. Thus, for more than twenty years now, organizational sociology has been in a kind of Kuhnian normal science phase. Research has gone on in incremental fashion within a relatively accepted contingency-systems paradigm. In many sections of the research community people have been getting on with the job.

In my own small way I have too. Working in a school of management, the contingency approach is the hub of much of my teaching, research and consulting. But having received a basic training in sociology I knew that things were not quite so simple. My early encounter with that discipline was in the mid-sixties, and I was introduced to professional sociology, a value-neutral science. As my reading and personal contacts widened, it became clear that this was a notion which was, and is, contested. With time, and especially with the eruptions of Vietnam, the Student Movement of 1968 and Watergate other conceptions have come increasingly to the fore. Sociology is now not infrequently introduced to students as an inherently critical, anti-establishment, social movement, and the idea of science is treated as a sham. Marxism, in all its variants, has become more emphasized. And the criticism of structural-functionalism and systems theory has become a familiar theme. If journal covers can be seminal, then this accolade must go to the July–August 1968 edition of the *New Left Review*, which carried a red banner emblazoned – 'Combat Bourgeois Ideas'. As Lenin taught, a task of the revolutionary cadre is to provide slogans. This one has resonated throughout much subsequent sociology. It was only a few years before this crusade was visited upon organizational sociology. Sociological discourse has come often to be preoccupied with the struggle between the world-views of structural-functionalism and conflict theory.

My first degree was from the University of Aston, in Birmingham, England. This afforded me the opportunity for close contact with several members of the Aston group, during their ground-breaking organizational research. To my knowledge, Aston is the only case of a style of macro-organizational research which has been identified by its University location. This is some testament to the collective spirit and relative modesty of the original team. Sitting at the feet of David Hickson, John Child, Jerry Hage, and Colin Fletcher, I had an opportunity to drink in their missionary zeal for an empirical, quantitative approach to organizational sociology. Later, as a researcher in the Organization Behaviour Research Group of the London Graduate School of Business Studies, I had the chance to work under Derek Pugh and alongside John Child, Roger Mansfield and Andrew Pettigrew. I extended the Aston approach into the study of trade unions and professional associations, with Malcolm Warner, and dealt with other Aston chestnuts such as size and technology. The Aston studies have now been worked on by many scholars, in widely differing types of organizations, and in many countries of the world.

Yet, even as the Aston and the related studies by Blau and Hage and their colleagues blossomed, there were growing signs of challenge, and of attempts to shake Organization Theory out of this approach, or any like it. The criticism that had been made of mainstream general sociology came to be deployed against organization studies. Initially these were mounted in terms of an espousal of methodological individualism, as applied to problems of reification; later the terms were more structuralist, and more Marxian. Those seeking to present their work done within con-

ventional organizational sociology were greeted with a steadily less sym-
pathetic reaction by their sociological peers. The cry in the seminar was
'. . . correlations prove nothing . . . ', '. . . you've got to talk about meaning . . . ', '. . . you've reified the organization . . . ', '. . . you've misunder-
stood Weber's ideal type analysis . . . ', '. . . this is too static, you are
ignoring change . . . ', '. . . surely you have to go outside the factory . . . ',
'. . . this is all ideology . . . '.

The consequences of this growing tide of criticism have been extra-
ordinary. Organizational Theory has come into disrepute in many
quarters. Though widely offered in courses, organizational sociology is
often treated in a superficial and scathing manner, which is light in understanding and heavy in critique. This process accelerated of late with the
publication of texts for students which introduce the subject to them by
means of exegesises which are highly theoretical and damning in many of
their judgements on the work of organizational scholars (Burrell and
Morgan, 1979; Clegg and Dunkerley, 1980). Thus a generation of students and teachers grow up with little knowledge of that literature, for
early in their development they are persuaded that the fundamental
assumptions of the subject are in error, and so deep study is hardly worth
the effort. At this point the negative judgements become self-sealing.
This is unfortunate in terms of the misrepresentation of the traditions and
achievements of this branch of learning. Where organization sociology is
being offered to students who have a need to know about organization for
their own work lives, the exposition-as-critique approach is a catastrophe, and a serious loss of educational value for them.

Given the importance of these issues, I have waited for some years for
signs of a reply. Yet this has been notable by its absence. If evidence were
required that organizational studies contains theoretical and empirical
work of both volume and breadth, then this has been amply furnished by
the many reviews of the literature (Hall, 1977; Hage and Azumi, 1972;
Etzioni, 1975; Child, 1977b; Khandwalla, 1977; Mintzberg, 1979; Kotter
et al., 1979; Hage, 1980). But the essence of the critical movement is that
such writings constitute little or no defence because they tend, if anything, to perpetuate the erroneous philosophical and theoretical assumptions, and the scientism which is being held up for ridicule in the critiques.
Accordingly, the criticism of fundamentals has gone largely unanswered
– and for too long.

While there is an increasing recognition of the multiple paradigm
nature of organizational and social studies, some of the discussants have
not fully appreciated the theoretical and philosophical nuances, and have
tried to interpret the whole debate as resolvable in empirical terms
(Hage, 1980; Ritzer, 1975). Perhaps the most graphic incident I observed
was in the Psychology Department at the University of Maryland. A visit-
ing Professor kept a whole room on the defensive while he tormented

them over their scientism. His arguments were mainly philosophical, and to every reply he had a ready riposte. Students of the brain were led into baited traps, which when sprung, impaled them on the nonidentity of 'the brain' and 'I' as predicates of sentences in ordinary language. To those versed in Winch (1958) and Ryle (1949), the ploys would have been instantly transparent. But the fifty-strong faculty and graduate students of that Psychology Department were operating in a dimension unfamiliar to them.

The present volume has arisen out of my conviction that the time has come to attempt to show that these sorts of criticism, as applied to Organization Theory, are largely wrong. I seek here to fill the lacuna in the literature by providing a rebuttal to the growing number of critical works. Hopefully, this may serve as rallying point for other students of organization and lead to a reassertion of our sub-discipline as purposeful, coherent and with its own criteria. A full volume has proved necessary in that, though the elements of criticism may be advanced segmentally, a true reply needs to be fairly comprehensive.

The concern herein is to consider many of the major, frequently used objections to conventional Organization Theory and the associated empirical studies. Accordingly, the volume tries to approach the issue of the coherency of the subject by an analysis at three levels; metatheory – the classes of theories such as structural-functionalism and conflict theory and their relationships to each other in the context of organizational studies; theory – the examination of specific organizational theories which are held to be inadequate in certain, delineated ways; and methodology – the research procedures used especially in comparative studies of organizational structure which are likewise subject to supposedly damaging critique.

I hope that this work will serve to caution the critics, who have thus far prosecuted their attack on organization studies unchecked. I trust that it will bring some comfort to colleagues in organizational sociology, though perhaps also give them pause on one or two aspects of their approach. I wish that those students and teachers caught in the cross-fire, who are at present uncertain of their stance in the debate, may at least reappraise the merits of organization studies.

Australian Graduate School of   LEX DONALDSON
Management in the University of   *May 1984*
New South Wales / Department of
Sociology University of Maryland
/ University of Aston Management
Centre

Acknowledgements

I should like to thank my many teachers. David Hickson gave me a patient and humanistic introduction to organizational sociology. Jerald Hage offered me the first glimpse of a theoretical mind in action, and he has also kindly provided me with continuing support in the form of a sabbatic leave spent in his department at the University of Maryland. John Child has ever been a conscientious teacher and an exemplar of scholarly thoroughness. He has recently hosted me on a study leave at the University of Aston where this volume was completed. Derek Pugh has provided the sense of a stable underlying scientific programme for the endeavours of many of us. Teresa Keil and David Podmore initiated me into sociology. Graham Chute and Michael Hall provided early familiarization with philosophical issues.

Philip Yetton and Mike Crawford have provided intellectual companionship in Australia. Jerry Hage and Frank Hull carried on much of this same role at Maryland. Bob Wood has performed this service both in America and Australia. My economic colleagues at the School have been a source of general stimulation and assistance: Chris Adam, Ric Dowell, Malcolm Fisher, Bob Marks and Peter Swan. The Australian Graduate School of Management in the University of New South Wales, by their generous grants of study leaves, enabled this volume to be completed. The successive Directors of the AGSM, Philip Brown and Jeremy Davis, receive particular thanks for that. The AGSM is blessed with an unusually helpful library service which has greatly eased the burden of an emigré sociologist; Pam Taylor deserves a special mention in this respect. Also an expression of gratitude is appropriate to June Ohlson.

I should like to thank those who were good enough to give their comments on earlier drafts of this book: Peter Blau, Stewart Clegg, John Child, Jerald Hage, David Hickson, Andrew Pettigrew, Derek Pugh, Malcolm Warner and Bob Wood. In the best traditions of classical management theory, the responsibility for the position taken in this volume rests solely with the author.

Throughout my labours of the past six years June Ohlson has been a constant, caring heart and to her this book is dedicated.

1

The attack on Organization Theory

With the growth of sociology since the end of World War Two, there has been attendant specialization, and a number of sub-disciplines have become established, such as urban sociology, educational sociology and, in particular, organizational sociology. The latter developed during the nineteen fifties and sixties, extending and elaborating its theoretical paradigm and refining its methods of study (Burns and Stalker, 1961; Etzioni, 1961; Blau and Scott, 1963; Woodward, 1965; Hage and Aiken, 1970; Hall, 1972). It seemed, during the middle sixties, to be becoming an established and accepted branch of sociology. However, within the last two decades, sociology has undergone strenuous self-examination, especially of the nature of fundamental sociological theories. In particular, structural-functional theories, such as those of Parsons (1951), were criticized as being static, postulating value consensus and being, in Mills' famous phrase, 'usable ideology' of a conservative kind. This position was contrasted with that of change-oriented conflict theories, such as those of Marx (Rex, 1961).

This line of attack has been extended into organizational sociology. Basic concepts such as goals, systems and structures, have been criticized in terms of their logical, philosophical and theoretical status. For instance, in a discussion of Etzioni's *Comparative Analysis of Complex Organisations* (1961), Burns (1967: 121) asserted that Etzioni's theory of the congruence between certain types of compliance system and certain types of involvement, is a tautology. This is the sort of attack developed by Silverman (1970) in his influential book, *The Theory of Organizations*, where central concepts of organizational sociology are argued to be erroneous philosophically, and deficient sociologically. The charge has been levelled that much of what purports to be scientific sociological analysis applied to organizations is, in fact, ideological. Critics of conventional organizational sociology have argued that a more 'sociologically adequate' mode of analysis can be found in other approaches, such as social action theory or radical structuralism. These are asserted to offer humanistic and change-orientated alternatives to organizational sociology.

The present work offers a defence of conventional organizational sociology. This is done by considering arguments such as those of Silverman (1968, 1970), Burrell and Morgan (1979), Whitley (1977), Davies (1979), Child (1972a, 1977b), Benson (1977), Turner (1977), Heydebrand (1977), Goldman and Van Houten (1977) and Clegg and Dunkerley (1980). Whereas the critics base their attack heavily on logical and philosophical argument, their own position is shown to contain inconsistencies and to be based, at times, on misunderstandings of philosophy. The theoretical positions of structural-functionalism and systems theory are argued to be neither illogical nor ideological, and to reflect concerns which are at the heart of the discipline of sociology. The social action approach is shown to be sociologically deficient, and to be inadequate as the basis of a humanitarian sociology. And radical structuralism is shown to be inimical to the study of organizations.

Over a decade has passed since the early critiques of those such as Silverman. One might have expected that such a blast against organizational sociology would have led to a rapid and energetic rebuttal. The more so in Britain, as this had seen the flourishing in the sixties of an organizational sociology in the work of Burns and Stalker (1961), Woodward and her associates (1965, 1970) and the Aston group (Pugh *et al.*, 1963, 1968, 1969a, 1969b). However, such an expectation was not fulfilled. Mouzelis (1969) and Fletcher (1969) replied to Silverman's 1968 journal article, but his reply was an even more thorough-going rejection of organizational sociology (1969). Etzioni, in the second edition of his *Comparative Analysis of Complex Organizations* (1975), defends his thesis against the charge of tautology, but his discussion of Silverman is brief and omits Silverman's central charges against the whole philosophical coherence of organizational sociology. More recently, Bradley and Wilkie (1980) have offered a critique of Radical Organization Theory as contained in the writings of Salaman (1978), Clegg and Dunkerley (1977) and Benson (1977). However, this is a short commentary which notes the lack of documentation for many of the accusations, the unfairness of several of the charges and the obscurity of much of the language used by the critics. Nevertheless, with the publication of the book by Silverman, *The Theory of Organizations* (1970 in Britain and 1971 in the United States), the ideas came into wide currency, and reached a large student audience as recommended reading by the Open University in Britain, and similarly, in numerous universities in several countries. Moreover, even in 1969, a leading member of the Aston group, Child, was citing the argument of Silverman approvingly, and wrote about the idea of supra-individual goals and processes as 'reification' and as 'quasi-metaphysical manoeuvres' (1969b: 27). Other prominent members of the Aston group have, in their review of that programme of studies (Pugh and Hickson, 1976), indicated his objections to work such as theirs, but have left the issue unresolved. The research group, formed around Joan Woodward at the Imperial College of Science and Technology in London, shifted their interest from technology, which was so central to Woodward's research (1965, 1970), in favour of an emphasis on power and ideology, watchwords of the new, critical sociology. Technology became for them, task analysis, which is concerned with decomposing the organizational work system into roles performed by individuals, and choices made by them (Abell and Mathews, 1973; Abell, 1975). This is a model quite consonant with the social action approach of Silverman. Hence, not only has there been no effective counter to the criticisms of organizational sociology, but the critique has, to a considerable extent, struck home, persuading not merely the wider sociological readership, but also some of those actively engaged in the study of organizations.

Others have commented upon the rising tide of criticism and its increasing effect. Writing in 1977 Whitley notes that: 'The number of publications criticizing "orthodox" approaches to the analysis of organizations has increased considerably in recent years' (1977: 54). And he further remarks that their content has shifted from being primarily concerned with technical problems, more to criticisms based on philosophical grounds. Davies, in 1979, in a review of the development of organization theory, has described its evolution from structural-functionalism and comparativism to the negotiated order view. Davies sees Silverman's critique as being particularly 'influential' (1979: 414). Indeed, Davies writes of medical sociologists in Britain coming to understand organization theory ' . . . almost exclusively via Silverman' (1979: 416). The year of 1979 saw also the publication of Burrell and Morgan's volume on *Sociological Paradigms and Organizational Analysis*. This work extends the critical discussion of organization studies methodologically, theoretically and philosophically, and introduces labels for the newer, rival approaches as radical humanism, radical structuralism and anti-organization theory. That same year saw a conference in Britain on critical and radical approaches to Organization Theory.

In the United States there has been a similar growth in criticisms of orthodox approaches to Organization Theory. The philosophical and indidivualist mode of attack has been deployed by Turner (1977) on Blau's (1972) theory of structural differentiation in organizations. A counter-orthodox approach to the study of organizations of a dialectical or explicitly Marxian kind has been offered by Benson (1977), Heydebrand (1977) and Goldman and Van Houten (1977). Many of these writings have been collected together in a Sage monograph on *Organiz-*

ational Analysis: Critique and Innovation edited by Benson *(1977). A* number of these critics (Burrell and Morgan, 1979; Clegg and Dunkerley, 1980) refer to the journal, the *Administrative Science Quarterly*, as a kind of bastion of orthodoxy. That journal has rightly become known for its rigorous, tough-minded and often quantitative research articles. Much of the mainstream research which the critics seek to correct has been published therein (e.g., Pugh *et al.*, 1978, 1969a, 1969b). Yet in recent years Karl Weick, known for his subjectivist, almost mystical writings on the *Social Psychology of Organizing* (1969), has been Editor. The *ASQ* has published more recently a review of its previous contents (from 1959 to 1979) by Daft (1980) which is critical of the quantitative tradition and is more approving of qualitative work. And now three of the key figures in the critical movement, Benson (1977), Morgan (1980) and Clegg (1981), have each published statements of their position in the *ASQ*. It would seem that the challenge to orthodoxy has breached the castle walls of positivism, and penetrated its keep.

In the everyday research literature of journal articles on organization, whether American, British or from Continental Europe, assertions that the contingency approach is deficient on fundamental grounds have become familiar (Budde *et al.*, 1982; Millar, 1978; Blackburn, 1982; Smith and Nichol, 1981). And the explicit critique of orthodox approaches to organizations is made by certain scholars writing from the European mainland (Schreyogg, 1980).

What was once a fringe counter-movement has become an incipient hegemony.

Yet there are many problems in the critiques essayed by Silverman and the like which need to be made plain. The implications of their new programmatics for organization sociology, whether social action or Marxian theories, present difficulties. The lack of effective counter-discussion, and the growing influence of this movement are undesirable, for the sub-discipline, for sociology and for society. In making this reply this volume seeks to halt this trend and to begin to reverse it.

It should be noted at the outset that the work is concerned only with the criticisms from outside of orthodox Organization Theory of its fundamentals (philosophical assumptions, theories, methods, ideological biases and so on). There are, of course, many other criticisms of organization studies in terms of certain parts of it. For instance, Starbuck (1981) has questioned the Aston studies in terms of their methods and contribution to knowledge about organization studies. Again, Schoonhoven (1981) has criticised contingency research for shortcomings in method and model specification. And the debate on the relationship between technology and structure continues (Eilon, 1977; Hickson *et al.*, 1978;

Blau *et al.*, 1976; Reimann, 1977; Reimann and Inzerilli, 1979; Gerwin, 1979; Reimann, 1980). This volume does not seek to address these more technical criticisms which seem to be from within the broad tradition of orthodox organizational analysis. Such a debate over details, specific theories and methods is part of the scientific approach to organizational sociology or organization studies. In the view of the present author, this discussion is healthy and is to be welcomed. Indeed the author has made a modest contribution to criticisms of this kind in his critique of the replicability of Woodward's findings on technology, organization structure and performance (Donaldson, 1976). The focus here is on those writings which purport to make damaging criticisms of the whole enterprise of organizational analysis as conventionally practised and which argue the necessity of replacing this approach by newer ones. It is this more radical strain of criticism which needs to be combated because it would eclipse or even destroy a valuable intellectual stream, and because it often mischaracterises that tradition and advances statements about organizational sociology which reflect muddled thinking.

This volume is principally a defence of Organization Theory. Since many academic labels suffer from ambiguity, and field definitions tend to be emotional, territorial issues for those involved, it is important to try and clarify terms of debate at the outset. The phrase, Organization Theory, is here being used in the way it is utilized in North American business and management schools. That is, the reference is to topics, such as organization structure, strategy, organization-environment and power and influence. These form a sub-set of what is taught within the subject known as Organization Behaviour (sometimes also known as Human Behaviour in Organizations). This latter heading includes also Managerial Psychology. More recently, there is a tendency to distinguish between these two components of Organizational Behaviour: Organization Theory and Managerial Psychology, as Macro- and Micro-OB, respectively. These are all no more than linguistic conventions, which seem to enjoy some shared meaning within certain sections of the international academic community. There is some sense to them, but equally anomalies are not hard to discern. For instance, whereas Organization Theory is mostly about 'big things' like corporate structure and strategy, much of the literature on influence is about how individual managers interact with each other and their private stratagems for advancing their interests (Pettigrew, 1973). Thus some of the analysis is at the individual or group levels, which is distinctive of Micro-OB or Managerial Psychology. Equally, studies of leadership style and intra-group communications of top management by managerial psychologists, inform issues of corporate strategy formulation and implementation (Argyris and Schon, 1978). Hence, level of analysis, while capturing much of the difference between Macro and Micro is not an exact discriminant. In this way Micro- can illuminate phenomena often dealt with in Macro-OB.

Much of what makes up Organization Theory are topics such as structure, authority, power, formal organization, informal organization, bureaucratization, professionalization, democratization and the impact of changes in size, technology, task, uncertainty and public accountability. Many of these subjects have been studied under subjects such as Organization Sociology or Industrial Sociology. These in turn draw on general Sociology and Anthropology, using concepts such as role which are common to sociological studies of the family and religion and across societies of the industrial and non-industrial types. Much of Organization Theory is derived from Weber's (1968) work on authority and bureaucracy. Thus much of Organization Theory is co-terminous with Organizational Sociology. This is one reason why power interactions between individuals are defined as within Organization Theory. While Organization Theory draws heavily on sociology, other disciplines also contribute. Much of Organization Theory is about coping with uncertainty and the information processing required thereby (Galbraith, 1973). This involves psychological concepts such as information processing capacity, search and scanning and decision-making.

The work of Thompson, March, Simon and Cyert has been very influential (Thompson, 1967; March and Simon, 1958; Cyert and March, 1963). And this clearly reflects economic notions such as the theory of the firm, as well as those derived from statistics and probability. For a time, the phrase Organization Theory seemed to be used to refer almost exclusively to March and Simon and the work of the Carnegie School. However, latterly, it seems also to be used to encompass the neo-Weberian tradition of theorizing about organizations. The term Organization Theory as used in this volume has this broader meaning and refers to theories of organizations, of both psychological and sociological disciplinary background. Organization Theory and Organization Behaviour are characterised by a primary orientation towards explanation and to being open in principle to learn from any discipline: sociology, psychology, economics, statistics and so on (Pugh, 1966). This is to be welcomed, though in practice much of extant Organization Theory, especially that discussed herein, is based either in psychology or sociology.

This volume then is a defence of Organization Theory. However, it needs to be made explicit that we are defending also the associated empirical enquiry. Every science has a theory of a more or less developed form and empirical studies which ascertain the validity, and need for refinement, of that theoretical structure. Macro-Organizational Behaviour is no exception to this. While Organization Theory is a term which is sufficiently understood to perform useful service in the title of a syllabus or a book, the subject does have an empirical arm. The area of study is not purely theoretical, nor should the emphasis on theory in the title of this volume be taken to imply any belief that it is, or that it should be so. On the contrary, there is an extensive literature, especially of field studies in actual organizations. Much of the ensuing argument is an assertion of the need to continue this tradition, especially of comparative studies. However, there is also a concern with theoretical matters herein. One issue is whether much of the empirical literature is theoretically adequate. Another is whether conventional theoretical frameworks, such as structural-functionalism and the contingency approach, are too limited to be useful. Several alternative programmatics, involving different theoretical frameworks, are offered by critics of the orthodoxy: Social Action Theory, Sociology of Organizations, Marxian Organization Theory and Strategic Choice. This raises several issues about the sociological adequacy of conventional Organization Theory. Many of the criticisms reviewed here are about the failings of organizational enquiries to meet the requirements contained in classical sociological frameworks. Our discussion will suggest that much of the extant literature represents a promising line of intellectual endeavour with social relevance. Moreover, the current literature is grounded in coherent theoretical frameworks. These frameworks include some which have strong roots in sociology. While sociological theory is a rich seam for organization theorists to mine, the test of validity for an Organization Theory is not whether or not it is subsumable under a classical sociological theory. This is consonant with the position, which was signalled earlier, that Organization Theory is multi-disciplinary.

Thus far we have defined Organization Theory by drawing on linguistic usage and subject boundaries. However, one might ask what is the distinctive characteristic of organizational phenomena. An organization may be understood as a set of roles oriented towards securing a goal (Barnard, 1938). It is any social system which comprises the coordinated action of two or more people towards attaining an objective. Organizations are purposeful systems. Most commonly they are corporations, schools, universities, armies, hospitals and like formal organizations. But they could also be two families arranging a picnic, or two neighbours helping each other fix a common fence, or a criminal gang making a robbery, or a band of guerillas making a revolution. While organizations of the former type usually have a legal existence, formal organization and formal boundaries, these characteristics are not necessary for the social system to be an organization. What seems to be distinctive of organizational studies is the phenomena of goal-oriented behaviour, coordination amongst individuals and other properties such as degree of differentiation, integration mechanisms, extent of concentration of power, authority, communication, legitimation, conflict and so on. This is what forms the subject matter. Contemporary statements of Organization Theory reemphasize these common underlying abstract variables (Mintzberg, 1979; Hage, 1980). These are what the writings on organization of Weber, Durkheim, March and Simon, Mintzberg, Child, Galbraith and Hage have in common. Sometimes they may be studies in empirical research projects which draw a sample of legal employing organizations (Pugh *et al.*, 1968). But this is not a definition of organization in theoretical terms. Organization, as the coordinated action towards an objective, goes on in the Ford Motor Company, which is a legally identified organization and a barbecue party, which is often a private assembly of friends. Conversely, in ordinary language people use the word organization to refer to the Ford factories, machines, products, toilets and employees, to everything which lies within the legal envelope. However, Organization Theory is about only a narrow sub-set of that phenomena, the organization structure and attendant social system. The interaction between the structure and the technology or personality of employees might well be studied. Yet many phenomena remain inside the organization which do not enter the province of organization studies, but which are studied in other disciplines, e.g. the way tax laibilties occur between stocks at different stages in the production process (raw, semi-finished and finished) may be of interest to an accountant, the connection between fluorescent lighting and employee eyestrain may be of interest to an ergonomist. Pugh (1973) has pointed out the way in which the lay meaning of organization needs to be distinguished from the term used in organizational behaviour. Thus, in Organization Theory, the reference is to abstract properties of social organization structure, formal and informal. This is often related to individual organizational behaviour such as turnover, absenteeism, job satisfaction and the like.

One consequence of the abstraction in the definition of organization is that it is applicable at several levels, and can be used to study more than one level simultaneously. Studies of organization are made at the level of the individuals' roles (Gerwin, 1979), at the level of sections, at the level of departments, at the level of divisions, at the level of subsidiaries and at the level of whole organizations. Sometimes enquiries are made at more than one level: as in Lawrence and Lorsch's (1967) study of departments and their coordination through interdepartmental and superordinate levels, Lorsch and Allen's (1973) study of divisions and the corporate level, and Van de Ven and Ferry (1980) have studied organizations at multiple levels simultaneously. Going upwards in substantive terms, Etzioni (1968) has applied an Organization Theory perspective to the study of societies. Here again, the approach focuses on coordination of different sub-units and strata towards goal attainment, and on the various mechanisms and processes for energizing and guiding societies. Employers' associations, national economic development councils, trade union congresses and, more generally, organizations which are made up of other organizations, may be studied through the framework of Organization Theory (Berry *et al.*, 1974). Different perspectives such as those from political science, economics, sociology and other disciplines may fruitfully be brought to bear on these super-organizations, as they may also on individual firms or individual workers. Thus it is not the case that Organization Theory studies organizations which other branches of learning do not. There is no one-to-one correspondence between Organization Theory and organizations as substantive entities which are never enquired into by other disciplines. What is at the focus of Organization Theory is a concern for the social organizational structure and its relationships to goals. But even here, other perspectives, not central to Organization Theory as conventionally practised, may usefully supplement that approach. For instance, valid knowledge about motivation and incentive schemes, which may be drawn from industrial psychology, would illuminate the connections between role behaviour, goals and performance (Lawler, 1976).

Having dealt with definition the discussion can now return to the attack on organizational analysis. Organization Theory has come under fire from two directions. On the one hand, it has been criticized for being too structural, and not concerned with explanations in terms of the acts of individuals and the meanings that they attach to their social transactions. On the other hand, it is attacked for being too concerned with the organization *per se*, and insufficiently concerned with the larger set of structures which shape and constrain the enterprise.

The first strand of criticism consists of critiques of structural theories used in the study of organizations. Those theories include cybernetics, structural-functionalism and the systems approach. Whilst varying in their emphases, they all share a readiness to conceptualize events involving organizations in terms of supra-individual concepts of structure, such as specialization of functions, centralization of decision-making, or adaptation to the environment – and talk of organizational goals. It is this kind of macro language which has come under criticism from the individualist wing of critics.

The concepts of organizational systems and goals are said to be reification, and thus to fallaciously impute to organizations a concrete existence which only their members really have. Moreover, intentions are ascribed to organizations, whereas only humans can have goals. Systems are seen as vague metaphysical notions. The concept of systems needs is considered to be vaporous. And the argument is made that, in fact, all this talk of objective analysis of organizations boils down to sociologists endorsing managerial views of the organization, and producing a language which mystifies other employees and helps keep them acquiescent. Similarly, structural-functional theory assumes equilibrium and value consensus. This makes it incapable of handling change and conflict. Hence structural-functional analysis of organizations is static and is just a rationale for the status quo. It explains present structures by saying that they are functional.

Individualistic critics distinguish this systems-level approach from one which focuses at the individual level and is concerned with individual behaviour, its meaning to the individual, his or her perception of the world and his or her value preferences. In particular, the alternative approach championed by these protagonists is the social action theory. This is asserted to be more 'sociologically satisfactory', and to be more appropriate to a sociology which dedicates itself to the aid of 'suffering humanity'. Further, by concentrating on the actor's perspective, it is said to lead to the analysis of contrasting perceptions and values which, in turn, lead to the analysis of the origins and manifestations of conflict. By contrast, the approach which focuses on structures and their functioning is said to gloss over these differing perceptions and values, to lead away from the analysis of conflict, and to lead to the view of organizational life as one of static equilibrating structures or systems. This view, it is asserted, minimizes the recognition of change and provides a language which veils the phenomena of change and conflict, and so furnishes a very useful ideology for those wishing to preserve the status quo. Moreover, Organization Theory posits rationality as a characteristic of formal organization. Sentiment and irrationality are ascribed to the workers. This serves as an excuse for efforts to manipulate them, in order to get them to accept managerial goals and views. Despite pretensions to science and objectivity, organizational sociology just presents management's views, and helps to pursue its interests. In sum, the organization structural approach is seen as static, somewhat metaphysical and ideologically conservative; and it is contrasted with an approach which emphasizes the individual and conflict.

Social action theory stresses the need to see all things from the viewpoint of the individual, rather than to make deductions from notions of some supposed social structure or society or political economy. Against the more determinate views of people as prisoners of a social system, individualism argues that people have free choice to act as they want. By seeing the human agent as potent, and by giving sovereignty to individual volition, individualism offers a humanistic alternative to positivism. In rejecting the idea of social science, causal laws are denied as impossible and generalizations are seen as, at best, severely limited in their compass.

In the extreme the position is the ideographic one: things can only be understood as singularities in their own terms.

This intellectual movement is buttressed by a number of arguments from philosophy. One is that meaning is specific to a symbol system, e.g. a language, and cannot be divorced from its context. For example, the moves of a pawn in chess only have meaning within that game. This points to the way that much of meaningful human action can only be understood through an examination of the rules or language used in that particular society, region or work-group. Explanation consists of stating the meaning in that specific context. Since the Social Action Theory is concerned to understand the meaning of action, it follows that generalizations will be limited to particular contexts, and that enquiry needs to use internal methods. This leads to a rejection of comparative methods, quantification, controlled experiments, standard variables, questionnaires and other tools of organizational sociology. In their place are advocated participant observation, qualitative methods, hermeneutics, historical and processual studies.

The critics argue that each individual social actor has his or her view of the situation, including a perception of what is in their interest. The Social Action theorists would have sociologists construct explanations in terms of the perceptions and values of different typical actors. This would allow recognition that the interests perceived by different groups of members in organizations will often diverge. Such differing interests form the basis for conflict. Often organizational arrangements represent compromises reached between these groups. The status quo is liable to be perpetually open to attempts to renegotiate the established order, as the fundamental differences of interest have not been reconciled, and remain as a source of tension. The compromises reached between groups reflect differences in their power. This is argued to be a better model for explaining both present structural arrangements and change.

The second main stream of criticism of orthodox Organization Theory comes from those who see in it a failure to locate the organization within the social structure of society. In particular, radical structuralists see the societal order as characterized by oppression and inequity and assert the need to examine organizations in terms of their role within this social system.

The neo-Marxians push further than the Social Action theorists with the concepts of interest and power. They are also concerned with conflict, and of the way in which conventional organizational sociology fails to reveal the role of organizations within the larger structure of domination in society. For them, key elements are the way organizations work to exploit and dominate many members of society, and the way the organizational entities fit within class, imperial and government systems. They argue that the interests of actors can be inferred from Marxian political economy, whether or not the actors see it that way. These are the objective interests, such as that of capitalists to maximize profit and minimize wages, and of the proletariat, the opposite. The further argue that power differences are themselves explicable in terms of a structure of domination, which relates to property differences and to exploitation. The phenomena of domination, exploitation, capital accumulation and so on interact to produce changes in consciousness, conflict and, ultimately, contradiction and massive social transformation. Neo-Marxians argue that theoretically useful sociological work on organizations has to study them within such a framework. For them Organization Theory is a tool of domination and subjugation.

It is the intent of this volume to enquire into the validity of these and related criticisms of Organization Theory. A number of these attacks will be shown to be false. Others will be seen to be only partially true. Theories of the structural-functionalist type will be argued to be cogent. And empirical studies using comparative, quantitative methods will be revealed as apposite. Alternative programmatics will be held to involve difficulties, and to be based, in some cases, on a displacement of certain topics of enquiry. While acknowledging the need for enhancement of the theoretical framework and for flexibility in definition of the objects of study in Organization Theory, the argument is made that this requires supplementing rather than supplanting conventional approaches. Equally, changes in method should take the form of refining rather than abandoning.

The following chapters are divided into two parts. In Part One, principal criticisms of Organization Theory are considered. The discussion commences with an examination of the supposed inadequacies in supra-individual organizational concepts, such as goals and system needs. Having established that this language is philosophically sound and is conceptually meaningful, the discussion turns to theories which deploy such notions, in particular, to structural-functionalism. In Chapter 3 problems supposedly inherent in this theory are discussed, especially when applied to the study of organizations. This raises the issue that paradigms, such as structural-functionalism and conflict theory, are incommensurable and that therefore synthesis is impossible and each approach in sociology and organizations must be continued in isolation. Chapter 4 seeks to show that this is not so in terms of theory. Next (Chapter 5) the charge is dealt with that the organization literature is atheoretical, an assortment of empirical results lacking even the cogency which following the structural-functional line would bestow. This involves probing the logical status of certain theories of organization. The view taken here is that structural-functionalism remains useful as a framework. Much of the empirical and theoretical literature relates to this metatheory. It is suggested that the failure to note this in certain critical commentaries relates to omissions or imbalance in the literature review. There is a tendency to emphasize sociological rather than organization theories. This raises the question of the relationship between sociological and organizational theory. Chapter 6 suggests that these two sets overlap but are not identical, and that Organization Theory needs to be recognized as legitimate in its own terms. In Chapter 7 the idea of the scientific study of organizations is shown to be widely appropriate, despite claims that certain topics, such as power, require alternative approaches. Chapter 8 considers the charge that Organization Theory suffers from managerial and conservative bias. The discussion brings out the way in which organizational analysis is not identical to managerial views, does not justify extant conditions as necessarily the most functional, and may constitute a criticism of certain organizations and their managements. Further, it provides one approach to the analysis of organizational change, and suggests when change would assist the organization reach its goals and what form they would need to take. The ensuing Chapter 9 examines the accusations that organization theories are ideologies of exploitation and domination. In discussing the charge of ideology, it is suggested that for a system of ideas to be ideological, it would need to be shown that it necessarily has this use, rather than that it may occasionally be so used. The critical literature provides no evidence of systematic ideological use, nor, even, of episodic use.

In Part Two attention shifts to four alternative approaches to the study of organizations which the critical literature suggests would be more fruitful. In Chapter 10, the Social Action Theory is examined. The discussion finds this to be misnamed and suggests the individual frame of reference approach as a more apt label. Problems are noted in that the approach tends to an atomistic view of social life, overstates individual volition, understates socio-economic determinations, ignores nonrational cognitive processes and tends to be used to construct explanations of limited generality. Chapter 11 treats the Sociology of Organizations approach. The call in that programmatic to widen organization studies by including more about the interaction between organization and the wider society is accepted. However, this should not lead to an abandonment or downgrading of the importance of continuing to study intra-organizational variables and their interrelation. The specific contribution made by such work in the past indicates the fruitfulness of that approach. In Chapter 12 perhaps the most radical (politically and intellectually) proposal is discussed, that for a Marxian Organization Theory. There remain disjunctions of subject matter and level of analysis between Marxism as a societal theory of change in socio-economic systems and theories about organizations. This precludes there ever being such a class of Organization

Theory. Several examples of purportedly Marıxian analysis of organization are discussed and shown to be compatible with orthodox treatments of organization. Attention turns in Chapter 13 to the programme for organization studies advocated in conjunction with the concept of Strategic Choice. This position is seen as the result of attempting to accommodate the conventional approach with that from Social Action. The formulation of Child (1972) advances criticisms of the orthodoxy, which are misguided. Upon closer examination Strategic Choice turns out to be an amalgam of contingency-design, Social Action and radical structuralist ideas which are not entirely consistent with each other.

Finally, in Part Three, a brief illustration of the usefulness of contingency theory in practical organizational design is provided. This outlines some principal findings from organization research and shows how they may be formed into a coherent model for guiding decision-making on redesign.

PART ONE

A reply to criticisms of Organization Theory

2

Organizational concepts

One of the earlier lines of criticism of organizational sociology has been of organizations as purposeful systems. Concepts such as organizational goal and systems needs and indeed the concept of the organization itself have been attacked as metaphysical and as mystifying. The critics have approached organizational life from a more individualist perspective. They have pointed out that organizations are composed of individuals who relate to one another. Moreover, these individuals by no means always share the same objectives or values. Thus the approach is one of individual reduction, that is to give an account of what happens in organizations in terms of what each person is seeking and how they transact with each other. This chapter will consider these attacks and will seek to show that organizational-level concepts are intellectually coherent and need to be retained in organizational sociology. The shortcomings in trying to approach organizational phenomena from a strictly individual level will be identified in a later chapter (Part Two, Chapter 10). And in a subsequent chapter of Part One (Chapter 9) the issue of the supposedly ideological characteristics of organizational concepts will be addressed.

Silverman (1968, 1970) argues that organizational sociology has embraced too uncritically a conception of the organization as a system with its own needs and goals. He finds such notions to be erroneous, and to divert attention away from the study of what is actually going on in organizations: that individuals with different views and differing values come together in an arrangement which is characterized by struggle and conflict between individuals and groups. Moreover, by adopting a systems view we are tacitly siding with the management and accepting that other employees must be kept in line, through persuasion and so on. Silverman rounds out his thesis by presenting some examples of how organizational phenomena may be more adequately understood in social action terms.

If Silverman had argued simply that the sociological study of organizations would benefit from more enquiry into the perceptions held by different members, then the author would be in agreement. But Silverman asserts much more than this, and his thesis is far less tolerant. It is that structuralist approaches are both deficient as theory and are tools for sub-jugation. Social action theory emerges from his discussion (Silverman, 1969) as the only alternative for sociological enquiry. Indeed, one of the principal forms of the argument by Silverman is to show how the concepts of systems-level analysis fail to be reducible to the concepts of action theory, i.e. the latter is used as the criteria for ascertaining the adequacy of the former.

Systems versus individual perspectives

Silverman begins his critique by noting that the system theoretic concep-tion of organizations posits that 'An organization is thought to have a goal which is something more than the sum of the goals of its members' (1968: 222). This attribution by Silverman to systems theory of goals, is accurate. Silverman then states:

> There are certain obvious difficulties in this position which, because it has been accepted as the 'conventional wisdom', have largely gone unnoticed. By treating the 'goals' and 'needs' of organizations as givens, it seems to us that we are attributing apparently human motivations to inanimate objects: in other words, we are reifying the organization. (1968: 223)

Again, in his book, Silverman writes:

> To use the concepts of organisational needs and of a system's self-regulating activities in any way other than as a heuristic device is inadmissable since it implies that the power of thought and action may reside in social constructs – this is sometimes known as the problem of reification. (1970: 3)

Systems theory does impute needs and properties, such as self-regulation, to systems (Miller and Rice, 1967). Silverman has made two charges against this: that human characteristics are being ascribed to the inanimate, and that this is reification. Each will be considered in turn.

Is imputing needs to systems at all the same as talking about human motivation? Systems theorists, in positing the concept of systems needs, are saying that organizations need to maintain the supply of inputs, such as raw materials or work, by employees. This is not the same as talking about the needs of an individual for water or food. The unit of analysis is different (i.e. the organization rather than the individual) and so are the needs. Systems theory tries to be applicable at several levels of analysis, so that the broad, theoretical categories such as latency or pattern-maintenance, may be applied at either the social system or the individual level. But the specific reference of these general requisites, or needs, will vary between levels reflecting the specific characteristics of the different units. For instance, human beings have sexual needs and erotic feelings, social systems do not; they have the requirement for biological reproduction of their populations in order to continue manning the system. The needs of organizations and individuals may have empirical connections, theoretical communalities, and be metaphors of each other, but this is far different from saying that they are identical. In other words, in asserting that Organization Theory attributes human properties to inanimate objects, it is Silverman who is reading this attribution into systems theory.

In laying the charge of reification against organizational sociology, Silverman is making a criticism whose meaning requires explanation. An answer can be found in the origins of this type of criticism. The starting point here is the philosophical anthropology of Marx, especially the younger Marx. Here the central paradox, or contradiction, is that man makes social institutions but then experiences them as alienated, that is, externally constraining, socially and historically imposed 'things'. This objectification, of what were originally purposive human actions, clouds the man-made-ness of social institutions, which forestalls the re-creation of institutions which have become exploitative or which otherwise no longer serve many of those who are subject to them (Berger and Pullberg, 1966).

This process is often referred to by the philosophical term, reification, which originally had the wider meaning of the fallacy of misplaced concreteness. This refers to the error of imputing ontology, literal existence as attested by touch, sight, smell, etc., to concepts such as atoms in physics, which do not have corporeal existence, yet which exist in the sense of being abstract postulates, or man-made fictions, which form part of a theory which can be found to be useful, if and when deductions from it survive testing. Hence, in the orthodox philosophy of science, the concept of reification has a meaning within the argument that science is a nomothetic, hypothetico-deductive activity. The point of the concept of reification is that it cautions against trying to attribute to concepts like atoms, unnecessary extra properties like corporeal existence, which they do not have because they are not that sort of 'thing'. It guards against the error of dismissing or disproving concepts like atoms because they fail tests such as touch. The notion of the reified concept safeguards the abstractions of the natural sciences from an inappropriate kind of dismissal based on a misunderstanding of their logical status. In the terms of the later Wittgenstein (1963), it points out that the language game of proving atoms in nuclear physics is different from the language game of proving the existence of tables in everyday life.

Consider now how the term, reification, is used by some of the critics of organizational sociology. Following the early Marx, they maintain that formal organizations are man-made entities whose human origins become obscured in their growth, a process which is helped by their description in terms such as 'system'. The reference to supra-individual activity, such as in adjusting to the environment or coordination or the needs of the organization for maintenance, are said to be reification, because, actually, everything that happens in organizations is done by humans. Whilst this latter statement is true: everything that happens in organizations is done by humans (apart from that which is done by machines whose programmes are, of course, written by humans originally), to say that describing this in structural language is reification does not follow. Whilst everything is done by humans, this statement misses out what it is about the doing that makes it organizational. Barnard defined organization as 'a system of consciously coordinated activities or forces of two or more persons' (1938: 73). Take coordination of two people towards task completion (like loading furniture onto a truck). Each carries out actions, but what makes this activity coordination is that they manifestly do the task better through lifting up at the same time (that is, through coordination). The adjustment of the behaviour of each to the other, coordination, and the accomplishment of an end which would be difficult (if not impossible) to achieve without human coordination, is what makes this a piece of organization. Barnard's definition emphasizes that even complex organizations are ultimately reducible to individuals coordinating to achieve some goal. Leaving aside the issue of the logical status of 'goal' for a moment, we can begin to see that what makes individual action organization is coordination of those individual actions (through mutual agreement or command or whatever); and reference to the fulfilment of some task (like loading a furniture van or building a hydro-electric station), which, in general, will tend to be of such magnitude that one individual unaided cannot accomplish it. Hence, the organizational dimension of human actions is the element of coordination. Now is this reification?

There is an old saw in philosophy: 'I have come to the University of Oxford. I have seen the students, the bicycles, the dons and the colleges, but I have not seen the University of Oxford. Where is the University of Oxford?' The answer is that the University of Oxford does not exist in the same sense that students, bicycles, dons and colleges do. The latter exist as flesh and bone and steel and brick, but the University of Oxford does not have that kind of existence. It 'exists' in the sense of granting degrees, appointing dons or of examining students. It is what turns flesh and bone into a student, that is, a member of the organization with certain delimited rights and obligations, and informal expectations. The language games of existence of a person or bicycle and of an organization, like the University of Oxford, are fundamentally different. This is the point of this basic exercise in philosophy.

Applying this to the preceding situation we can see that the language games of the existence of human individuals and of organizations are different. This need not be an invidious distinction. An entity, with the properties of breathing, thinking and feeling, exists in a different way from an entity whose properties are coordinating towards fulfilment of a task. To refer to organizations as supra-individual abstract concepts is no more silly than talking about atoms in physics, or the legal system in Britain. To class such talk about organizations as reification is to reveal, not a sophisticated awareness of contemporary philosophy, but a misunderstanding of it.

Using the term reification in the philosophy of science is to emphasize that scientific theories are distinct from objects in ordinary life. The utility of the concept is to defend esoteric language from dismissal. Neo-Marxians counterpose man as creator of human institutions with man as the mystified beholder of such institutions when they have become Sedimented. For neo-Marxians, theorizing about the operations of human institutions in systemic, supra-individual language is reification. Hence neo-Marxians have taken the concept of reification in the opposite way. In the philosophy of science, the concept is used to defend the esoteric and the intangible, in neo-Marxism the same word is used to castigate the supra-human.

Some order may be brought to the discussion by deleting the term reification from the neo-Marxians critique and rephrasing their objection in sociological, rather than philosophical, terms. This would lead to the following restatement of their essential thesis: concepts such as system and structure should be avoided because they add nothing to the explanatory power of sociological theory, and because they mystify members of society, thus keeping them enslaved. The first part of this statement is that systems thinking does not contribute to sociological theory, and the second part is an empirical generalization about the effects of certain ideas on people (discussed further in Chapter 9). The former statement, when expressed plainly, would make even a Marxist quail, for the history of Marx's own theorizing is of the increasing elaboration of a systems model of economic structures (feudalism, capitalism and socialism) their laws of development, internal contradiction and transformation (Marx, 1973, 1969, 1954). A categoric rejection of systems thinking is not compatible with Marxism. Nonsystemic individualism is logically possible as a position within sociology, but its fruitfulness as an explanatory device would seem extremely limited. The development of sociological theory has seen the construction and refinement of frameworks which utilize the concepts of system and structure, such as the division of labour and rates of economic growth in Durkheim (1964), and the systems and structure of bureaucracy and capitalism (Weber, 1968). To dismiss systems approaches in Organization Theory by the accusation of reification is philosophically and sociologically naive.

The foregoing discussion should guard against the rejection of all supra-individual concepts as being inherently wrong. Yet while this may be recognized by many, there are still certain collectivity-level notions at which they would baulk. One of these is the notion of organizational goals.

Organizational goals

The issue about goals is a particularly delicate one, easily confused. The critics of organizational sociology accuse sociologists of using the concept in a way which does not recognize its problematic nature. Silverman contends that talk of goals ascribes volition and purposeful action to organizations which only humans can have, and is, therefore, guilty of reification or anthropomorphism. By contrast, social action theorists would chart the differing goals of each actor, and in this way make explicit the conflicts and compromises ongoing in organizational life. Whilst it is true that only humans can define goals (ideal future states), and that organizational goals are defined by humans, what makes the goals organizational is the process of their authorization and institutionalization. This latter process ensures that goals, once understood and shared, and perhaps backed by detailed plans and schedules, can survive the death of most of their architects. The process of authorization involves the organization giving its legitimacy to the objectives (just like the University of Oxford grants degrees). This makes the objectives the property of a supra-individual 'entity'. The institutionalization process, similarly, makes the objectives the property of the supra-individual collectivity. Hence, once again, Silverman, in charging reification, is confusing the language games about individuals with those about supra-individual collectivities.

Goals and goal-setting involve consciousness, and this happens in the minds of humans. But this does not mean that organizational goals are nothing more than the objectives of each individual in the organization. To argue this is to evade what it is that makes goals organizational – that certain objectives become authorized and institutionalized. At this point we can speak of the goals of the organization. The thinking up, formulating and arguing over goals is all done by humans but there is a collectivity-level process which has to happen before these statements become organizational goals. Workers and managers in General Motors will have their preferences for what it should do, so will the consumers of its products. But these preferences only become goals at the point that the top management and board of directors of General Motors authorize them and approve capital expenditures and other decisions to implement strategy, e.g. to have smaller, more fuel-efficient cars. Ordinary language recognises this difference between the members and the institutions and records this by using the words 'GM' or 'it' as the subjects to which are predicated policies and actions. In everyday life people use these phrases without confusion. Once again, Silverman is mistakenly seeking to reduce to individual action the acts of collectivities.

Turning to the issue of goal-attainment, slightly different considerations apply. If the goal of an organization can be operationalized in observable terms, that is, making so much profit, curing a certain disease, or defending certain territory, then one can examine the organization to see whether or not it attains that goal. Non-human servo-mechanisms hunt for, and attain, their targets independently of human intervention (though of course humans normally set the targets or define a target-setting mechanism). Once the concept of a goal can be expressed as an operationalized concept, then goal-attainment is not an exclusively human faculty.

This leads to the question of how to operationalize the goal concept. For the social action theorist, an operationalization is always suspect because it selects a measure out of a set of diverse, often ambiguous and somewhat conflicting aims of individuals. The structural perspective points out that not all of these aims are authorized and institutionalized. The social action theorist says that this is exactly the point, and this reflects the domination of others by the ruling elite of the dominant coalition. The structural reply is that this may often be so. Identifying the actual goals of an organization from the aims held by individuals does involve abstraction, but it is not arbitrary. It is not just at the whim of the external analyst to select goals out of the individual aims, it is a task for empirical research to find what objectives are authorized and institutionalized. One may find that certain objectives are only weakly authorized (that is, inconsistencies exist in the statements by authorities; compliance is only weakly enforced; powerful groups prevent full adoption of the programme) or equally that the institutionalization is far from complete (tolerance of substantial deviation from corporate purpose in certain sub-units, imperfect understanding of top management's objectives throughout the membership, scarce resources committed away from, rather than towards, goal-attainment). Organizations vary empirically in their degrees of authorization and institutionalization of their goals, just as they vary in the contents of the goals. This phenomenon, however, can only be understood from within the structural perspective, for concepts such as organizational authorization and institutionalization, though involving human action, are properties of the supra-individual collectivity, that is, the unit of analysis is the organization, not the individual.

The kernel of Silverman's charge is that organizational sociologists treat goals as unproblematic. However, the modern systems theory treats the aims of organizational activity as anything but this. Organizations are viewed, in this model, as an integrated set of sub-systems operating in an environment with which it is interdependent (Pfeffer and Salancik, 1978; Taylor, 1976). The organization transacts across its boundaries bringing in supplies, energy, manpower, capital, technology, legitimacy and regulation and in exchange gives finished products and services, wages, dividends, cash, innovations, taxes and cooperation with superordinate bodies. These transactions are all necessary to its continued, long-run existence. Structural-functional theory posits that there is some minimum level of fulfilment of each of these transactions below which it cannot drop without impairing its ability to sustain the other transactions. This is a complex multi-output model. Each of the distinguishable class of recipients, termed stakeholders, will tend to have their own peculiar evaluations of the output of the firm; that is, the shareholders may look for one thing: profits; the workers look for another: outputs, wages, employment, satisfying work, etc. Such a stakeholder model was propounded by Cyert and March in their *Behavioural Theory of the Firm* published in 1963, five years prior to Silverman's article. These different stakeholder views can be described in the language of Social Action Theory as the values of the actors. Modern organizational sociology, far from disguising the plurality of evaluations, makes it explicit in the systems organization-in-environment model.

The first preferences of the stakeholders do not all become the goals of the organization. The organizational goals represent a sub-set of this diverse set of would-be objectives for the organization. The goals selected usually involve a trade-off between the preferences of the differing stakeholders, e.g. the workers and their unions do not get as high wages as they would like, the general manager of a product division does not obtain the priority on corporate investments that he would like (Hage, 1980; Bower, 1970). The selection of goals is done in the main by top management. Indeed, this process of determining priorities between rival claims for resources and attention, is one of the cardinal and distinguishing tasks of the highest level of management (Ansoff, 1965; Christensen *et al.*, 1978; Mintzberg, 1979; Pfeffer and Salancik, 1978; Taylor, 1976). The actual goal which they set represents a selected and edited version of the competing claims of the stakeholders.

Taking goals as given does elide the differing preferences of constituents and the process whereby they are accepted or discounted. If the interest is primarily in the plurality of preferences and their quasi-resolution, then this requires study in its own right. But where the question is the effectiveness of the organization, then the criteria are those contained in the goals. And the goals are the goals *of the organization*.

Silverman continues: 'Instead of attempting to establish empirically the conceptions of ends and needs held by its members, we begin with a priori notions of an organization's "needs" and then examine the processes through which it secures them' (1968: 223). Again he is correct in saying that systems theory deals in a general, *a priori* conception of systems needs, rather than in empirically finding out what varied objectives are held by the actors. But he is wrong to see this as mistaken. For systems theory deals in supra-individual processes and needs, not the needs and objectives of the actors. Once again Silverman fails to recognize that the conceptual distinctions need not imply that conceptions distinguished are inferior, one to another. They are just different. The defect is Silverman's in not acknowledging that there is nothing logically or theoretically wrong in having sociological theories which deal at different levels: systems theory at the systems level, and individual theories at the individual level. Because Silverman approaches systems theory from the paradigm of Social Action Theory he perceives conceptual operations which do not fit that framework as necessarily erroneous.

Silverman goes on: 'It seems doubtful whether it is legitimate to conceive of an organisation as having a goal except where there is an ongoing consensus between the members of the organisation about the purposes of their interaction' (1970: 9). Here Silverman is saying that organizational goals are nothing more than the purposes of their constituent individuals, and as such become the goals of the organization only if and when the individuals concur in their objectives. This is individualistic reductionism. It omits what it is about organizational goals that makes them organizational, i.e. that they have been authorized and institutionalized. The concept of organizational goals in the systems approach is not that of consensus and does not presume consensus. In the discussion of coercive compliance systems by Etzioni (1975) the goals of these organizations, such as concentration camps, are not held to be shared by their coerced inmates.

Silverman continues: 'This can only divert attention away from "why" questions and towards "how" questions; away from causes and towards consequences' (1968: 223). The distinction here between 'why' and 'how' questions is a prelude to his subsequent argument that sociology requires answers to 'why' questions and that these can only be found at the level of the actor, i.e. by understanding the motivated action of individuals. But it is by no means acceptable to posit that the goal of social science is answers to 'why' questions rather than to 'how' questions. A central point of the philosophy of science is that in any science explanations of 'why' questions are answered in 'how' terms, i.e. by explaining events by reference to regularities in causal relations between variables. 'How' answers tell us the causal mechanics of phenomena, and thereby provide scientific explanation (Toulmin, 1962). Such explanatory theories may be in terms of the motivations of individuals, and may thereby provide some answer to the lay question of 'why', but there is no restriction in social science in general to this sub-set of theories. Certain branches of sociology, such as interpretative sociology, do make such a restriction. Silverman argues for this narrow conception and this will be considered subsequently. The immediate point is that answering 'how' questions gives causes.

Conclusions

Thus the organizational-level concepts such as systems needs and organizational goals are not infected with the kinds of intellectual error which their critics have claimed. They make a distinctive and integral contribution to organizational analysis and cannot be supplanted by individual-level concepts.

3

Structural-functionalism in the study of organizations

Structural-functionalism has received considerable criticism as a theoretical framework for the study of organizations. In particular it is attacked as implying consensus on values by their members, as being tautologous, as lacking objective criteria of survival, as emphasizing consequences rather than causes, as assuming equilibrium, as being unable to explain change, and as having no place for endogenous change. Each of these issues will be considered in turn.

Silverman characterizes structural-functionalism as positing a 'normatively integrated organizational "system" ' (1968: 233). Despite the frequent accusations of its detractors, structural-functionalism does not posit complete consensus on values in society, and postulates other mechanisms as providing societal cohesion, such as systems integration (Lockwood, 1964). Solidarity achieved through interdependence in society works by having distinct occupational groupings which are not all like-minded one with another (Durkheim, 1964).

As noted earlier, in Chapter 1, it has been said of Etzioni's typology of the congruencies between compliance systems and individual states of involvement, that is a tautology. Each of these elements, however, has been defined independently and the statement that they tend to go together is an empirical connection of them, a testable proposition. Moreover, whilst the theory states that they will tend to be observed together and to be in equilibrium, it does not claim that this will always be so. States of incongruency are described as possible, but as producing a strain and therefore lowering the survival probability of the organization. Hence the tendency towards empirical correlation of compliance and involvement has exceptions to it specified, and these are predicted to be relatively less effective in functioning, and less likely to survive. Now, these last two are empirically testable propositions. In the first edition of *A Comparative Analysis of Complex Organizations*, Etzioni (1961) stressed the differential survival outcome of incongruency. In the second edition, emphasis is given to the concept of measuring systems ineffectiveness and to discussing studies which have operationalized these concepts (Etzioni, 1975). These studies show that organizations which score highly on the attainment of their goals tend to score highly on the other systems' requisites, such as adaptation, etc. These studies provide empirical support for the compliance theory, and also for the more general notion of organizations as social systems. Hence the Etzioni theory provides an example of how a high-level theory of the structural-functional type, whose initial exegesis concentrates on analysing the congruent (equilibrium) state, nevertheless contains clear implications for states of disequilibrium, which can be operationalized, tested and found to be valid. The career of Etzioni's theory might be taken as a cautionary tale: dismissed as a tautology, then refined and operationalized, and finally, attaining some degree of confirmation empirically.

Care is needed about dismissing theories of the organicist type simply because they may sound slightly truistic or tautologous. Many pieces of theoretical or paradigmatic writing tend to have that tone. It is inherent in the abstraction of the language, but it does not necessarily mean that it cannot be tested and confirmed by follow-up research.

The example of operationalizing functional requisites, and showing that they are indeed requisites of continued systems functioning, answers the charge that conceptions of systems needs are all, inherently, so vague as to be metaphysical. Silverman (1968) makes play of this in his critique of Selznick's theoretical scheme of organizational functioning. Once again, what has been done is to take a theoretical exegesis which necessarily contains, at its core, several highly abstract conceptions, and, by noting their abstract quality, to seek to disparate the whole approach as vacuous.

Silverman stresses his argument about the arbitrary nature of systems needs statements by asserting that one criterion often used, survival, is so loose as to leave the issue ambiguous: 'If the only test of whether a need is real is if the system cannot survive without meeting it, then what do we mean by "survival"? How are we to judge whether the system has "died" or merely changed?' (1968: 232). Business firms do go bankrupt, armies are defeated in battle and religious organizations dwindle in membership. Organizations that lose all members and resources are dead. Organizations which are tending that way are in ill-health. There is nothing vague or metaphysical about this, it goes on all around us.

As has been seen in the last chapter, an observation of Silverman (1968: 223) is that structural-functionalism focuses attention on consequences rather than on causes. Structural-functionalism is primarily concerned with explaining the existence and continuity of structural elements, in terms of the contribution to the rest of the system. It does not explain the origins of particular forms, but rather the reason for their continuity and increasing appearances in the populations of societies, and their increased development within particular societies. As in natural evolution, selection is explained by survival value, but the genesis of the varieties from which the selection is made lies outside the theory (Aldrich, 1979). This variation in human societies may be due to random fluctuations, accidents, improper socialization, creativity, choice, and so on. However, once they are in existence, the consequences of differing organizational forms, in terms of their survival value and performance, have causal influences on organizational structure, through feedback loops. These are key elements in models of organizational change of the structural-functionalist variant. Thus consequences are causes in structural-functionalism.

It is often said of structural-functional theories that they assume equilibrium. This seems to be a partial truth which has been subject to misinterpretation. Structural-functional analysis has at its core a model of a social system which, when in equilibrium, has sufficient interchanges between the sub-systems to sustain each of them, and thereby maintain the social system. Equilibrium is thus a state which is not devoid of movement, for the flows move between sub-systems, but is one in which the overall social system in its environment is stationary. Change takes the form of internal adjustment to reach equilibrium. This is normally conceived of as caused by external changes in the environment to which the social system must adapt. This usually entails adjustment of one or more sub-systems, leading, in turn, to adjustments of the others until equilibrium is re-established at a different position within the environment. This is the paradigm of structural-functionalism.

Note that each of these terms is defined relative to the other: sub-systems *vis-à-vis* systems, equilibrium *vis-à-vis* maintenance of existence. This is not because the elements are tautologous but because they are elements of a paradigm. Note also that these are not testable propositions, a paradigm cannot be tested directly, only its utility can be critically assessed by the degree of success that lower-level deductions have in withstanding attempts to falsify them through empirical testing. The equilibrium 'assumption' is part of the conception of the paradigm, but it does not mean that structural-functional or systems theorists assert that every collectivity under study, even if they treat it as a system, is thereby assumed to be in equilibrium. It may well be in a state of disequilibrium attendant upon some exogenous change which is still being worked through. The structural-functional imperative alerts the analyst to systematically examine the adequacy of the performance of different functions, and to look for dysfunctional strains resulting from inadequacies in the performance of these functions. This is not merely an arcane point. If structural-functional analysis had no conception of a state of disequilibrium, of not being in a position to continue systems functioning, and if it really did hold that all systems were, *de facto*, in equilibrium, then it would preclude the study of dysfunctions. It is the existence of dysfunctions, and their comprehension within a structural-functional analysis, which is the motive for many of the studies in organizational sociology. The aim of many such studies being, on occasion, to produce more specific knowledge about organizational design in order to avoid some of these dysfunctions in the future. If the structural-functional framework ruled out states of disequilibrium, *a priori*, then no such studies would be possible within that approach.

Having dealt with the charge that structural-functionalism assumes equilibrium, consider the accusation that structural-functional analyses, nevertheless, often, in practice, posits equilibrium. This idea is negated by the many studies of dysfunctions in organizations, such as the now classic studies of bureaucratic dysfunctions (Merton, 1949; Gouldner, 1954; Crozier, 1964). Each of these postulate pathological cycles, detrimental to efficient goal-attainment. Note in passing that each offers causal explanations of how people and structures interact to produce consequences contrary to the intentions of the actors. It is axiomatic to structural-functional analysis that contrasts between states of equilibrium and disequilibrium can identify ineffective designs and illuminate change processes.

Change in organizations is treated by structural-functionalism within their broad theoretical scheme. Organizations face the requirement of meeting their systems needs (such as for adaption, goal-attainment integration and latency). These require certain transactions with the environment and particular internal structures. As the environment changes so the structure of the organization and its goals will, usually, require modification to maintain compatibility with its niche and to ensure continuing satisfaction of the system's needs. There are two main mechanisms for this organizational change. The first occurs at the level of the population of organizations and is a change in its average characteristics through the differential survival rate of those organizations which fit the current environment, and the culling of those which do not. This is the population-ecology model of organizational change (Aldrich, 1979). The second occurs at the level of the organization itself. Here the organization alters its goals and structures to fit the changing circumstances. For instance, management may see that in the extant business climate there would be gains, such as enhanced profit or lower risk, to be had from diversifying its product range. They implement a plan of diversification, through acquisition or internal creation of new product lines, and then need to change their structure to manage this new more diversified corporation, from the Functional to the Product Divisional types. This new match between situation and structure will often come about by deliberate adaptation, that is by management consciously choosing a structure which is a better fit than the old one. However, some adaptation may come about through random processes, i.e. a change is made which happens to turn out to produce a better fit. In adapting to the new situation the company may have to adopt a structure such as a divisional system or a matrix which it has never used before. However, usually there will be other companies in the same society which have such structures. So the former company can learn from them and need not invent all the elements of the newer system. Thus many of the ideas about alternative organizational forms exist already.

The particular contribution of structural-functionalism to the explanation of organizational change is to point out which forms are best suited to which situations; and to identify the pressures which will lead a firm to change, that is which combination of context and structure will constitute a mismatch, a state of disequilibrium. The general structural-functionalist model of change is that it will occur when organizations disequilibriate and will be a shift to a condition of equilibrium. For example, Hage (1974) explains change in a hospital in structural-functional systems terms. A number of new medical specialties were introduced into the teaching hospital. A more organic structure was required for effective functioning when there was more knowledge complexity. After a process of change the structure shifted and became less mechanistic. The structural-functional model deals with the origins of change as conditions of disequilibrium. It does not necessarily give an account of change in the sense of who in the organization will argue for change, who will oppose it and which party will win. Thus it does not give the sort of information which a power-conflict model will. Nor does it necessarily say specifically from where the information about new structural types will be drawn. A knowledge of power alignments or the way certain experts filter information into an organization would enhance the explanation. However, the structural-functional perspective does offer certain suggestions to the explanatory effort: that change is initiated by disequilibrium, will not stop before a new state of equilibrium is reached and that certain combinations of situation and structure constitute such states (for an example see Chapter 14). It suggests a developmental sequence of transition through a sequence of successive stages of equilibrium attendant upon changes in the organization in size, product diversification and knowledge complexity. Thus the paradigm contains the possibility of predicting when organizational change will occur and towards which new form. Structural-functionalism in the study of organizations does contribute to the explanation of change. What it does not do is offer an account at the level of individual actors, their differential preferences and power. Thus the approach is distinguishable from that implied by an individualistic perspective. While recognizing the contribution which an individual-level approach makes, the potentiality of the structural-functional perspective for the study of organizational change needs to be acknowledged.

Silverman notes that many of the theoretical formulations give emphasis to external factors as the sources of change. Silverman depicts this as inadequate because it 'precludes' (1968: 231) the endogenous sources of change in organizations:

> The treatment of how pressures for change arise within organizations would require a systematic analysis of the conflicts of interest that may exist and of the balance of power that structures their outcome. (1968: 231)

This is the familiar charge that the systems-in-environments model does not deal with endogenously caused conflict, such as occurs when the dissatisfaction of employees with their effort-bargain erupts, after a period, in overt conflict such as a strike. But are such events really omitted from the framework of structural-functionalism and systems theory? A consideration of this question requires a discussion of the concept of exogenous change in systems theory.

A certain amount of criticism has attached to the notion in the structural-functional paradigm that change comes, initially, from outside the social system. This has been taken as excluding immanent changes resulting from class conflict or similar inter-group strife. In the Marxist version of social change from class conflict, this is in turn caused by changes in the relations of production (property and other economic relationships), which are in turn causally related to changes in the means of production, the technology of manufacture, etc. These changes are within society if this is taken to mean the physically defined, geographically-bounded nation state. However they are outside the social system which is the analytically defined abstraction of the social relationships. Technology, climate, imported goods, and even population are physical properties impinging on the social system of the society, but they are not inside the social system, they are outside it. Similarly, changes brought about by new ideas (religion, science, etc.) are to be classified as emanating from the cultural system of the society (or any other society). Once again, their impact is on the social system from outside. Once these terminological points are made clear, much of the controversy over the notion of external origins of disequilibrium is shown to be misplaced. Almost all of the major and classical sociological theories of change involve, in these terms, disequilibrating forces on the social system from outside; technology in Marxism; industrialization in Durkheim's writing. Systems perspective, with its notions of endogenous and exogenous, does not preclude either Marxian or Durkheimian types of social theory.

Whilst the logic of the structural-functional position may not have been prosecuted fully enough in organization studies (this is discussed further in Chapter 5), the idea of the contrast between effective and ineffective structures is basic, and so, of necessity, is the empirical study of disequilibrium as well as equilibria. Hence, the charge that structural-functionalism disregards disequilibria and change, could only be true to the extent that structural-functionalism denies its own logic.

Structural-functional and systems theories posit an equilibrium from which an organization may be displaced only by external impetus (Parsons, 1951). But they also insist that any disturbances take time to work through to equilibrium. Hence, in the case of ongoing hostility in industrial relations, the strike is not a sudden ('immanent' in Silverman's terms) move from equilibrium during the period of relatively latent hostility which preceded it. There were strains in the latency sub-system (the distrust between workers and managers). Hence the oft-given example of purely endogenous change, on-going industrial relations struggle, is not incompatible with structural-functional or systems theory. The analysis of such events in such language may seem strange, the language unfamiliar and there may even be nothing gained in explanation of these particular events by making such a transformation. But the point for the present argument is that such phenomena are compatible with the structural-functional or systems model.

Silverman develops his theme with regard to the treatment of power:

> Similarly, power is to be treated as 'the generalized capacity to mobilize resources in the interests of attainment of a system goal'. Thus we are not to be concerned with the causes of the distribution of power, only with the consequences (for the system) of its use. (1968: 229)

The definition precludes consideration of the ways in which power can be used to further the interests of the holder. But it is questionable whether the definition quoted has had much impact on organizational sociology. Perhaps the most influential formulation is that of Weber (1968), for whom power is defined in interpersonal terms. It becomes authority through legitimation by being granted through the due processes of rational-legality. At this point the power exercised is presumably in the interests of the organization, or so the incumbent authority would judge. However, in the Weberian framework, power *per se* is interpersonal and it may or may not be seen as being wielded in the interests of the wider organization, and the framework makes explicit who does that judging: the official and his superiors. This conceptual scheme has been used in practice by organizational sociologists to analyse the way in which bureaucratic officials use their power and the apparatus of bureaucracy to protect themselves (Crozier, 1964). Again, another major conception of power, derived from the Weberian, is that of Blau who sees its origins in exchange and dependency. Using such a conception in empirical studies, power is explained as arising from differential expertise between employees (Blau, 1973). A further explanatory theory stresses coping with organizational contingencies as a source of power (Crozier, 1964; Hickson *et al.*, 1971; Hinings *et al.*, 1974). This latter is inherently based upon the systems model, for it is the system which determines which contingencies are important. Thus the systems- and structural-functional-based conceptions of power differ from that quoted by Silverman, and explain causes as well as consequences, in terms of vertical distribution, horizontal distribution, rational-legal, expertise, professional, exchange and other bases.

Conclusions

A number of the criticisms of the structural-functionalist approach to the study of organizations have been reviewed and shown to be false. Structural-functionalism does not assume that organizations are integrated through the values of their members; there are systemic means to attain adequate integration. There is nothing inherently tautologous about such structural-functional organization theories and they can be testable. As part of this, the survival criteria are particularly open to verification. Equilibrium is a key notion in the theory but there is no assumption that all organizations are actually in this state. Structural-functionalism conceives of organizations moving from equilibrium through disequilibrium to new states of equilibrium. This is part of the way in which the theory analyses organizational change. Thus phenomena of change and dynamics have a place within the structural-functional perspective. Whilst much of structural-functionalist enquiry is concerned with the functional consequences of structures, these feed back to cause structural change. Much of the analysis of change is concerned with exogenous stimuli and the account given differs from that offered in terms of the struggle between rival interest groups. While the latter is a useful contribution to the understanding of change there is no need to disparage the insights about change coming from the structural-functionalist paradigm. This implies that a fruitful approach would be to draw on both perspectives simultaneously and synthesize their knowledge in the study of organizations. However, certain commentators have argued against this as being either impossible or undesirable. Accordingly, the discussion turns now to the issue of the reconcilability of the structural-functional and conflict paradigms.

4

Paradigm incommensurability

The current theoretical analyses of sociological and organizational work classify them into a number of distinct theories such as structural-functionalism, power conflict and social action. Since each of these offers partial illumination of organizational phenomena it might seem reasonable to employ more than one simultaneously in order to give added explanatory power. Hage (1980) has called for this in the study of organizations. This might seem to be an eminently sensible way to resolve many of the issues raised by the critics. However, within the critical literature there are express warnings against such attempts at 'emasculation and incorporation within the functionalist problematic' (Burrell and Morgan, 1979: 397). The study of theory has led not a few to the view that theories reflect world-views which are not merely distinct but are mutually exclusive. They are seen to contain at their base assumptions which are irreconcilable one with another. And from Kuhn (1970) is taken the notion that if different theories are each paradigms then intercommunication between them is impossible.

In championing Social Action Theory, Silverman (1968) is not merely saying that it is sometimes useful to approach certain phenomena in this way, and that this can be added to the results of structural enquiry for a better understanding. Silverman equates each of these positions to the immanent or transcendental views, respectively. He then asserts the imperative that: ' . . . we must decide whether an "Immanent" or "Transcendental" model is more appropriate for the analysis of social systems' (1968: 231).

Fletcher (1969: 113) suggests that the issue should be resolved by seeing which of the two approaches is more useful as an explanatory device, and that the relative superiority of each approach may vary according to the phenomena to be explained. Such a position rests on the orthodox philosophy of science, and Silverman, in his reply, explicitly eschews this:

> According to Fletcher, 'Organicist theories are best challenged by an empirical contest: that is to discover the proportion of the variance in the

same variable that can be attributed to competing independent variables' (113). I think this misunderstands the nature of the assumptions upon which models are based. Models, as I understand them, rest on a series of meta-theoretical arguments which are not susceptible to empirical test. Variables are, therefore, not something 'out there' which competing models are used to explain; instead, one's perception and definition of a variable depends on the model being employed. The 'needs' of Systems, to take one example, only becomes a variable within the terms of a certain analytical framework. 'The choice of syntax and vocabulary', as Laing has put it, 'are political acts which define and circumscribe the manner in which "facts" are to be experienced'. (1969: 420)

Silverman disavows eclecticism because he rejects the notion of the resolution of theoretical debate in science through empirical testing. Yet it is just such a doctrine which has been one of the cornerstones of the ideas of tolerance and pluralism as values within social science. Again, in his reply to Mouzelis (1969), Silverman explicitly states that the approaches of social action and structural-functionalism are not complementary but competing. For Silverman each enshrines a separate world-view, including a distinct epistemology for the social sciences:

> Mouzelis' argument is rather different. He appears to acknowledge the status of Structural-Functionalism and Action as models but suggests that they should be regarded as 'not mutually incompatible but complementary' (111). In support of this conclusion, he points out that both are capable of explaining conflict, change and (presumably) stability. Now I do not deny that this is so. However, it seems to me that this strengthens the case for regarding them as competing rather than as complementary frames of reference. The positivist Systems perspective equates the natural and social worlds and purports to show how transcendental systems define Man's behaviour. The action perspective, drawing on Weber and Schutz, points out the socially constructed, meaningful nature of social life and emphasizes a separate logic for the social sciences. The 'major obstacle to the growth of sociological theory' to use the phrase with which Mouzelis begins his remarks, may well arise in the attempts to impose a false unity on these two approaches, often ignoring the fundamental questions raised by the differences between them. (1969: 421)

Silverman goes on to cite Berger and Luckmann's *The Social Construction of Reality: A Treatise in the Sociology of Knowledge* (1966), and quotes approvingly from Dawe that: ' . . . the conflict between the two approaches rests "upon two central problems which represent conflicting social and moral concerns" (the problems of order and of human control)' (1969: 421).

In the case of Burrell and Morgan (1979), they discern four fundamental philosophical dimensions which underlie sociological and organizational analysis: ontology (nominalism *v.* realism), epistemology (anti-positivism *v.* positivism), human nature (voluntarism *v.* determinism) and methodology (ideographic *v.* nomothetic). They analyse and classify sociological and organizational work in these terms. This involves a consideration of the fundamental logic of these positions and of the way it unfolds in, and guides, empirical enquiry. The philosophical dimensions lead to a fourfold typology of sociological paradigms according to two underlying dimensions of subjective-objective and regulation-radical change: radical humanism, interpretive sociology, radical structuralism and functionalist sociology (Burrell and Morgan, 1979: 23). These in turn underpin four types of organizational analysis: anti-organization theory, interpretism, radical organization theory and functionalist organization theory. They explicitly disavow the evaluation of one paradigm in terms of another (Burrell and Morgan, 1979: 395). Burrell and Morgan are concerned, they state, only with the analysis of each paradigm in its own terms (1979: 35). Burrell and Morgan see the four paradigms as exclusive and not reducible to one another. They can each be developed but no merging is possible. They are explicit that this should not be taken as a call for synthesis as the distinct paradigms are irreconcilable. An attempt to combine them would only lead to the subordination and incorporation of one paradigm to another:

> In essence, what we are advocating in relation to developments within these paradigms amounts to a form of isolationism. We firmly believe that each of the paradigms can only establish itself at the level of organisational analysis if it is true to itself. Contrary to the widely held belief that synthesis and mediation between paradigms is what is required, we argue that the real need is for paradigmatic closure. In order to avoid emasculation and incorporation within the functionalist problematic, the paradigms need to provide a basis for their self-preservation by developing on their own account. Insofar as they take functionalism as their reference point, it is unlikely that they will develop far beyond their present embryonic state – they will not develop coherent alternatives to the functionalist point of view. This conclusion is firmly in line with the perspective we have adopted throughout this work in suggesting that the paradigms reflect four alternative realities. They stand as four mutually exclusive ways of seeing the world. One of the major conclusions prompted by our journey through the realms of social theory, therefore, is that organisation theorists face a range of choices with regard to the nature of the assumptions which underwrite their point of view. For those who wish to leave the functionalist orthodoxy behind, many avenues offer themselves for exploration. (Burrell and Morgan, 1979: 397).

This is congruent with the philosophical-theoretical position taken throughout their volume. If implemented it would mean that the four paradigms would continue being developed in parallel. The literature on organizations would be subject to the factionalism of relativism without hope of integration. And indeed this is what Burrell and Morgan are arguing for. The implication they draw for the institution of organization studies is that it needs to eschew integration based on synthesis or eclecticism:

> Theories which seek to incorporate different levels of analysis do not always give the all round view which is sometimes sought. They may merely serve to strengthen and reinforce an approach which is, in essence, very narrowly founded. This is an issue which has considerable relevance for the organisation of research activities within social science as a whole. Multi-disciplinary research teams, panels of advisers, grant-awarding bodies and university departments are growing in both numbers and importance, a development which is helping to broaden what are seen as the limited perspectives which have characterized the past. The nature of our four paradigms, however, clearly illustrates that the problem of obtaining an all round perspective is much more far reaching than this.

> The path to the future is wide open. It is clear that the choices available to organisational analysts are extremely wide. (Burrell and Morgan, 1979: 401)

The implication is that social enquiry will continue as a set of litera-tures proceeding in parallel but with no reconciliation or unity. Such a position follows from their premise that paradigms are irreconcilable:

> . . . the four paradigms are mutually exclusive . . . A synthesis is not possible, since in their pure forms they are contradictory, being based on at least one set of opposing meta-theoretical assumptions. They are alternatives, in the sense that one *can* operate in different paradigms sequentially over time, but mutually exclusive, in the sense that one can-not operate in more than one paradigm at any given point in time, since in accepting the assumptions of one, we defy the assumptions of all the others. (Burrell and Morgan, 1979: 25; emphasis as in original)

Burrell and Morgan base their notion of paradigm (1979: 24) on that of Kuhn (1970). But is Burrell and Morgan's notion of paradigm consistent with Kuhn's conception? Central to Kuhn's definition of paradigm is the idea of incommensurability, i.e. that each paradigm is the way of seeing of a distinct community of scientists and that this prevents them from under-standing and communicating with the others. Burrell and Morgan classify Kuhn's view of science as within the ambit of phenomenological approaches to the philosophy of science. This refers to the notions of paradigms as ways of thinking which structure the perceptions of those individuals and groups who hold them (Burrell and Morgan, 1979: 255). While this element is there in Kuhn's formulation, to locate Kuhn within a discussion of phenomenology is to misunderstand his work. Kuhn stresses that science is a cumulative business of study, theory construction and empirical testing. In that sense he is at one with conventional philosophies of science (Popper, 1945; Toulmin, 1962). His particular point is that this is a process characterized, historically, by discontinuities and by discussion which is only partially open. Kuhn does not argue that in the long run truth tends not to triumph, only that the road can be an uneven one in the short run. Kuhn's contribution is essentially about the historical social processes in science, it is not a reformulation of the philosophy of science. It enriches but does not replace the account offered by Popper and Toulmin. In the 'Postscript–1969' to his second edition of *The Structure of Scientific Revolutions* Kuhn explicitly disavows relativism:

> Later scientific theories are better than earlier ones for solving puzzles in the often quite different environments to which they are applied. That is not a relativist's position, and it displays the sense in which I am a convinced believer in scientific progress. (1970: 206)

While reaffirming the idea of scientific paradigms as rival gestalts often subject to incommensurability in their attempts at intercommunication, Kuhn is at pains to distinguish his thesis from that of science as a subjective and irrational activity. He insists that there is a role for reason in arguments between paradigms (Kuhn, 1970: 199). Further such reasoning and argument are part of the process which leads to the acceptance of a new theory and the development of knowledge within the scientific collective. Likewise criteria employed in theory choice include those which feature prominently in the orthodox philosophy of science ' . . . accuracy, simplicity, fruitfulness and the like . . . ' (Kuhn, 1970: 199). Nor is the incommensurability between paradigms total or permanent. The processes of translation, persuasion and conversion are all evoked by Kuhn, though the latter, being a 'gestalt switch' (1970: 204), is less frequent for individuals. Kuhn's thesis thus remains that scientific development is marked by discontinuities, and that the collective makes the transition more often than do individuals, but it is far from arguing for untrammelled subjectivism, relativism, complete incommensurability, or paradigms as permanently irreconcilable. While in Kuhn's model the paradigm communities remain fixed and in opposition for some time, it would appear that they eventually intercommunicate and become mutually resolved, after generations perhaps. The paradigms may remain distinct but the community gains an ability to work with their different languages, to communicate and to utilize them in a complementary way. At least this appears to have happened in the case of physics, the example used by Kuhn (1970). In the long run even paradigms may become modalities in the open discussion within the scientific community. If this can happen in physics why not in sociology?

Thus Burrell and Morgan have overstated the extent to which Kuhnian paradigms are mutually exclusive. On the Kuhnian analysis this is true for certain periods but eventually some transcendent comprehension of rival theories is possible. It is a misappreciation of the notion of paradigms to see in them assumptions which make each contradictory to the other. This may well hold for the divergent philosophical dimensions which Burrell and Morgan deploy (1979: 1), but it is not true for theories in science even when they are sufficiently differentiated to be labelled paradigms in a Kuhnian analysis. Thus use of the term 'paradigm' by Burrell and Morgan is no proof of their doctrine of paradigmatic isolationism.

Turning to sociological theories, is it cogent to see them as necessarily isolationist? Is there something in their subject matter which leads them to such irreconcilability?

On the logical compatibility of functionalism and Radical Structuralism

Burrell and Morgan argue that synthesis is not possible between their sociological paradigms. In particular, functionalism is depicted as being incompatible with radical structuralist change-orientated models:

> . . . the factional and catastrophic models emphasise and reflect an underlying view of society characteristic of the radical structuralist as opposed to the functionalist paradigm. Whilst functionalists may be able to incorporate and use these models within the framework of their analysis, taken to their logical conclusion the two models belong to a quite different reality. They stress how social formations have inbuilt tendencies towards radical change rather than the maintenance of a regulated order. (Burrell and Morgan, 1979: 400)

However, this conclusion follows uneasily from their earlier discussion in which theories of the systems type are ranged along a continuum from those emphasizing order and stability, the mechanical, to those emphasizing conflict and change, the catastrophe theories (Burrell and Morgan, 1979: 67). The modern statement of functionalism is of a relatively open and flexible framework, which does not presume that everything is functional for everything else. This kind of fallacy is explicitly disavowed by Merton (1949) in his now classic exposition. Likewise, the postulate that every structure has a function is not made. And the possibility is raised explicitly that certain structures create strains for other elements in the society. This is discussed in terms of dysfunctions. It is explicitly noted that such strains and dysfunctions may be sources of change in the social system. Once one has the notion that the outputs of one sub-system may be dysfunctional for other parts then the essential notion of conflict has been introduced. If the theory goes further and postulates that the flows between the parts are such that the continuing functioning of the system will produce increasing dysfunctions which will eventually overstrain the system, causing breakdown and subsequent reorganization, then the ideas of contradiction and crisis have been stated, in systems rather than Marxian terms. Indeed, Merton has argued for this theoretical convergence in his statement that the structural analysis of society involves the stipulation:

> *That* structural analysis in sociology involves the confluence of ideas deriving principally from Durkheim and Marx. Far from being contradictory as has sometimes been assumed, basic ideas drawn from their work have been found to be complementary . . . For examples, the basic concepts of 'contradictions' in the one and of 'dysfunctions' in the other . . . (1975: 32; emphasis as in original)

The logic of functionalist enquiry is a three-step process between two levels of analysis, system and sub-system, which goes: system, sub-system and system. In neo-Marxian (as opposed to purely social action approaches to conflict) the same three-step process is followed. The main elements of the capitalist system are charted, as in Marx's *Capital* (1954), where capital and labour are distinguished. The routine operation of capitalism is then shown to be detrimental to first the labouring classes and then to the capitalist classes. These problems culminate in economic crises which combine with social antagonisms between organized social classes to tear the capitalist system apart. Hence both functionalism and Marxian radical structuralism deal in analyses which combine the explication of the interactions of systems and sub-systems, and use the notion of circular chains of functions and dysfunctions to explain continuity and change. Marxism is at a lower level of analysis than functionalism as it is mainly concerned with certain historically specific structures, feudalism and capitalism, and their change. As such it should be seen as a sub-type of structural-functionalism which deals with those historical issues and which posits crisis and revolutionary change as the mechanisms of transition. To state this is to do exactly what Burrell and Morgan warned against: incorporating radical structuralism within the functionalist framework. Yet it seems that logically they are a sub-set of structural-functional-cum-systems theories. When Burrell and Morgan depict the five types of systems theories on the order-change dimension (1979: 67) it seems that they were correct in portraying it as a continuum with no watersheds sharply separating categories. It is a generic way of thinking with some differences in emphasis. Again the case is made for functionalist absorption by noting the isomorphism between the key functionalist concepts of system, function and change and the core radical structuralist ones of totality, structure, contradiction and crisis. Merton writes that his structural analysis:

> . . . connects with other sociological paradigms which, the polemics not withstanding, are anything but contradictory in much of what they sup-

pose or assert . . . recent work in structural analysis leads me to spheres of agreement and of complementarity rather than to the alleged basic contradictions between various sociological paradigms. (1975: 30)

In order to demonstrate that structural-functionalism and conflict theory are fundamentally compatible in their concepts, let us take two propositions quoted by Burrell and Morgan, one each from the functionalist and radical structuralist paradigms, and show how each can readily transliterate to the other. As a capsule statement of the axioms of functionalism let us take Radcliffe-Brown's statement, and call this proposition 1:

1. The concept of function as here defined thus involves the notion of a *structure* consisting of a *set of relations* amongst *unit entities*, the *continuity* of the structure being maintained by a *life-process* made up of the *activities* of the constituent units. (1952: 180; quoted in Burrell and Morgan, 1979: 52, emphases as in original)

As a basic statement of Radical Structuralism let us edit two statements from Rex's schema and call this postulate 2:

2. [S]ocial systems may be thought of as involving conflict situations at central points . . . The existence of such a situation tends to produce not a unitary but a *plural society*, in which there are two or more classes . . . The activities of the members [of the classes] . . . must be explained by reference to the group's interests in the conflict situation. (Rex, 1961: 129; quoted in Burrell and Morgan, 1979: 353, emphasis as in original)

To show that they are not incompatible logically let us show how proposition 1 can be transposed into proposition 2 without breaking the laws of logic. This can be largely accomplished by introducing just four propositions, and done completely with six propositions:

3. The set of relationships between unit entities, includes relationships which are positive, in that they aid the recipient unit entity in its continuity and development, and relationships which are negative, in that they impair the continuity and development of the recipient unit entity.

4. Where relationships between any two unit entities include a negative relationship this will be called a situation of conflict.

5. Unit entities involved in conflict situations with each other will be termed classes.

6. Situations of conflict between classes are endemic in social systems (i.e. negative relationships between unit entities are frequent and chronic).

7. Social systems may be thought of as involving conflict situations at central points. The existence of such a situation tends to produce not a unitary but a plural society, in which there are two or more classes.

8. The behaviour of members of unit entities is explicable in terms of the relationships between the unit entities.
9. For classes in conflict the behaviour of the members is explicable in terms of their class interest in the conflict.
10. The activities of the members of the classes must be explained by reference to the group's interests in the conflict situation.

Hence the proposition of Rex, number 2, can be deduced from Radcliffe-Brown's statement, number 1, with the addition of just six other propositions. Of these 3 is an important conceptual point, about flows between entities being either positive or negative. Propositions 4 and 5 are just language respecifications. Proposition 6 is an important theoretical point. It is a key assertion of neo-Marxism and radical Weberian positions. It is necessary to include this to meet Rex's statement that conflict occurs at central points, i.e. conflict does not merely exist, it is highly salient. With these four statements, involving the addition of only two new premises (3 and 6), proposition 7 can be deduced which is the structural heart of Rex's conflict theory. The rest of Rex's statement is a stipulation that members' behaviour should be explained in terms of this structural conflict. It is really just a specification that the explanation made at one level of analysis (classes) is to be used at another (individuals). This is done here through making this transformation explicit in proposition 8. Proposition 9 completes this transformation by labelling the significance for the individual actor of negative relationships (class conflict) as class interest. These two propositions allow 10 to be deduced from 7.

To summarize, propositions 4, 5 and 9 are just statements of terminological conventions. Proposition 8 is a statement that what holds at one level holds at another. The new premises are contained in 3 and 6: proposition 3 is compatible with the contemporary functionalist framework of Merton. Proposition 6 is the sole radical structuralist premise. Once proposition 3 has been granted the only point at issue is whether negative relationships between unit entities are a pervasive and persistent feature of the social system. This is a theoretical point but it is also one which is empirically testable. What is the balance of positive and negative transactions between classes in capitalist societies? How far does it vary between societies of the capitalist type? Is it changing with respect to time? These then are issues which can be illuminated by empirical social analysis. The point at issue here is that the difference between Radcliffe-Brown's statement and Rex's, when stripped of terminological differences and the like, is one about the pervasiveness of negative linkages in the social system. This is a matter of degree. It is not a fundamental category difference. The positions of Radcliffe-Brown and Rex are not identical but neither are they based on diametrically opposite concepts, and they can be accommodated within the same (structuralist-systems) framework. They are not logically incompatible.

In sociological theories of society, accommodation of the functionalist and radical structuralist paradigms is logically possible and achievable in substance. The questions arise as to whether such a resolution of functionalist and radical structuralist paradigms is either possible or desirable in organization studies. Each will be considered in turn. While the major explicit purpose of Burrell and Morgan (1979) is the delineation of sociological-philosophic theories and the implications of each for the study of organizations, the radical structuralist approach, in their formulation, is equated with the neo-Marxian programmatic, i.e. societal-level analysis, in which there is little interest in organizations, *per se*. But this is based on the equation of systems models of the 'factional' and 'catastrophe' type with neo-Marxian theory. It would seem that such models in social science are not so restricted. Theories of organization exist which deal with factionalism and catastrophes, two terms which Burrell and Morgan (1979) use to identify radical structuralist models. The way ethnic and other ascriptions promote factions within work-groups has been dealt with for several decades in industrial sociology (Miller and Form, 1964). The tendencies to factionalism in management stemming from rivalries over career (Burns and Stalker, 1961) and education (Dalton, 1959) and producing the internal politics of organization (Burns and Stalker, 1961; Pettigrew, 1973) has been recognized in the literature on organizations. The models of organizational pathologies resulting from inter-group rivalry or personal frustration are quite customarily analysed as vicious cycles in organizational sociology and psychology (Crozier, 1964; Argyris, 1964; Walton, 1969). There is a management literature which deals with the dynamics of corporate collapse involving financial and economic contradictions (Argenti, 1976). The theoretical gambits of factionalism and contradiction are by no means confined to neo-Marxians or radical Weberians. Burrell and Morgan (1979) equate factional and catastrophe models with revolutionary social programmes. However, there is nothing in the logic of factional or catastrophe models which require that they take a societal rather than an organizational focus, and they have been utilized in substantive work on organizations.

Moreover, they have been used in synthesis with functionalist theorizing about organizations. In Crozier's (1964) study of French organizations the bureaucratic model of functioning is explicated jointly with the analysis of cleavages between status levels and resultant dysfunctions of inadequate vertical communications. Burns and Stalker (1961) locate their discussion of political processes within their analysis of the different structures, mechanistic and organic, which are necessary in conditions of low and high technological and market change, respectively. They go on to suggest that political activity is greater in organic structures due to absence of hierarchically imposed role definitions and consequent greater room for manoeuvre and potential for conflict. Further evidence of the fruitfulness of using functionalist and conflict perspectives on the study of organizations is the work of Hage (1980). This analyses organization structures in terms of their functioning and their internal conflicts. Thus functionalist analysis, with its emphasis on structures, contributive processes and contingent variation can, and has been, combined with perspectives emphasizing dissensus, antagonism, combativeness and counter-productivity.

However, there remains one area of difficulty in attempts to reconcile Radical Structuralism with functionalist Organization Theory. This is the divergent levels of analysis. Radical Structuralism is at the societal level and much of the concern of Organization Theory is at the organizational level. To qualify as Radical Structuralism an organizational analysis would need to establish significance in terms of radical change at the societal level.

At this point the reconciliation falters. For to take this step involves accepting the principle that organizational analysis must show a meaning in terms of conflict and change in the wider social system. Some analyses may do so. But to acknowledge this as a desideratum is to deny organizational phenomena as fit topics of enquiry in their own right. Organizational studies would be subordinated to the programmatic of Radical Structuralism.

This raises the issue of whether the prime focus for organizational studies should be the society rather than the organization. The discussion will turn to this presently (in Chapter 11). It would seem that there is no valid reason why organizational studies, in its entirety, must adopt Radical Structuralism as the master framework. Thus the research agenda and problem focus of Radical Structuralism and functionalist organizational enquiry are not identical. But this reflects a divergence of values, social position and political world-view rather than being based on logical incompatibility or incommensurability between scientific paradigms. For instance, Marxian social critics sometimes explain the occurrence of the crisis of capitalism in Britain before certain other capitalist countries, in terms of the inefficiencies in British industry through poor organization because of the class-stratified nature of the companies. This explanation draws, in part, on the kind of organizational analysis made by Crozier (1964). Thus Marxian structuralism is compatible technically with organizational-level research. Again, the continuation of domination in capitalist and state socialist countries has been related to the effectiveness of the internal security forces. Here the intra-organizational characteristics of the police are being placed within radical Weberian structuralism.

Divergences between organizational analysis and Radical Structuralism will remain because of different foci of attention and social visions, but this is not due to purely intellectual barriers to reconciliation such as paradigm incommensurability. Organization studies is not condemned to the fractionation and pluralistic ignorance of paradigmatic separate development. Synthesis of functionalist and conflict perspectives in organization studies is possible and has begun. In terms of organizational-level analysis, the paradigms are capable of synthesis, and have been so combined.

Conclusions

The notion of the irreconcilability of paradigms in Organization Theory has been shown to be inappropriate. This has involved a scrutiny of the 'received Kuhn' in order to breach the idea that paradigms in his thesis are permanently non-intercommunicating. Kuhn is shown to adhere to the conventional philosophy of science view that as science progresses it comes to transcend any particular paradigm. In practice, scientific paradigms become commensurable and this opens the door to the possibility of synthesis. The sociological theories of structural-functionalism and conflict theory have been shown to be logically compatible, each can be derived from the other. One of the fundamental axioms of sociological theory is that social phenomena can be explained in terms of the interactions between sub-systems. Both structural-functionalism and Marxism are built on this axiom and, indeed, the latter is a special case of the former theory.

5

Inadequate theory and methods

Whereas organization studies is sometimes criticized for drawing on theories such as structural-functionalism which are felt to be misguided, a further criticism is that the subject does not even do justice to the structural-functionalist paradigm. Thus research into organizations is seen as frequently failing to live up to the standard required for an enquiry to be genuinely about structures and their functioning. The origin of this problem lies in deficient methods founded in erroneous scientism. Going further, critics have asserted that organization studies is largely devoid of theory and, even, that what purport to be theories are not really. In this chapter each of these points will be considered sequentially.

In discussing the functionalist paradigm Burrell and Morgan conclude that 'there is room for a questioning of assumptions with regard to ontology within the bounds of the functionalist paradigm' (1979: 398). They write:

> Organisation theorists frequently treat the existence of organisations in a hard, concrete sense as taken for granted. They assume that there are real phenomena which can be measured through the nomothetic methods which dominate empirical research in this area . . . The notion that one can measure an organisation as an empirical facticity is as extreme as the notion that organisations do not exist. (Burrell and Morgan, 1979: 398)

Their critique here displays lines of continuity with Silverman (1968, 1970) in his charge of reification against organizational constructs. And it is noticeable that Burrell and Morgan use this term repeatedly in their volume (1979: 53, 160, 196, 201, 218, 287, 312, 324, 374). They go on to characterize present methods as reflecting such misconceptions:

> The implications of this issue can perhaps be most forcefully expressed by suggesting that there is a need for organization theorists to adopt methods of study which are true to the nature of the phenomena which they are attempting to investigate. Our review of the dominant orthodoxy within organization theory has shown that a large proportion of empirical research is based upon highly objectivist assumptions. The tendency in much empirical research has been for methodologies to

> dominate other assumptions in relation to the ontological, epistemological and human nature strands of our analytical scheme. The wholesale incorporation of methods and techniques taken directly from the natural sciences needs to be severely questioned. The problem of developing methods appropriate to the nature of the phenomena to be studied remains one of the most pressing issues within the whole realm of social science research. (Burrell and Morgan, 1979: 398)

Likewise the theory used in functionalist organization analysis is seen as being deficient in terms of structural-functionalism in sociological theory. Burrell and Morgan describe the evolution of structural-functionalist models (1979: 49). This involves a recognition of the functioning of societies as a set of processes. These take the form of relations between people which in turn make up the social structure. Such was the framework laid out by Radcliffe-Brown (Burrell and Morgan, 1979: 51). Such reasoning led him to argue that the study of functional processes (social physiology) has to accompany the study of structures (social morphology) (Burrell and Morgan, 1979: 52). This is then used by Burrell and Morgan as part of an attack on structural-functionalism as practised in empirical research, as being over-concerned with structures to the detriment of an analysis of functioning:

> In defiance (or at least ignorance) of his warning that 'the social structure as a whole can only be observed in its functioning', the notion of structure has become increasingly reified as some social theorists sought to identify its key elements. The 'search for structure' has led to an increasingly hard and indiscriminate application of the models and methods of the natural sciences to the study of social phenomena. In an extreme though pervasive form, much of contemporary structural functionalism manifests itself in terms of a host of empirical snapshots of reified social structure. In an attempt to focus upon, define and measure 'structures', the notion of functional process – so central to the conceptualisations of both Malinowski and Radcliffe-Brown – has been lost. There has been a swing to a highly objectified and static view of social reality – towards a positivism of an extreme, narrowly empirical and, indeed, atheoretical form. (1979: 53)

In an accompanying footnote Burrell and Morgan (1979: 109) make it clear that organizational research exemplifies this pathology. It is linked to methodological strictures that empirical work is too static, concentrating on snapshots and synchronic comparisons. This is a more familiar criticism of research in organizational structure, but when related back to Radcliffe-Brown's theoretical framework it is used by Burrell and Morgan to assert that the approach is theoretically inadequate:

> Many theorists working under the banner of systems theory, for example, have concerned themselves with the measurement of structures, with the social morphology of systems. There are many prominent examples within the field of organization studies. The work of the Aston

group of researchers, for example, Pugh and Hickson (1976), Richard Hall (1972) and almost any issue of *Administrative Science Quarterly* present excellent illustrations. Their systems models are constructed around *structural* notions such as size, configuration, centralisation, technology, environmental domain, etc. . . . these lines of development are open to the same sort of evaluation and criticism which we have discussed in relation to structural functionalists who have focused upon social morphology and social physiology. The social morphologists have tended to emphasize structure at the expense of process and, along with the social physiologists, have tended to provide explanations of social affairs which are geared to providing explanations of the *status quo*. Both have largely ignored or underplayed the third set of problems identified by Radcliffe-Brown – those of social development. System theorists who base their work upon mechanical and organismic models are not well equipped to explain situations in which the elaboration and change of basic structures are the essential features of the phenomena under investigation. They find difficulty in handling the problem of morphogenesis and discontinuous forms of change which lead to system disintegration, disappearance or destruction. (1979: 64)

Thus the structural-functional approach to organizations is attacked as not even cogent in terms of structural-functionalism. Burrell and Morgan complete their cameo of modern organizational analysis of the structural kind by linking its intellectual decline with concerns for applications:

Fostered by utilitarian demands for pragmatic theory and research geared to piecemeal social engineering – political, managerial and the like – theoretical insights have been largely submerged under a deluge of empirical research. (1979: 57)

Burrell and Morgan's volume is highly critical of the structural organizational analysis, notwithstanding their espousal of the doctrine that each paradigm has value in its own right. The reply mounted here will consider in turn each of their criticisms: objectivist philosophical assumptions, the inadequate methods, the inadequate structural-functionalism and the atheoretical nature of organization studies.

Burrell and Morgan base their philosophical analysis on four fundamental distinctions (about 'ontology, epistemology, human nature and methodology') which combine to form two frequently encountered positions: the subjectivist approach to social science (nominalism, anti-positivism, voluntarism and ideographic) and the objectivist approach to social science (realism, positivism, determinism and nomothetic) (1979: 3). To classify nominalism with anti-positivism and subjectivism is strange, since one of the leading exponents of positivism, Popper, defines this as being nominalist. Popper (1945) distinguishes nominalism from essentialism. The latter tries to answer questions about the essence of things. The former, nominalism, accepts that these may remain unknowable and that the task of science is to explain patterns in the symbols we perceive, admitting that these may only be surface manifestations of deeper entities. This then leads to the philosophical doctrine of coherency. Scientific explanation is the finding of regularities in phenomena and bringing them 'together' through a symbol system, a theory, which makes what may seem to be disparate phenomena related and thus coherent (Toulmin, 1962). It is often contrasted with the doctrine of the correspondence theory of truth, which holds that science is about finding the correspondence between phenomena and their abstract symbolizations. Modern philosophers of science tend to hold to the view that the coherence doctrine is a valid account of science whereas the correspondence theory is not. Burrell and Morgan (1979) use nominalism to mean subjective perceptions and distinguish this from realism which means, in their work, the doctrine that the social world exists apart from peoples' perception of it, and that it has existence in the same sense as natural objects. Thus they characterize the nominalism–realism distinction as a dimension of ontology, as they define and use that term. Philosophers of science have been at some pains to point out that scientific theories do not give ontological status to their concepts (Toulmin, 1962). Concepts are constructs, i.e. artificial and man-made efforts to understand the buzzing world of phenomena. Particle physics is the study of vapour trails in chambers, whether the particles exist in an ontological sense is an irrelevant question. Constructs in science do not have to pass tests for tangibility ('can you see it, touch it, smell it') to be legitimate elements in a scientific argument. Realism is an extra-scientific doctrine which is not implied in sociological theories which posit a social world independent of the immediate perceptions of individuals. Researchers who characterize organizations as having collectivity-level properties of structure such as centralization or formalization (e.g. Pugh and Hickson, 1976; Hage, 1980) are not thereby attributing ontology to their constructs. Such researchers are nominalists. Nominalism is the accepted doctrine in social science, certainly of the conventional, positivist kind. When Burrell and Morgan diagram the objectivist approach to social science and locate it at the realism end of the nominalism–realism continuum their schematic is confused (1979: 3).

Similar remarks apply to the second component of realism in the definition of Burrell and Morgan. They write of the realism–nominalism continuum as contrasting: ' . . . whether "reality" is of an "objective" nature, or the product of individual cognition; whether "reality" is a given "out there" in the world, or the product of one's mind' (1979: 1). Burrell and Morgan equate realism with the imputation of physical existence to the social world: 'Realism, on the other hand, postulates that the social world external to individual cognition is a real world made up of *hard, tangible* and relatively immutable structures.' 'For the realist, the social world has an existence which is as *hard* and *concrete* as the natural world' (1979: 4; emphasis added). Considerable debate in philosophy has revolved around the issue of whether what is known is anything other than the content of one's own mind. Since almost all sociological doctrines take it as axiomatic that there is more than one actor in the world, they are logically incompatible with such philosophies. The usual rendering of the problem in social philosophy is less extreme and may contrast the subjective perceptions of social actors with the idea of a transcendent reality. However transcendent notions of society or organizations or social class as existing in a literal sense, as do persons or tables, is a doctrine in little use in sociology. Society and organization, as with social forces, or causal factors or anomie, are constructs. They are man-made postulates which have some utility in clarifying our experience of the world. The phenomena which make them up, in a concrete sense, are the actions and perceptions of individuals: people communicating, trading, ordering, coercing and loving each other. The notion of society or the organization as a machine may be used as a metaphor, but this is not to be taken literally.

The tradition which emphasizes external constraint, as in the early Durkheim (1938), is talking about norms which exist (before) and which determine the actor, but they are carried by, and acted out by, other actors. For the single individual, social constraint is out there, independent of the person, and therefore thing-like, but it is made up of the actions of others. It does not exist above and outside like the moon. Again, Durkheim's notion of collective consciousness can be understood as a shared way of thinking common to members of a society. In that sense it transcends the individual, but in that sense only. This is the customary interpretation of this issue within contemporary sociology.

In making their analysis Burrell and Morgan (1979) misrepresent philosophy and the philosophical basis of sociological theory. To talk of the philosophical discourse about reality which ranges from solipsism through to transcendentalism is to cover a range which sociological theory does not embrace. It is based on a more limited range of that dimension. Burrell and Morgan are being too philosophical in that regard. Hence the continuum of nominalism to realism is one that is largely irrelevant for understanding and discriminating between social theories. The whole discussion of realism by Burrell and Morgan is superfluous to an analysis of functionalism in sociology or in organization studies. Their exegesis of the philosophical basis of sociology and Organization Theory, which is supposed to clarify, contains at its core a misunderstanding of both philosophy and social theory.

It follows also from this that by not appreciating that nominalism is integral to any science, including social science, they underestimate the importance in scientific research of establishing patterns in data, of revealing regularities in evidence which seeks to associate variables. The interpretation of such patterns involves theory. But the discovery of regularities serves as a stimulus to theory building and helps to delimit it to sensible channels. Moreover testing between rival theories involves further research to see exactly which of the differing, theoretically expected patterns are seen in the data. What Burrell and Morgan (1979) have provided is a view of social knowledge which dwells on the theoretical moment but which pays scarce attention to the empirical moment.

The argument of Burrell and Morgan, that functionalist organization studies is based on objectivist philosophical assumptions of an extreme and questionable kind has been shown to be misguided. The discussion now turns to their assertions that the 'objectivist' methods employed are inappropriate to the object of study, organizations. A consideration of this also necessitates an examination of the third major line of criticism of Burrell and Morgan: that organization studies does not do justice to structural-functional theory. Both of these propositions will be treated together in this exposition. Clegg and Dunkerley (1980) are similarly concerned about scientistic approaches to organizations which mistakenly treat structures as objects and attempt to prove their existence through statistical tests.

Clegg and Dunkerley assert that the Aston studies are a 'fetishistic exercise in objectification' (1980: 260), based upon seeking to prove the existence of organizations through Guttman scaling (1980: 260). And that this is apiece with science as a manipulative activity (1980: 257).

Their criticism is that in order to attain control organizations must first be objectified (Clegg and Dunkerley, 1980: 258). This is done through researchers seeking to show that organizations exist through using Guttman scales. Clegg and Dunkerley show, however, that Guttman scales are only devices for checking the ordinal ordering of data in any particular set (1980: 259). They hold that this means that such scales are not really scientific measurement, and that the task of devising general measurement procedures has fallen into error (1980: 260). There are several problems with this criticism. First, it is not clear why control in actual organizations is predicated upon, or assisted by, researchers convincing themselves that organizations are objects. For members of organizations their structures (i.e., the rules, authority levels, records, etc.) do stand as Durkheimian facticities, external to them and constraining them. But this would hold regardless of whether researchers somehow accord ontological status to organizations. The impact of the organization on a member would be appreciated by a Roman soldier, long before organizational research existed.

The Aston researchers sought to use Guttman scales to check that items formed into scales had the properties that such scales possess, i.e.

they lay along an underlying dimension which attained the ordinal level of measurement (Pugh and Hickson, 1976; Galtung, 1967). In the event, their scales mostly did not attain the high standards of reproducibility normally advised for Guttman scales and they were mostly treated as additive indices, a more ordinary kind of scale (Mansfield, 1973; Galtung, 1967). Their claim to being acceptable measurement rests mainly on the fact that they have revealed broadly similar patterns of correlation across diverse studies (Pugh and Hickson, 1976; Pugh and Hinings, 1976; Hickson and McMillan, 1981) and that they have not been shown to be any more unreliable or biased than the other main measures of structure, such as those developed by Hall (1963). More importantly for the present discussion they show signs of a useful degree of generality (Pugh, 1981). They were devised so as to be general in the referent of their items, that is to tap bureaucracy across a range of organizations and have been employed in that way, though necessitating some modification in some types of organizations (Pugh and Hinings, 1976; Hickson and McMillan, 1981). But none of this has ever been suggested by the Aston researchers as proving that organizations exist. The existence of more than one dimension of structure has been claimed (Pugh *et al.*, 1968, 1969) based on lack of correlation between some major structural scales, but this has been the subject of controversy (Child, 1972b). The postulation of the existence of a dimension means that patterns in data can be parsimoniously represented by an underlying factor. The dimension need not literally exist in an ontological sense. The postulate is a mental construct of the researcher which makes observed data more coherent. The discussion in the Aston literature about the existence or not of dimensions of organization structure, such as concentration of authority (Pugh *et al.*, 1968), is to be understood in these terms. It is not a claim to have empirically demonstrated organizations as ontologically existing. This interpretation is raised by Clegg and Dunkerley (1980) but appears to be a misunderstanding by them.

Burrell and Morgan (1979) develop their critique of contemporary comparative studies of organization structure by criticising them in two ways. First they say that they are too static, second they say that they are of structure when they should be of process. The distinction between structure and process is one which is often drawn today, usually to make a criticism of contemporary methodologies, the implication being drawn that alternative forms of enquiry are needed to capture process. The theoretical argument is made that it is through processes that organizations function, come into being, continue and change. Before accepting this argument it is worthwhile going back to the central arguments for the development of the structural approach to both organizations and sociology. This rests on the recognition that interactions between a person and others make up social and organizational life. These are often subtle, usually intangible and often changeable phenomena. However, certain relationships recur, and display regularities and patterns. Moreover much (though not necessarily all) that is consequential for questions of social stability and change, organization functioning and performance has to do with these processes. It is these recurrent patterns which are called a structure, as in social structure and organization structure. This is the structural paradigm. The long-run evaluations of this notion hinge on how far such an approach does explain questions of social stability and change, organization functioning and performance. At a lower level such patterns in process are conceptualized as variables such as centralization, specialization, communications and so on. The operational indicators of the concepts are admitted by their users to be imperfect and over the decades improvements are made. Contrast Whisler *et al.*'s (1967) index of centralization of decision-making as inequality of salary distribution with the Aston scale which measures how close to the centre decisions are taken (Pugh and Hickson, 1976). The concern in the comparative literature for measuring structure is not an oversight or a second best for the study of process. It is a deliberate implementation of the structural paradigm.

Burrell and Morgan's (1979) point is that modern organization research favours the study of structure over function. If this is true then it is a damaging criticism of organization studies in so far as it claims to be structural-functional. The accusation that organization studies is static and too structural refers to the practice of measuring different aspects of structure (such as specializations, centralization and so on) at one point in time in a set of organizations and then statistically relating these structural variables to each other by correlations and the like. At first glance it may seem reasonable for commentators such as Burrell and Morgan to see in this a neglect of the study of functioning. Yet one of the motives for using such a research design is to establish whether the variables are associated in a stable way. For example, size has been shown to relate to degree of specialization. When such associations, as reflected in correlations, are seen to exist not just in one data-set in one study, but in many different data-sets, then this is evidence for positing that the association is not adventitious but is a necessary connection. Size has repeatedly been shown to correlate, quite strongly, with specialization (Pugh and Hickson, 1976; Pugh and Hinings, 1976). This is evidence in support of the proposition that specialization is an elaboration of structure as size increases which helps the performance of the organization. In structural-functional terms it is asserting that the processes of individuals playing out roles in a way which recognizes specializations between them is functional for the continuity of the organization. Hence, the static correlation, when replicated, is interpreted by a model of the structural-functional kind. Structure is being understood as a stable pattern of relationships between people which provides a contribution to functioning. The latter refers to processes whereby people know what is expected of them and their colleagues and can therefore do their job, become knowledgeable in it, and understand interdependencies between themselves and others leading them to communicate and to dovetail their activities. In other words the social system is able to attain its objectives, socialize and motivate members, accomplish learning, cohere, survive and perhaps flourish. The interpretation is exactly one derived from the structural-functional perspective on social life. Many studies take aspects of the formal structure as the elements of structure to be so analysed (Blau, 1972; Rumelt, 1974).

Critics may contend that this imputes too much, that replicated correlations do not prove that the structures have the functions postulated. Such propositions based on correlational studies are to be understood as hypotheses for further empirical testing. The question becomes does increasing specialization or differentiation with increasing size in fact help to maintain adaptions, goal-attainment, integration and latency? This requires a further type of analysis, but one which remains within the structural-functionalist paradigm.

In the work of Hage the functioning of structures was examined in terms of the outputs of the organization, more particularly, the rate of adoption of programmes offering new services to clients of health and welfare establishments. The enquiry was conceived in order to directly test the functional consequences of different structures (Hage, 1980). Drawing on the work of Burns and Stalker (1961), a formalized theory of innovation was constructed (Hage, 1965) in which the rate of innovation was dependent upon organizational structure variables such as the amount of knowledge and expertise possessed by the staff (termed complexity) and degree of formalization of roles. Subsequent tests of this theory through cross-sectional and longitudinal studies have substantially confirmed the hypothesis (Hage and Aiken, 1967; Hage and Dewar, 1973) and led to a refinement and extension of the theory (Hage, 1980). Thus, within conventional organization studies one finds that the functioning of structures has been researched in fulfilment of the structural-functionalist programmatic. The brief discussion of the work of Hage and Aiken by Burrell and Morgan (1979: 163) describes their research as measuring and explaining organization structure and omits any reference to their investigation of the functional outcomes of structures.

In other, mainstream research this issue is pursued through an enquiry about performance (Woodward, 1965; Lawrence and Lorsch, 1967; Khandwalla, 1973, 1974; Lansley *et al.*, 1974; Rumelt, 1974; Child, 1975;

Grinyer *et al.*, 1980; Lenz, 1980). The theory, within the contingency approach, is that it is the degree of appropriateness of the structures (i.e. the extent to which the extant structures are those which are required by the state of contingency factors) which determines the adequacy of functioning as revealed in turn by the performance indicators. If the proposition connecting size-specialization is valid then the expectation is that those companies which increase their specialization in proportion to their growth in size should display superior performance to those which do not. The former may be operationalized as firms which cluster close to the trend line of specialization on size, and the latter taken as those which deviate from this. This is the form of trivariate analysis of structure/ contingengy/performance which is a key stage in contingency analysis, for which Woodward's (1965) work stands as an exemplar and which has been followed in subsequent studies (Lawrence and Lorsch, 1967; Khandwalla, 1973, 1974; Lansley *et al.*, 1974; Rumelt, 1974; Child, 1975; Grinyer *et al.*, 1980; Lenz, 1980). Hence the imputation of functioning is a hypothesis which is tested empirically.

Many comparative studies which employ a structural-functional interpretation do not examine the functional outcomes of structures (Blau and Schoenherr, 1977; Blau *et al.*, 1976). To this extent their assertions about consequences for effectiveness remain conjectural. The results of such work constitute propositions to be tested in studies which investigate performance and functioning. Studies which do no more than correlate context and structure remain useful as preliminary work. If the results of a series of such surveys shows that context and structure are associated, and that this replicates and generalizes across many studies in diverse settings, then this suggests that there may be a causal connection and that this may be of a structural-functionalist kind. Thus enquiries into context and structure are suggestive for possibly fruitful lines of research into context/structure/functioning relationships.

While the limitations of correlational studies of context and structure need to be recognized the resolution involves further prosecution of the structural-functionalist programmatic by research into structure/ contingency/performance relationships utilizing comparativism, cross-sectional data and statistics. There is nothing inherent in these elements of method, which when combined together, and with theoretically meaningful hypotheses, precludes their illuminating functioning.

This raises the issue of whether the performance variables used in the empirical studies correspond to the adequacy of functioning in terms such as adaption, goal-attainment, integration and latency. In several empirical studies the performance variables are financial measures such as profitability or growth in sales (Lawrence and Lorsch, 1967; Child, 1975; Rumelt, 1974). These would appear, *prima facie*, to be indicators of goal-attainment, but their correspondence to adaption, integration and latency would seem to be less direct. Other variables, such as the market conditions, would seem to affect a company's profitability, in addition to the internal adequacy of the functioning. Hence the empirical correspondence of company financial performance to functioning seems problematic. Another approach is to take as the performance indicator job satisfaction (Likert and Likert, 1976). This seems to have a more direct connection with functioning, but only to part of what would be classified under latency: individual motivation and tension release. Hence this seems to be too narrow to stand as an index of functioning. It suggests however that an expansion of such indicators across the categories such as adaption, goal-attainment, integration and latency would produce the desired set of measures. These would be variables which intervene between structure and ultimate criteria such as profitability. The inclusion of such measures into the above-mentioned trivariate relationship of structure/contingency/performance would enable direct testing of structural-functionalist interpretations. Such an approach in the case of size-specialization would mean that the proposition would be investigated by examining whether other companies deviating from the trend line of specialization on size, were indeed lower in terms such as adaption, goal-attainment, integration and latency. It might transpire that the fit of specializations was consequential for integration but not, or less so, for latency, or had the opposite effect. This would elaborate our structural knowledge in a way which was in keeping with the programmatic intent of the structural-functional perspective. Some attempts to treat the measurement of performance have been made in this way (see Etzioni, 1975). It seems fair to say that such an approach has not been well institutionalized within organization studies to date. An attempt to be more conscious in the application of the structural-functional perspective would lead this way.

Thus some part of the difficulties in organizational research, as in the tendency to date to demonstrate only relative weak performance consequences of the hypothesized specialization on size relationship, and other propositions emerging from attempts to operationalize bureaucratic theory, may relate to theoretical deficiencies in the approach to performance measurement (Child, 1975). Hence the charge that organizational research has been narrowly operationalist and not always sufficiently theoretical would seem to be partly valid, at least in respect to the performance issue.

What of Burrell and Morgan's other argument, that such studies neglect change and systems' disintegration? The contingency approach is that for effective performance, structure has to fit the contingencies (size, product diversity and so on). If there is a mismatch this will set up pressures for change in either structure or contingencies to restore effective performance. These pressures may be off-set in the short run and in certain circumstances (Child, 1972a). But over the long run there will often be change towards congruency, i.e. adaption, or the organization will not survive (Aldrich, 1979). Etzioni (1961), in the first edition of his *Comparative Analysis of Complex Organizations*, laid stress on survival as the consequence of congruency between organizational compliance systems and the involvement of their participants. In the second edition more attention was paid to the satisfaction or lack of satisfaction of functional requisites (Etzioni, 1975). Thus the mainstream of organizational structure research utilizes models which do have implications for organizational change and they do specify conditions under which systems disintegrate, i.e. chronic and severe incongruency. It is therefore misleading for Burrell and Morgan to state that they 'have largely ignored or underplayed' change (1979: 65). Such models predict when change will arise (i.e. where there is incongruency) and the form it will take (i.e. moves towards congruency).

Many empirical studies have been made of samples of organizations at one point in time in order to observe patterns of association of their structural variables. However, a snapshot measure, when repeated over time, provides data on structural change. Indeed it is a requirement for describing changes in structure. Further, longitudinal studies are a necessity in order to directly test causal paths. Latterly, certain scholars have made longitudinal enquiries (Inkson *et al.*, 1970; Dewar and Hage, 1978; Rumelt, 1974; Channon, 1973; Dyas and Thanheiser, 1976; Suzuki, 1980). Thus present comparative methods are not inherently static and have been used to document change and examine underlying patterns of causation.

It remains true that such work has often not dealt explicitly with the processes of change in terms of the mobilization of differing factions of varying amounts of power (Child, 1972a). However, structural analysis does offer explanation of the circumstances under which incongruency will often arise, what are likely responses of powerful elites, what the extant distribution of power will be in the organization, which change attempts will realize their goals and what the resultant distribution of power will be (Hage, 1980). While some of this work has developed latterly as a conscious attempt to meet criticisms of the kind mounted by Burrell and Morgan, it represents the culmination of a long line of structural-functional enquiry (Hage, 1965; Hage and Aiken, 1967; Hage and Aiken, 1970; Hage and Dewar, 1973; Hage, 1974; Hage and Dewar, 1978). Comparative studies of organization structure can, and do, illuminate the processes of functioning, systems change and, potentially also, disintegration.

Before leaving the critique by Burrell and Morgan (1979) of supposed deficiencies in the research procedures used in functionalist organization research, one further criticism requires rebuttal. At one point in their review of the empirical literature they characterize the research in the following way:

> There is scarcely an organisational variable which has not been measured in some form and even correlated with itself in the objectivist search for 'significant' relationships which eventually will prove 'determinate'. The 1976 and early 1977 issues of *Administrative Science Quarterly*, for example, contain objectivist research on the familiar topics of technology and structure, size and structure, structure and effectiveness and structure and environment, as well as many objectivist articles on the traditional human relations issues. (Burrell and Morgan, 1979: 163; italics as in original)

When a variable is correlated with itself and the results are presented as significant findings a substantial error of methodology has been committed. To accuse organizational scientists in general, and *ASQ* contributors in particular, of making such errors is a serious charge. When given currency in the literature through books such as Burrell and Morgan's this sort of criticism can be used to dismiss empirical studies of organizations.

Burrell and Morgan exemplify their charge, as follows: 'It can be argued, for example, that in attempting to correlate the technology and structure of organizations, researchers are examining two aspects of the same variable – viz. the method of control' (1979: 223). Burrell and Morgan do not furnish any further proof of this assertion. Studies which relate organization structure (e.g. functional specialization, number of departments) to the degree of automation (Blau *et al.*, 1976) are not doing this. In the case of the studies in the Woodward (1965) tradition it might be argued that her technology variables reflect the way manufacturing is organized in the sense of managerial choices over the size of batches and so on. While such a variable is, in that sense, about organizational structure, relating it empirically to other variables, such as span of control at the first-line supervisor, is not in error, as the two variables are different components of organization structure. There is nothing tautological about testing for empirical associations between different aspects of organization structure, providing each is analytically and operationally distinct. Both may be modes of control but this in itself does not produce the fallacy of definitional dependency.

The mistake of correlating a variable with itself is usually easy to spot and rectify. However, there have been occasions when this error has passed through into the organizational literature in a more than trivial way. This has occurred in studies of the administrative component. This is the ratio of the administrative or support workers to total number of employees in an organization. Interest focuses on them to see whether organizations become either 'more bureaucratic and top heavy' or 'more economic in their administrative costs' as they grow in size. This has led to a series of studies which relate the administrative ratio to size (e.g. Blau, 1972; Blau and Schoenherr, 1971; for a review of studies see Freeman and Kronenfeld, 1973). While this is a reasonable intention, early researchers have done this through simply correlating administrative ratio with size. Since the denominator of the administrative ratio is size, this means that size is being correlated with the inverse of itself (i.e. the denominator). This is an artifactual negative correlation. Size is also being correlated with the numerator (the number of administrators). The observed correlation is the resultant of these two: the artifactual, negative correlation ($r = 1.0$) and a real correlation (of varying value). This is unsatisfactory and erroneous, and has led to the recommendation to use other techniques such as regression which provide meaningful results, free from the problem.

The exposition of this problem of definitional dependency in the administrative component literature (Freeman and Kronenfeld, 1973) has led to the results of the early works containing this problem being viewed as inadequate. At least some of the later work in the literature on this topic has consciously avoided this pitfall (Child, 1973) – though not all, some subsequent studies perpetuate the problem (Blau *et al.*, 1976). This illustrates one of the recurrent themes of this volume, that the scientific process, of the discovery of truth through open dialogue and knowledge culmination in a literature, does in fact operate in organization studies, albeit imperfectly and not instantaneously. If organization research were simply the kind of acritical, unself-conscious, nonintellectual activity as the detractors depict, then one would find only the surface rhetoric of science. Yet for those familiar with the details of its working, what is revealed is a process which is scientific in substance.

A further series of criticisms of research procedures used in comparative studies of organizational structure has been introduced by Whitley (1977). Whitley makes a critique of the methods used in the Aston studies. He writes: 'Furthermore, it is assumed that the identified structures are crucial aspects of work organizations, crucial in accordance with contextual variables and affect organizational performance' (1977: 55). To say this sounds as if the Aston studies made sweeping and unjustified assumptions about their structural scales. Yet a large part of the research published since 1968 is an empirical test of the relationships between the structural variables and context, and also the relationship with performance. The former have generally revealed strong results (Pugh and Hinings, 1976), the latter weak ones (Child, 1975b). Whitley is characterizing as some preposterous claim what has in fact been the subject of careful study. The Aston approach to structure does not *assume* such relationships, it has investigated them.

Whitley continues:

> In short, the authors consider that, because differences between the organizations' positions on the five primary dimensions are inferred from statistical manipulations of responses, 'real' differences which indicate major attributes of organization have been located. (1977: 55)

Whitley refers in a derogatory way to statistically manipulated responses (1977: 55), but he does not explain what is wrong with the particular manipulations done in the Aston studies. The published results (Pugh *et al.*, 1968) show very clearly that the organizations studied did vary in their scores on the primary dimensions, i.e. there are real differences. Also, the five primary dimensions are major in the sense that they are about different aspects of structure, such as specialization and centralization, which theories of organizations (Weber, 1968) have distinguished and treated as key terms. By any reasonable standard the measures reveal real differences on major aspects of structure. This can be claimed without denying that there will be some measurement error and without claiming them to be exhaustive of all theoretically important aspects of structure.

Whitley (1977) advances the epistemological stricture that gathering structural data from key informants implies the referential theory of meaning. Since Whitley sees this as philosophically dubious, the notion of asking managers about 'organization' founders. Here Whitley is drawing on the shift in philosophy towards the work of the later Wittgenstein (1963). This argues that the meaning of words is not that they are labels for things, but rather that they are used within language games. The meaning is the piece of behaviour and interchange, including verbal behaviour, which accompanies it. This is contrasted with the notion that meaning is a process of a symbol referring to, or standing for, some thing. Applying this to organizational life, Whitley argues that: 'Similarly, "organization structure", or, indeed, "organization", does not refer to a "thing", but rather obtains its meaning and significance from the framework within which the term is employed' (1977: 55). Here we see an argument broadly similar to that of Silverman (1968, 1970). Organization is a problematic concept, and a cogent approach to organizations would have to consider a more micro-approach which focused on linguistics in human interaction. Here the key notion is that the concept of organization as an entity is incompatible with a language game paradigm of meaning. Organization only has meaning within the extant language games. And Whitley writes:

> In the case of the analysis of organizations, this would be derived from the theoretical purpose and structure behind the study itself. It would

then have a technically specific meaning which would be based on a particular framework and intellectual tradition. There is no reason to expect such meaning to resemble managers' conception of the same term. (1977: 55)

Hence interviews are confounded because they confuse language games. This presumes that the terms of 'organization', 'organization structure' and so on are used differently by researchers and managers. This is an empirically testable proposition. Whitley presents no evidence that the terms differ so much, and that the actors are so incapable of reaching agreement that communication is vitiated. While some such differences exist, the terms used by theoreticians such as specialization and centralization have developed out of the lay conceptions of managers, to aid their problems, and so have a great deal of commonality. Moreover, definition of terms, such as what is meant by 'the organization' (the plant, the division, the corporation, etc.) is a customary part of interviews and questionnaires which employ the term. For instance, Van de Ven and Ferry (1980) are careful to define these referents in terms meaningful to respondents in their questionnaire studies of organizations. Further, most of the Aston questions do not ask the informant about global things like 'the organization structure'. They are about specific things like: 'Is there a written job definition for the Chief Executive?', or 'Who is the most junior person on whose decision action can be taken to decide a new product or service?' The aggregations of a large number of such nitty-gritty questions produces the scores on the main scales of structure. In practical, operational terms the meaning gulf between researcher and manager is less than Whitley asserts. The language game theory of meaning does not place organization studies at an impasse.

In summary, many of the aspects of contemporary empirical, organizational research are useful, and are compatible with a theoretical approach from structural-functionalism. These include conceiving of organizational, as distinct from individual properties, the use of variables, operational definitions, synchronic data, statistics, hypothesis testing and causal models. Further developments of diachronic studies, measurement refinement, theory construction and so on are needed, but these will complement not replace the features listed previously. While this discussion concurs with Burrell and Morgan (1979) to the extent that modern organization research could be more firmly based on structural-functional theory, in contrast to them, the need is seen here to continue to utilise scientific methods and an analytic treatment of structure. Moreover, contemporary studies of organization structure are by no means incompatible with the study of processes of the kind which feature in structural-functional frameworks.

However, some critics maintain that leading organization research programmes such as Aston or the series of studies by Blau and his colleagues are devoid of theory. Clegg and Dunkerley (1980) criticize the Aston studies as being merely empiricist, and not scientific, for they say, they simply relate observations and seek to show their generality, rather than explain them through a theory. Likewise, Whitley writes of the Aston studies that: 'The whole research study exemplifies the dominance of naive inductive empiricism as a methodological ideal in the field of organizational studies' (1977: 55).

Whitley (1977) briefly sketches the early work of Pugh and his colleagues beginning with the 1963 paper. However, this review is soon terminated with the 1968 article by Pugh *et al.* These are key articles but they are also early ones and cannot be reasonably taken as a basis on which to evaluate the Aston studies.

He notes that: ' . . . the theoretical approach became less relevant to the research itself as the work proceeded. The search for reliable scales and indices of dimensions of organizational structure evolved into the central area of concern' (Whitley, 1977: 55).This is a fair statement of the difference between Pugh *et al.* (1963) and Pugh *et al.* (1968). But as a statement of general trends it is false. Two articles in 1969 concentrate on explaining structure by reference to context, and by offering a taxonomy of structures (Pugh *et al.*, 1969a, 1969b). And then, the series of papers by Child (1972, 1973) explicitly sought to reassert theoretical concerns, and indeed refer scathingly to a tendency for earlier Aston papers to rely on statistical procedures rather than theoretically derived models in the analysis of data.

The use of factor analysis by Pugh *et al.* (1968) to extract underlying dimensions from the primary dimensions may be characterized as inductive. Yet this procedure has been heavily criticized by Child (1973a) who has sought to downgrade the importance of such inductive tools in favour of hypotheses derived from theory. As Starbuck notes (1981), there has been little subsequent reliance on the results of factor analysis. Within the ranks of the Aston school there are self-correcting mechanisms to guard against naive inductivism. It seems fair to say that the Aston studies over-relied on techniques such as factor analysis at certain stages in their development. But this has been corrected by a more explicit concern for theory even within their own number. Many scientific literatures seem to go through periods of over-concentration on data-patterns or on theory, and the right balance between all these elements takes time to establish. To dismiss the whole Aston research approach as 'naive inductive empiricism' is unwarranted.

Blau's theory of structural differentiation in organizations (1970; Blau and Schoenherr, 1977), has been called into question by Turner (1977). The thrust of the criticism is that it is not really a theory and does not add anything to lay, commonsense explanations. Benson cites Turner's critique approvingly in his article: 'Organizations: A Dialectical View', in support of his own criticism that work such as that by Blau is in error because ' . . . the research itself is drawn into the presuppositions of the order under study' (1977: 11).

Turner (1977) mounts his attack in a way which is philosophically quite technical and potentially very damaging. As he notes the idea of a causal nexus between size and complexity underlies classical sociological theories from Durkheim to the contemporary (Turner, 1977: 20). Accordingly, if the work of Blau is seen to be seriously deficient then not only is a well-known example of organizational sociology inadequate but a principal strand of organicist sociology is suspect. Indeed such is the intention of Turner as his conclusion is a call for interpretive approaches to sociology (1977: 33). The critique is mounted against Blau from the standpoint of the philosophy of science and from ordinary language philosophy. In particular, the claim of Blau to offer a scientific sociological explanation is challenged by purporting to show that Blau's work is not a theory, and that the account he offers is based on, and reducible to, the 'plain man's' account (Turner, 1977: 20).

Turner shows that to qualify as an explanation the propositions must be deduced from more abstract theory statements. He criticizes some versions of the theory of Blau (i.e. 1970) for being deficient as regards deductive structure (Turner, 1977: 23). This hinges on the problem, as Turner sees it, that the higher-level principles speak of differentiation whereas the lower-level, empirically tested hypotheses, are of a variety of things such as the number of branches, occupational positions, hierarchic levels and so on (1977: 24). Therefore, argues Turner, the former proposition does not subsume all the operational indicators and one or other of them might not hold and the theory proposition would not say which would not hold. Thus the purportedly universal theory proposition is just a summary in a logical sense. The proposition is implied by the hypotheses rather than implying them. Thus the hypothetico-deductive structure collapses (Turner, 1977: 24). Yet differentiation as used by Blau and other sociologists, as a conceptually based delineation of roles, does imply separation into branches, occupational positions and hierarchical levels, i.e. it is a more abstract concept which subsumes all of these. Blau defines differentiation explicitly in such a way that it includes all the operational indicators and yet is a conceptually defined class with boundaries:

> A dimension of differentiation is any criterion on the basis of which the members of an organization are formally divided into positions, as illustrated by the division of labour; or into ranks, notably managerial levels; or into sub-units, such as local branches, headquarters divisions, or sections within branches or divisions. (1970: 203)

And the theory statements made by Blau are claims that all these forms of differentiation are subject to them. Therefore the theory is hypothetico-deductive and the proposition implies the hypotheses. Moreover, forms of differentiation other than those measured by Blau have been shown to conform to these propositions, for example, Child (1973b) finds the same tendency to increase differentiation with size at a decreasing rate for Functional Specialization.

That differentiation refers to a class of variables which are not exhaustively enumerated *ex ante* does not preclude this from being a term which needs to be understood in terms of a body of theory such as that by Blau, and having its lineage in classical sociology such as Durkheim (1973). Moreover, propositions about these lower-level observables are deduced from higher-level statements which deal in phenomena which are not measured within the studies. Blau explicitly refers to other underlying, unmeasured concepts which form part of the higher-order explanatory postulates from which the hypotheses are derived. Intra-unit homogeneity is produced by differentiation and reduces the administrative component required to coordinate within the unit, while the inter-unit heterogeneity is also raised by differentiation and this requires more coordination thus increasing the administrative component (Blau, 1970: 217).

Thus it would seem that Blau's formulation does meet the requirements of the philosophy of science to be judged to be a theory.

Turner's next point is that laws in science refer to chains of causation which cannot be interrupted or reversed. Therefore for Blau's theory to be law-like it must be ineluctable (Turner, 1977: 24). At this point Turner introduces the 'partially hypothetical example' (1977: 24) of the Florida state legislature setting limits on the maximum ratio of administrators to teachers in the schools under their jurisdiction. After some years of operation the ratio is depressed below what it would otherwise have been despite increases in students and teachers. Thus the working of the size-administration causal chain in Blau's theory has apparently been altered. This means that the causality has been interfered with through human intervention, yet if this were a genuinely scientific theory how could this be for: 'The legislature could not successfully legislate against the laws of gravity, or impose regulations on the tides' (Turner, 1977: 25).

Faced with this argument Blau's theory begins to look like some kind of pseudo-science. However, Turner's objection hangs on a particular interpretation of Blau's propositions, as contextual determinism rather than as contingency-design. If they are seen as the former then the size-administration proposition is a causal path(s) in which size determines (directly and indirectly in Blau's theory) the number of administrators. If size increases the administrative component must rise, i.e. it is inevitable.

But this interpretation is to divorce Blau's theory from the wider meta-theory of structural-functionalism. The increase in administrative intensity with growing size is necessary to solve the problem of coordinating larger organizations. If the administrative component does not also grow then integration declines and performance deteriorates. In order to avoid this most organizations, over the long run, do in fact increase their administrative component with their size. Thus we have the frequently observed associations (Blau, 1972; Child, 1973b; Reimann, 1979). However, this is not inevitable, for it is contingent upon several conditions, such as the availability of the funds, the permission of superordinate bodies, the inclinations and beliefs of senior management and so on. In the 1972 version of this theory Blau states that large size is a necessary but not a sufficient condition for differentiation (1972: 22); thus the size-differentiation connection is not inevitable. He lists several other conditions for differentiation to increase with size. These include: ' . . . if management is interested and capable of furthering effective operations' and also the proposition that differentiation, through creating more homogeneous sub-units, does increase effectiveness (Blau, 1972: 22). Thus Blau's propositions are to be understood within the structural-functional perspective as specifying structural patterns for performance, which may not always be met, but which through processes of adaptation and survival are recurrent and frequently observed in empirical studies. The legislature, or other human agencies, can intervene and stop the size-differentiation or other linkages. But when they do they will produce organizations with problems of coordination and performance. That is the element of the theory which is ineluctable. Structural-functional theories of the contingency sort are immediately deterministic in the consequences of match between contingency and structure on effectiveness, rather than in the supposedly cause-effect connection between contingency and structure (i.e. contextual determinism). Turner's scenario of the Florida state legislature is not a valid objection to according the status of scientific theory to the work of Blau.

Turner continues his critique by contrasting the explanation offered by Blau with that which would be given by a 'plain man' (1977: 27). Such a fellow would describe these phenomena by reference to the motives and reasons of organizational participants. These descriptions would use similar conceptual terms to Blau, such as divisions and sections, with the same meanings (Turner, 1977: 28). And would explicate the administrative practices used by participants which produce the curves and generalizations to which Blau refers (Turner, 1977: 31). However, Blau's theory is in no way superior to the plain man's account, as it adds nothing to the explanation, for the generalizations about curves and so on ' . . . are conceptually constructed of facts which have already been explained' (Turner, 1977: 31) by reference to participants' practices.

The criticism about Blau's theory adding nothing to the plain man's explanation raises once again the issue of individual reductionism. Participants undoubtedly can offer a variety of reasons as to why differentiation increases with size in their own, and others', organizations. Reference to these particular and various administrative practices helps to answer questions about how organizational change comes about at the level of the actors involved. They would form part of an interpretative explanation at the level of the motivations of the typical actor. Even more specifically, they provide answers to the everyday questions asked in ordinary language: 'Why have more administrators been hired in this organization?' 'Because there are more employees to manage now.' But explanations at this level of individual motivation and action is not what theories such as Blau's seek. They are conceived within a structural-functional metatheory and wish to understand recurrent structural forms by reference to the constancies of functional requisites, such as the need for coordination, and to the empirically variable circumstances. They try to explain generally observed co-variations between contingencies and structure in terms of objective requirements for viability and effectiveness. The explication of this is one of the ways that structural-functional theories add something to explanation, for the propositions describing the curves, such as size-differentiation, are deduced from higher-level premises which deal in the requirements for coordination and so on. Turner notes that there are these 'further reasons' behind the hypotheses but incorrectly states that these are attributions of reasons to individuals when they are really systems imperatives of organizations (1977: 26). This confusion allows Turner to see the explanatory basis of the theory as lying in individuals' motives which form part of the argument for claiming that Blau explains that which has already been explained. However, in defining his subject matter as formal structure Blau counterposes it to the results of individual motivations, and thus sees structural phenomena as not requiring explanation at the micro-level: 'Formal structures exhibit regularities that can be studied in their own right without investigating the motives of the individuals in organizations' (1973: 203). In keeping with this, the fundamental premises of the theory are organicist imperatives and the processes of theory construction, testing and evidence gathering occur within a scientific endeavour.

Thus Blau's theory is a genuine explanatory effort distinguishable from the plain man's accounts and not reducible to them. Such a validated theory would add greatly to the plain man's understanding of organizations, and would give him enhanced certainty about likely patterns and requirements for effectiveness.

In conclusion, the critique by Turner uses philosophical concepts to probe the adequacies of Blau's theory of structural differentiation. Despite Turner's contentions the work of Blau emerges as genuinely

theory-like, offering explanation by reference to functionalist imperatives, implying determinacy and being conceived within a scientific
approach. This promises knowledge of a kind which is an advance on the
beliefs of individuals as contained in ordinary language.

Conclusions

Contemporary comparative studies of organization structure such as that
by Aston (Pugh and Hickson, 1976; Pugh and Hinings, 1976) and Blau
(1970; 1972; Blau and Schoenherr, 1971) have been explained in theoretical terms. Much of this theorizing is of the structural-functional kind.
Many of the studies are cross-sectional but longitudinal studies are now
developing by repeating these comparative studies across time. Both synchronic and diachronic studies are leading towards an understanding of
the way structure is necessarily connected to situational variations in
terms of the requirements for effective functioning. Further refinement in
methods and theory, and more extensive data collection are needed.
However, this will need to build on, rather than to replace, many of the
characteristics currently existing in that literature: the use of comparative
methods, standard operational measures, variables and statistical
analysis.

One reason why organization studies is sometimes seen as lacking in
theory is the fixation upon sociological theories to the neglect of organizational theory. While there are linkages between these two bodies of
thought, such as in the common threads connecting structural-functional
theories of society to those of organization, there is a need to recognize
the separate identity of the latter. This raises the question of how far
organizational theories are separable from sociological theories and
whether this is desirable and legitimate. The next chapter will discuss this.

6

Relationship of Organization
Theory to Sociological Theory

Organization studies are criticized for being theoretically inadequate. This is sometimes said with reference to their employment of a framework such as structural-functionalism which is felt to be inherently limited. This has been discussed in Chapter 3. Again, organizational research is sometimes criticized as not really being satisfactory structural-functionalism, and this was discussed in Chapter 5. Going further, critics sometimes suggest that the study of organizations is atheoretical and this also has been considered in Chapter 5. Such theory as deployed in organizational studies is seen, on occasions, as being a rather inferior variant of sociological theory. The position being taken in this criticism is that Organization Theory should be closely related to Sociological Theory, and that the latter is to be used as the criteria for judging the former. This chapter continues the discussion, which was begun in the preceding chapter, of the accuracy of the depictions of Organization Theory in the critical writings and goes on to reflect upon the strength of the connection between sociological and organization theories, and asks how far need explanations of organizational phenomena be derived from sociology.

Burrell and Morgan write that in organization studies 'theoretical insights have been largely submerged under a deluge of empirical research' (1979: 57). However, the charge that organization analysis as a whole is atheoretical has to be considered against the curious omissions in the review by Burrell and Morgan (1979). The leading positions in sociological theory are given systematic exposition, as in Marx, Weber, Pareto, Durkheim. In several cases this takes the form of a line-by-line quotation of the sociological models, as in Dahrendorf, Rex and Silverman (Burrell and Morgan, 1979: 12, 196, 197, 210, 352, 353, 354). By contrast many major organization theories are given little or no exposition: March and Simon, Cyert and March, Thompson, Perrow or Hage. Those organization theories which are given prominence are the more sociologically oriented ones, related to mainstream sociology often through the topic of bureaucracy, as in Merton, Gouldner and Selznick. In the case of Blau, his exchange theory is reviewed (Burrell and Morgan, 1979:

88), but not his theory of structural differentiation (Blau and Schoenherr, 1971; Blau, 1972). Discussions of theoretical frameworks of organizational works are quick to subsume them into the framework of sociological theory. This is done via the link of common, related or antecedent concepts. Theory is identified as sociological theory and little consideration is given to specifically Organization Theory.

Burrell and Morgan spend about twenty pages (pp. 160–80), in a book of over four hundred pages, on major branches of contemporary research. They write: 'Our discussion of objectivist research on organizations since Woodward's study can be no more than illustrative. We shall confine our attention to the most promising pieces of work, directing the reader interested in obtaining a more encompassing view to issues of the *Administrative Science Quarterly* over the last ten years or so' (1979: 162).

The culmination of Burrell and Morgan's brief discussion of mainstream organizational research is a contingency model of organizations (1979: 178). In essence this is a variant of the organic-mechanistic thesis which is elaborated to the point of differences in sub-systems, which are exemplified by functional departments. The model presented by Burrell and Morgan of contingency theory for 1979 is essentially Lawrence and Lorsch's model of 1967. Much work in the empirical and theoretical literature has gone into identifying other contingencies and their structural implications. Any true contemporary summary of contingency theory as it existed in 1979 would have had, in some way or other, to include the contingencies of size (Pugh and Hickson, 1976; Pugh and Hinings, 1976; Blau, 1972), diversification (Stopford and Wells, 1972; Channon, 1973; Rumelt, 1974; Dyas and Thanheiser, 1976), public versus private ownership (Pugh and Hickson, 1976; Pugh and Hinings, 1976), and democracy (Donaldson and Warner, 1974a; Donaldson and Warner, 1974b). Yet it is in keeping with the sparse and inadequate treatment of the empirical literature by Burrell and Morgan that all of this is absent. Moreover, the Lawrence and Lorsch model has received important qualification by Lorsch and Allen (1973), who point out that it holds only in organizations which are highly interdependent. In conditions of low interdependence the propositions about differentiation and integration no longer apply. The work of Lorsch and Allen is crucial for modern organizational studies as it stands at the interface of the analysis of two different contingencies: uncertainty and diversification. It contains a theoretical interpretation which accords well with ideas of earlier organization theorists such as Thompson (1967). Yet it is not even in the bibliography of Burrell and Morgan (1979: 414–15). Further, there is neglect in the review by Burrell and Morgan of other theoretical conjunctions in contemporary empirical research.

The core achievements of organizational sociology to date are codified in theories such as the axiomatic theory of Hage (1965), the theory of structural differentiation of Blau (1972), the theory of bureaucratic control of Child (1972, 1973), and the theory of interdependence and coordination modes of Thompson (1967). All of these are subsumable under structural-functionalism (see Hage, 1980). Hence the charge that organization studies is atheoretical rests on a highly selective review by Burrell and Morgan (1979) which does not do justice to the field. Moreover, their approach considers Organization Theory from the perspective of Sociological Theory rather than in its own right.

This raises the issue of whether theory, in the sense of Burrell and Morgan, and others, that is as Sociological Theory, should be given a central place in organization studies. The set of classical sociological theories may inform organizational analysis but they should be accorded no priority over more specifically organizational theorizing. The final test should be the empirical one of explanatory power. This raises the issue of what is to be explained. Here the argument from sociology tends to concentrate on phenomena which are sociologically interesting. This usually means that they relate to the classical writings. Such topics would include bureaucracy, alienation, anomie and power. Going further, critics of Organization Theory often assert the desirability of studying sociologically important phenomena such as domination, ideology, social stratification and economic contradictions. By so doing they are, quite consciously, raising the focus of interest from the organization to the wider society. This brings the topics investigated more firmly into line with the concerns of classical sociology (and more particularly of Marxism). Yet this sort of assimilation of all social science enquiry into classical sociology needs to be questioned.

An equally legitimate approach is to take those problems which concern people working inside organizations, such as how to make organizations more effective, efficient, innovative and fulfilling for their members. Burrell and Morgan write of these as 'pragmatic' and 'managerial' concerns. Pragmatic they are, and managers certainly seek answers to them, but so too do workers, union officials, governments, bankers and taxpayers. Many workers and lower-level employees show a very keen interest in the question of whether their organization is structured and run as effectively as it could be. How to get more service from existing health and welfare organizations without having to increase taxation is a vital issue for governments and citizens around the world. Travelling in Britain in December 1979, I found it difficult to meet anyone who did not have a theory as to why British Leyland was failing as a profit-making car company. The desire for valid cause and effect knowledge about organizations, their structure and functioning, is in widespread public demand. In terms of this writer's values, organization studies should seek, *inter alia*, to answer such questions. Does this pragmatic orientation condemn such studies to be atheoretical?

Recalling the logical definition of theory as a body of coherent propositions with some degree of abstractness, the answer is in the negative. Knowledge of organizations will be contained in propositions about cause and effect (e.g. Hage, 1980). This is necessary for the pragmatic reasons of understanding in order to control organizations. As such it is likely, and indeed present practice suggests, that knowledge will lead to sets of propositions (e.g. Blau, 1972; Hage, 1980). The connections within and between such sets will need to be consistent otherwise understanding, prediction and control will be vitiated. Hence any useful multi-proposition model of organization must strive to meet the consistency requirement which is such an important desideratum of a theory. Finally, for the propositions to be of more than limited applicability (i.e. they work for IBM but not Ford) they must abstract enough to provide a general framework. Hence the requirement for pragmatic usefulness once expressed through the programmatic idea of science-building leads directly to the goal of theory construction. Hence organization studies should be pragmatic but it should not be, and is not, atheoretical.

But is organization studies theoretical in the sense of reflecting the concerns of classical sociology? It is in part, in that those classical notions inform the theorizing (see Hage, 1980). But the acid test is the empirical explanatory one. There should be no prior commitment to mimicry of classical sociological concepts. How much impact has classical sociology had on organization studies in fact? Hage (1980) has provided a discussion which indicates the linkages between Sociological Theory and Organization Theory. Accordingly the discussion here will seek to do no more than strike a balance by showing aspects of discontinuity between the two.

Several well-known organizational theories have been depicted as following from classical sociological ones. Burns and Stalker's (1961) mechanistic-organic ideal types have been described as Durkheim's (1933) organic and mechanistic but with the names altered and swapped to opposite polarities. Both schema have a polar type where integration is achieved through roles defined within a division of labour: Burns and Stalker's mechanistic and Durkheim's organic. Both share a type with integration based on shared values: Burns and Stalker's organic and Durkheim's mechanical. But social consciousness in the organic type (Burns and Stalker, 1961) is seen as highly differentiated as specialized, technical knowledge. This is not the same as the shared folk imagery of Durkheim's mechanical type. Again, the division of labour in Durkheimian organic types has evolved, the division in Burns and Stalker's mechanistic organizations is imposed by hierarchic authority.

No matter which ends of the two continua one contrasts they are conceptually distinct. It seems much more straightforward to see Burns and Stalker's work as the evolution of theories of organization. The mechanistic is the bureaucratic type with its advantages (orderly specializations, efficient handling of the routine) and its acknowledged dysfunctions (stifles initiative of incumbents). The organic is the human relations model. Decision-making is based on free discussion, expertise and internal commitment. It is seen as most appropriate for complex, novel situations. Hence an unfolding and resolution of a theoretical dialogue within organization studies seems to offer a sufficient account of the genesis of Burns and Stalker's work. Durkheim's work may have had some influence but it would seem erroneous to depict a one to one correspondence between the schemas.

The work of Lawrence and Lorsch (1967) is also seen as being based on Durkheim's (1964) analysis of the forms of social solidarity. Lawrence and Lorsch (1967) write about differentiation and integration. Durkheim wrote about differentiation in society, especially in the economic sphere, and of the problem of creating social coherence between the resulting separate occupational communities each with their distinct thought ways. There are echoes of this in Lawrence and Lorsch's model of organizational departments specialized functionally, each with their own perceptions and interpersonal styles. But the pre-existing management theory has placed great emphasis on the phenomena of specialization and of coordination attained through a variety of means. These means are elaborated in Lawrence and Lorsch's work into their variable modes of integration: through hierarchy, rules and procedures, coordinating committees, liaison individuals and coordinating departments. Note that they are all techniques possible within an organization. Durkheim's mechanisms are different and are societal: economic interdependence and syndicalist government. And it is crucial to Lawrence and Lorsch's theory that the appropriate integrative mechanisms will not necessarily exist in an organization and are sometimes absent. This provides the rationale for their analysis as a contribution to the design of organizations, i.e. their rational construction by the management. Once again core components of the framework are distinct. The Lawrence and Lorsch work seems to be more of a refinement of managerial theory, enriched by the understanding that organizational subcultures often form along the lines of functionally specialized departments, and of the varieties of coordination mechanism used and prescribed in contemporary organizations.

The basic theoretical proposition, that more differentiation requires more integration accords with Durkheimian concerns. Though here, later research by Lorsch and Allen (1973) has shown that this generalization breaks down for organizations with low levels of interdependence. The implication of Durkheim's analysis would be that, since interdependence is itself a source of integration, low interdependence, which is accompanied in practice by high differentiation, would need a high degree of integration through coordinating mechanisms. Yet the research and theory points to the opposite conclusion (Lorsch and Allen, 1973). The organizational level does not conform to the societal-level, classical generalization. The reader may feel that these last remarks demonstrate the futility of straining the analogy between societal and organizational phenomena. Indeed they do. But they make the point that sociological theory while sometimes a useful input to organizational analysis is not an unerring source of illumination. For a further discussion of the lack of correspondence between Sociological and Organization Theory see Donaldson (1976: 255), on the claim by Zwerman of the Marxian nature of Woodward's contribution.

Displaying the link between sociological and organizational theory as closer than it actually is does a mischief by sustaining the myth that organizational analysis is dependent upon social theory. The implication of such a model is that organization studies, in order to increase its explanatory power, needs to pay more attention to classical sociology theory.

Conclusions

Our contention is that organization studies will be best served by resisting the seduction of becoming completely assimilated into the approach of general sociology. Concepts, findings and methods should be drawn on selectively, but complete integration should not be accepted *a priori* as a desirable goal. The conclusion to this question is to affirm the desirability that organization studies be: pragmatic in its cardinal values, concerned with feasible change, socially responsible and responsive, and concentrate on the generation of valid and useful theories of organizations.

7

The possibilities for scientific study of organizations

Much of the discussion around conventional organization studies raises what is perhaps the most fundamental question in social science – Is a science of social affairs possible? More specifically, in this context, can there be a science of organization? Does not the very treatment of the subject matter by a scientific approach preclude real understanding? Is not the application of methods of the natural sciences inappropriate to the study of human interaction? This often leads to argument against the use of nomothetic and statistical approaches and the advocacy of processual or historical modes of enquiry.

Child (1972a) writes of the necessity for explanations of structure to attend to the political processes of change. Pettigrew (1979; 1977) has called for greater use of qualitative methods in the study of culture and for a processual model of strategy formulation. Daft (1980) criticizes the use of quantitative methods in organization studies and cites benefits from more qualitative approaches. In this chapter we shall seek to assess the validity of these criticisms. This will require a consideration of the role and purpose of science in the study of human affairs. The scientific mission will be defended against the idea that the analysis of ordinary language is a sufficient source of wisdom, and also from the relativism of the Sociology of Knowledge approach. The discussion will then focus on topics which are sometimes seen as incapable of a scientific treatment: change and power politics. While qualitative and historical studies are seen as making a valuable contribution, comparative and quantitative studies are argued to provide a distinct, complementary addition to knowledge. This involves an appreciation of the importance of causal inference and generalization. Correspondingly, the compatibility of change and power political phenomena with structural models is stressed.

One of the most thorough-going rejections of the programmatic of building a science of organizations is advanced by Turner (1977) on philosophical grounds. In his critique of the theory of structural differentiation of organizations of Blau (1970), he states that the idea of a superiority in the scientific status of certain explanations is based on a picture of science as dealing in 'hard' data as contrasted with the subjectivity involved in lay accounts. This, Turner contends, is a 'misleading' picture of the physical sciences and neglects the fact that such subjective judgements are what individuals employ in making moral decisions, the most important ones (1977: 29). In this way the accounts and methods used in ordinary language are held to be generally of equal status to scientific results and, in the specific case of Blau's theory of structural differentiation, more satisfactory.

To take these points in reverse order, the fact that individual subjective judgements may be the stuff of evidence in ordinary discourse and even of moral action, does not mean that it is equivalent to, or similar to, scientific evidence. The elements of method, such as measurement, sampling, controls and standard operating procedures, have been devised in order to reduce the subjective component in observation, such that scientific data are those on which there is a high degree of intersubjective agreement between trained scientists (Popper, 1945). Of necessity many areas of life remain outside this arena including many which are important, such as morals. The intention of social science is to examine social phenomena in the scientific way. Such scientific knowledge of social matters as may be produced will be superior to lay beliefs in that the former will better meet the criteria of validity according to the epistemological canons of science. The attempt by those such as Blau to create scientific laws in the study of organizations is part of such a programme. To the extent that they do in fact fulfil the requirements of scientific knowledge then they would be entitled to claim a status superior to lay accounts. Whatever the long-term verdict of the scientific community may be on his particular theory of differentiation, Blau's work is an attempt at science and deserves to be acknowledged as in a different, and in some ways putatively superior realm, to that of participants' views.

Turner's discussion exemplifies the tyranny of ordinary language philosophy. All explanations are reduced to lay accounts. The existent explanations exhaust the limits of understanding. Any ambiguity or confusion or disagreement left at the end of everyday discourse will continue. The whole notion of transcendent forms of discourse and of knowledge such as science is eschewed. Turner (1977: 20) quotes approvingly the formulation of ordinary language philosophy by Austin (1970):

> Our common stock of words embodies all the distinctions men have found worth drawing, and the connexions they have found worth making, in the lifetimes of many generations: these surely are likely to be more numerous, more sound, since they have stood up to the long test of the survival of the fittest, and more subtle, at least in all ordinary and reasonably practical matters, than any that you or I are likely to think up in our arm-chairs of an afternoon – the most favoured alternative method.

To juxtapose this philosophy, as Turner does (1977: 20), to empirical sociology and to suggest that this is a viable alternative method for this subject is to advocate a doctrine which is conservative, anti-scientific and anti-sociological. It is precisely the shortcomings in ordinary discourse which have led to the attempt to surpass this with specialized studies and language games, such as physics, economics, sociology, and organization studies.

Another philosophically based denial of the programmatic of science in social studies is that which argues that the task of theory is not to replace established theory with another, more complete, explanation, but merely to criticize. This idea is drawn from the Sociology of Knowledge (Willer, 1971) which argues that knowledge is determined by the social structure of relationships and reflects it. The theories and paradigms to which individuals subscribe are determined by their social position. Further, the established ideas tend to be the ideas of the establishment, the ideas which buttress the dominant class. The inconsistencies, inadequacies, errors and faults in these ideas are revealed by the critical theorists who occupy a structural position such that the contradictions of the established order become transparent to them (Mannheim, 1936). These contradictions presage massive structural changes to come in which the fundamental structural relations will be changed. In the new society, relations will be different and hence ideas will be different. In the present society, however, actors can only glimpse some possibility of what the transformed society will be like. Therefore, a complete new theory is impossible. All that is possible at present is a critical dialogue with the established theory, which points out contradictions in the theory and in society, but such work will always be intellectually incomplete and unfinished as the social structure constantly changes. The task of the social theorist, then, is to criticize theories, especially their ideological significance, their explicit or implicit justification of domination or exploitation. This definition of the sociological activity takes sustenance from the sub-title which Marx (1954) chose to give to his *Capital*: 'Critique of Political Economy'. That choice of words is seen as being paradigmatic rather than adventitious.

Against this, the first thing that needs to be said is that it is a departure from what has normally been taken to be a sociological approach to social phenomena. The origins of sociology as contained in the work of Durkheim and Weber are contrary to such a dialectical, relativistic conception of sociology. Certainly, sociological analysis constantly reveals the relativity of the perceptions of actors in the system, but it nevertheless goes on to make statements about social process (for example, forms of solidarity, the growth of bureaucracy, etc.) whose truth or falsity is determined by the sociological observer, not the subjects. Sociology often records relativism but it transcends subjectivism in its analytic results. Despite the invitations offered by Berger (1973), sociology is not reducible to mere relativism. Hence, it has a venerable and legitimate knowledge-construction moment. Moreover, the position of a purely critical sociology assumes the truth of certain propositions about the determinate relations of knowledge and social structure – propositions in the Sociology of Knowledge – which have not been shown to be true empirically. For instance, it is not well established that a person's ideas are determined by his or her social position. Or again, if the established ideas are the ideas of the establishment, how can it be the case that book-shops in bourgeois societies such as America, Australia and Britain bristle with works by Marx and Lenin? Whilst the activity of critical sociology, by eschewing attempts at theory-building of an elaborate kind, may seem to be modest, its premises are based on strong generalizations which go beyond what have been established as sociological findings.

It is sometimes argued, either explicitly or implicitly, that the use of sociological analysis is descriptive rather than causally explicative. The word 'account' is often used as the description of the act of sociological analysis. This term has been borrowed from philosophy, and contains within it the assumption that sociology is about describing the world (especially, of course, actors' actions) rather than explaining it.

Or again, protagonists of Social Action Theory may say that they are explaining it, in the sense of understanding the interpretation placed on his or her acts by the actor. This is now quite a common statement about the limits of sociological ambition. It is often justified by reference to Weber's interpretative sociology. But Weber (1968) stated the aims of interpretative sociology, as combining understanding at the level of the actor with the complementary understanding at the level of science. By this Weber explicitly meant the use of scientific methods and the testing of causal theories (1968: 10). Some sociologists may wish to settle for a purely descriptive approach. However those wishing to pursue causal analysis have a clear precedent in the writings of the classical sociologists: Durkheim, Marx and Weber. The argument of this volume would be that organizational sociology should continue to seek causal knowledge in addition to description.

The argument for description is often linked to the assertion that sociology contains no causal laws. Even if this were so at present it does not constitute proof that such laws may never be discovered. The only way one can see if a phenomenon is capable of scientific explanation is to see whether or not laws can be found by going through the scientific activity of study, theory construction and theory testing, many times. Equally, the fact that certain subjects such as sociology or climatology have, to date, developed a poorer body of knowledge than modern physics is no proof that it will always be so. One cannot predict the future contents of human knowledge (Popper, 1945).

Science aims at the construction of valid general theories which provide causal explanations. These paths of causation provide information about why things are as they are, that is explanation. And they tell us what would need to be done to bring about a new state of affairs, that is they provide guidance for realistic social change. The causal paths, usually conceived of as one variable influencing another, give a picture of the temporal sequence of change. For instance, in Child's (1973a) model of bureaucratization, increasing size, such as numbers of employees, leads to the hiring of more specialists in administration (experts in accounts, e.d.p., market research, etc.) and they then generate more rules and regulations and more documents and paperwork, thus increasing the level of bureaucracy in the organization. Thus the scientific theory involves events occurring in a sequence over time. It is not static, and it does talk about change. Moreover, the generality of the model is potentially very great. The concepts which form the model are terms like size, functional specialization, standardization and formalization. These are potentially applicable to any formal organization in any society. Empirical work suggests that these concepts are applicable to a wide range of organizations in a wide range of industrialized and industrializing societies (Pugh and Hinings, 1976; Hickson and McMillan, 1981). And that at least some of the relationships which feature in theories of this kind are generalizable across classes of organizations and nations. The generality of scientific models is very attractive to those seeking understanding. A general theory, once validated, allows one to explain phenomena in a whole host of settings by the same underlying mechanisms. For instance, the notion that bureaucratization is caused by size seems to hold in manufacturing organizations, retail stores, service industries, hospitals and trade unions (Blau, 1972; Child, 1973a; Donaldson and Warner, 1974b; Blau *et al.*, 1976; Pugh and Hinings, 1976; Hickson and McMillan, 1981).

Structural explanations are often contrasted with explanations at the level of interpersonal interaction. The latter are said to be superior because they show the conflict and struggle between individuals and between interest groups. To say that size or technology cause standardization or centralization is described as inadequate because of this lack of reference to events at the more human level (Silverman, 1968, 1969; Child, 1972a; Benson, 1977). Hence the call for the study of political processes and history. The human interaction and negotiation level is examined in studies which often use case-study or qualitative methods. They describe one party attempting to influence another and the outcome in terms of particular decisions, shifts in power and changes in structure (Pettigrew, 1973). However, it may be that these phenomena are not incapable of study through a nomothetic approach. Work in that tradition would see the human drama as a set of variables intervening between context and structure. To return to Child's model (1973a) of bureaucratization, the degree of bureaucracy in the organization is determined by size with the causal path going via the development of administrative expertise. These experts are the architects of the new enhanced bureaucracy and the direct effect of size is to swell administrative specialization (the level of functional specialization and the level of qualifications of these specialists). Thus, one does not need to go outside of a causal modelling or nomothetic approach to capture key elements of human interaction consequential for structural change. By staying with and refining the orthodox type of theory the resulting knowledge gains in potential generality and in connecting up the empirical regularities such as size-specialization and specialization-standardization.

Radical structuralists are interested in power in organizations. Students of management process are also concerned with this topic. They have essayed an approach which has a number of affinities with that of social action theorists. Moreover, they have joined in the criticisms of organizational sociology by advocating a change in methodology from quantitative nomothetic enquiries to qualitative, intensive, hermeneutic studies.

Pettigrew (1973) champions the case studies of interpersonal (and intergroup) struggles within organizational contexts, as the way forward in the study of power and decision-making. What he offers are naturalistic descriptions of power and influence plays. The success of each influence attempt is explained in ethnographic detail by reference to the potency of some particular power resource, for example, information control. But a scientific explanation would require addressing issues such as whether information control is usually so effective, and whether actors in such a situation usually deploy their potential power. Case-study accounts such as those of Pettigrew leave open questions of causal inference and generalizability (Blalock, 1961; Galtung, 1967). They are extremely valuable in giving insights which lead to theoretical propositions to be tested in more methodologically rigorous work. Such research methods involve the opposite of clinical case studies: standardized instruments, multiple units of study, and statistical analysis. An example of this kind of careful enquiry into the determinants of power distribution inside companies is the work of Hickson and his associates (Hickson *et al.*, 1971), in which they relate the distribution of power inside organizations to differential coping with key uncertainties. This line of work was suggested by the qualitative case-study research of Crozier (1964). The naturalistic, microscopic, case-study approach produces interesting, and readily intelligible material about power and conflict, but it does not address the sociologically significant questions of general patterns of causation.

Orthodox approaches are often criticized for neglecting power phenomena and for being incapable of handling them. There may well be some aspects of power and political process which orthodox approaches cannot handle. However, it seems that many aspects can be studied scientifically and brought within the evolving nomothetic body of knowledge. Some of the work which has been done in this regard may well have been prompted by criticisms of orthodoxy of having neglected the study of power and process. To that extent some criticism may have had some validity in the past and served a useful function. However, what seems questionable is the belief that conventional methods and paradigms are incapable, even with extension, of handling power and process aspects, especially those important for explaining structure and change in organizations.

Power varies in the extent to which it is legitimised and so becomes authority, and there are a number of ways in which this legitimacy may be bestowed: traditional, charismatic, rational-legal and expert (Weber, 1968). Again, the bases on which power rests differ situationally and include: position, sanctions, expertise, referent and exchange dependency (French and Raven, 1960; Pfeffer and Salancik, 1978). These constitute the foundations of interpersonal transactions and are realized and honoured or contested in interaction between people. Thus they are phenomena at a human or anthropomorphic level. However, the stuff of human interaction is distributed in patterned ways. There are regularities which enable this to be spoken of as structures and in the organizational world they relate closely to the formal organization and its mission. It is not the case that the phenomena of power and process is all so special that it cannot be captured through procedures kindred to those used in the scientific approach to organization. Conventional research using quantitative methods has shown that the amount of influence possessed by a member is a function of their level in the hierarchy of authority, with higher levels having more. This holds across different nations, including capitalist and state socialist societies (Tannenbaum and Cooke, 1979).

Organizations whose lower-level participants submit voluntarily to authority, that is as clients rather than employees, are more likely to use expert power in dealing with them. Organizations whose lower-level participants are compelled to participate against their will are more likely to use coercive power on them (Etzioni, 1975). Power is distributed horizontally across organizations, between departments of the same *formal* level, according to which copes best with the most critical contingency or problem facing the organization, and which cannot be readily substituted by other individuals or groups accessible to the organization (Hickson *et al.*, 1971; Hambrick, 1981; Pfeffer and Salancik, 1978). This coping with critical contingencies also tends to lead to that department providing the next chief executive of the organization (Pfeffer and Salancik, 1978). Which contingency or problem is judged as most critical is partly a reflection of the environment but is also mediated by the elite in terms of their choice of strategy from amongst available options (Hambrick, 1981). Thus the distribution of power within an organization reflects its formal structure, task uncertainty, mission, environmental demands and strategy. Thus power phenomena can and have been incorporated into comparative structural studies of organization empirically, conceptually and theoretically.

As the foregoing indicates, formal organization affects but does not completely determine power relationships. The conventional literature abounds with discussion of how formal authority is sometimes undercut in practice by other bases. A frequent example is expert authority which can allow those at lower hierarchical levels to resist or influence those who are formal superiors. For instance, hospital administrators often have problems with obtaining compliance from the doctors (Hage, 1974). However, this does not constitute a critique of conventional Organization Theory for while there are many studies of formal organization, it is not suggested that these nonhierarchic bases of power and authority do not exist. Indeed the conventional organization studies literature has given much emphasis to expert power and authority for at least two decades (Blau and Scott, 1963; Blau and Meyer, 1971; Blau, 1973).

Another sense in which orthodox views might be seen as insufficiently sensitive to political phenomena is the notion of political ploys or stratagems. Observers of the political process who have used more qualitative or anthropological methods point out that it is not mere possession of a power base but how one uses it (Pettigrew, 1973). To have information and access to the powerful is one thing, using it effectively is another. This involves tactical issues of timing, interpersonal finesse and the gambits of the sophisticated gamesperson. Pettigrew (1973) charts how one manager was successful in influencing top management to buy the computer he preferred. His influence was based on control of information, access to the elite, coalitions with certain subordinates, judicious attendance at certain meetings and moves to block access to the elite by individuals who posed threats. The information control was based on his formal position which allowed him to filter information going to top management from rival computer manufacturers. The access to the elite was facilitated by his being formal superordinate of the other manager who favoured another computer firm, and the successful suppression of direct contact between the top management and that subordinate was legitimated by appeal to the principle of working through the proper lines of command. Thus structural determinants underlay much of the political action. However, there is still a sense in which an individual incumbent could have played his cards well or badly.

Kenny and Wilson (1984) suggest that these more individual power ploys are the ones most used by managers dealing with their peers, i.e. those over whom they have least formal authority. This seems to open up an arena of choice of individual volition and of indeterminacy which does not sit well with models of structural determination. A more dramatic case points up the issue more sharply. Kenny and Palmer (1980) describe events in an Australian company where a subordinate manager was able to take over the role and power of his boss. The subordinate began the episode with low position power and low expertise relative to the super-ordinate. Despite this, he was able to virtually turn the tables. Much of this was done by taking an active, communicative stance to others in the company especially those at even higher levels than the immediate superior. This was reinforced by helping to solve their problems (the strategic contingencies theory of intra-organizational power applies here). Kenny and Palmer (1980) ascribe much of this success to a very different personality between the two: extroversion and introversion of subordinate and boss, respectively. Thus it may be here that personality may be a determinant underlying this process. This would suggest that models of structural change would benefit by the incorporation of select personality variables in addition to the other independent variables of hierarchic position, critical contingencies and so on.

It may remain true that some part of political processes cannot be explained by the prior state of variables. This would constitute a realm of indeterminacy and human freedom of choice. However, the exact scope of this can be ascertained only by pursuing the programme of orthodox research and seeing how far power and political phenomena are explicable by reference to contingencies and pre-existing organization structure. Moreover, this is doubly so because the interest is not usually in political processes for their own sake but rather in as far as they are consequential for structural change or similarly macro-organizational phenomena. This necessitates that studies examine structure and the like and relate these to the political processes. Thus reasons both of theory and of research objectives suggest that an appreciation of political processes will need to be pursued within a framework which builds on existing conventional work on organization. As the discussion has indicated, the concern for comparative methods and quantification therein will not preclude adequate performance of that task.

Child (1972a) writes of the need for greater study of these political processes in order to more fully understand structural determination. And

Schreyogg (1982) states that this will require a paradigm shift in order to take place. The political elements, such as the power and preferences of the different groups, will need to be ascertained. These can, in principle, be measured alongside of the other variables such as the contingencies (size, task, uncertainty, etc.) and the structure (specialization, centralization), and then added into a multivariate model to predict change in structure. The work of Abell (1975) and his colleagues on charting different groups in organizations, their preferred outcomes to decisions and their power is suggestive of a measurement approach here. Tannenbaum (Tannenbaum and Cooke, 1979) and his colleagues have developed techniques for measuring power as have Hinings *et al.* (1974) and Heller (1971). The possibilities for combining value and structural variables in predictive models is exemplified by Hage and Dewar (1973). They showed that structural variables (such as complexity and formalization) together with elite values towards change, predict the rate of innovation in subsequent time periods. The analogy would be to use structural and value variabales to predict structural change. Thus the study of political processes especially those consequential for organizational structural change can involve extensions to the theory and methods used in conventional organization studies but it does not need to abandon orthodox approaches.

Conclusions

It is by no means established that science is impossible in the study of organizations. Many of the existing approaches are used for reasons which continue to be sound. There is a positive role for case studies and qualitative methods. The study of power, politics and change are seen as compatible with scientific, quantitative and comparative approaches. The development of knowledge in organization studies has, and will, come about through the enhancement, rather than abandoning, of scientific approaches. We reaffirm the commitment to valid general causal laws as the goal in this, as in any other branch of the social sciences, rather than to an appreciation of uniqueness.

8

Conservative and managerial bias

One of the more central accusations against organizational studies is that it takes a biased view tending to side with management against the workers, and conservatives against radicals. This, it is argued, is fundamental given the theoretical approach taken by organizational students.

Managerialism

One of the lynchpins of Silverman's argument is that, in using the concepts of systems and their needs, the analyst is drawn to an acceptance of the views of the management, and to social interventions of a doubtful kind:

> So we begin to distinguish 'formal' from 'informal' organization and to attribute rationality to the former and non-rational affectivity to the latter. Then we proceed to look for ways in which people can be made to see how their goals are really indistinguishable from system goals: to make the personality fit the role, rather than the role adjust to the personality. Thus the positivist orientation, which is the first to claim its value-freedom, degenerates, as did its founder, into what we may politely call 'value-relevance'. (1968: 223)

Again, Silverman makes clear that the sins of the Human Relations Movement have been committed by structural-functionalism:

> With solid theoretical reasons and with, no doubt, the best of value-free intentions, the functionalist view of the characteristics of a system seems to us to have become as involved in managerial aims as the earliest Human Relationists. If the strictures about 'cow sociology' apply equally well to both, it is because each has taken management's problems as their problems: productivity in the case of the latter, 'adaptation' and 'integration' in the case of the former. (1968: 229)

And such terms as integration are, for Silverman, synonyms for domination:

> Thus 'integration', for instance, is not first a system need but a group need. It is the problem of groups who desire to maintain the *status quo* in an organization and their places within it; it has 'functional' conse-

quences for some, 'dysfunctional' for others (who, by being 'integrated may have forgone the chance of attaining their ends). (1968: 232)

At the core of Silverman's arguments one finds again, his discomfort with the concept of organizational goal:

A disturbing consequence of all this is that, by accepting the system's 'goal', we are pushed inexorably towards a view inseparable from that of management. For management's problems, the survival and adaptation of the system, have become our problems. (1968: 223)

It is true that systems theory is concerned with survival and adaptation, and it is certainly true that managers are concerned with this. But not only are the theorists' and managers' respective views logically separable, but they are often separated in practice. The theory posits survival and adaptation as systems needs, and the concrete functioning of the system (especially as compared with other systems, and with itself over time) is examined in order to discern what structures are most conducive to survival and adaptation given different environmental exigencies, and to learn what kinds of adaptation are most appropriate. This is done by examining the empirical structures and adaptation attempts by managers, some of which are successful (i.e. are shown to be functional for the system) and some of which are unsuccessful (i.e. the dysfunctions are shown to outweigh the functions). Some attempts at adaptation and survival authorized by managers will be revealed by research to be maladaptive and to lead their organization towards extinction. For instance, minute division of labour among lower-level employees to secure higher rates of productivity may lead those employees to have dissatisfaction with their jobs, which may lead them to quit (Likert and Likert, 1976; Argyris, 1964). A high rate of employee turnover leads to inefficiencies through extra training and recruitment costs, and through general disorganization by inadequate socialization of members. This in turn leads to lower levels of productivity. The managers initiating this chain of events did not intend to bring it about, but their behaviour caused it. The social science analyst points out the dysfunction of this structure. In this way, though both manager and analysts are concerned with systems effectiveness, their viewpoints are distinguishable. The concrete meaning attached to adaptation and survival by managers and theorists-as-researchers, is not identical. For this to be so, the understanding by managers of what is implied for their organization to survive and adapt, would have to be infallible. If this were so, there would be few significant dysfunctions for sociologists to study. Also, there would be little incentive for those in Schools of Management interested in refining prescriptive theories of organization, such as the writer, from so doing, since all present organizations would be perfect and managerial knowledge complete. Once again, Silverman's method is to essay similarities at a textual level which misrepresent disparities of substance.

Hence the systems needs, such as those for survival and adaption in the systems theory, are not at all the same as the goals to which managers hold, or even to those objectives which are empirically operating in a given organization. The objectives authorized by senior managers, and which have become institutionalized in the organization (i.e. resources are allocated towards tasks which aid their fulfilment, performance is assessed and sanctioned against these criteria, etc.), may, from the standpoint of systems theory, neglect or run counter to certain essential functions. A management may authorize goals of high financial return and seek to pursue them through ruthless personnel policies. The resulting levels of tension and anxiety down the hierarchy may produce levels of conflict, defensiveness and employee turnover which so disrupt efforts at routine production and operational problem-solving, that the financial return from the unit declines in the medium term. This would be the case of the functional requisite of goal-attainment operating in a way which was incongruent with the requisites of latency (employees' commitment and anxiety), integration (interdepartmental conflict), and adaptation (lack of flexible problem-solving). Empirical studies which have sought to operationalize each of such requisites in concrete organizations have found, as structural-functionalism would predict, that under-emphasis on one type of requisite in practice is dysfunctional, i.e. impairs the operational performance of the system (Etzioni, 1975). Thus for goals to be attained successfully attention must be paid to ensuring satisfactory levels of the requisites of latency, integration and adaptation. This indicates that the objectives as set by historical individuals, top managers of organizations, are not the same as the needs of the system as revealed by structural-functional analysis. If and when organizational structural-functionalism becomes all-knowing, and if managers accepted and completely implemented it, then their objectives and systems needs would be identical, but we are presently far from either condition.

Again, in discussing the problems of identifying systems needs, Silverman asserts that because this is difficult the analyst will in fact come to embrace the position that whatever exists is functional:

> We have noted how difficult it is to ascribe 'ends' or 'needs' to systems. Very often, it seems to us, what has passed for objective analysis has largely stemmed from the value commitments of the observer to the *status quo*. How, for instance, am I to defend my conception of system 'needs' against that of someone else. (1968: 232)

Yet the theoretical expositions of modern structural-functionalism explicitly caution against imputing functions to everything that happens to exist. In his classic formulation, Merton (1949) expressly warns against this as a fallacy to be avoided, and illustrates this by reference to the inanity of supposing that because gentlemen's suits have buttons on the cuffs that they serve a function. It is the task of structural-functional analysis to examine whether the elements that presently exist have functions or whether they are dysfunctional, and indeed to assess the net balance of their functions and dysfunctions for the system. Functionality is not assumed at the beginning of the enquiry. If it could be there would be no need for the analysis. A world-view which assumed that what is, ought to be, has no requirement for empirical enquiry. Structural-functionalism is not doctrinaire conservatism. Part of Silverman's confusion may stem from a failure to appreciate that systems needs are theoretical entities. They are generally applicable to all social systems, or, at least to classes of them. Silverman tries to approach systems concepts from his concept of the ends of the actor, which, for him, are empirically ascertained in each situation. Applying such logic to the notion of systems needs would imply that one empirically established this for each system. Yet this is not what the concept means in the systems approach. Therein it is a theory, based on empirical observation and reflection, about what all social systems need in order to survive. Thus the concept is deployed from outside the particular empirical case, and this reduces the extent to which the analyst makes judgements.

It is not the case that the analyst defines needs by picking one or some out of the differing objectives pursued by the workers and managers: profits, wages, an easy life, etc. There is by no means consensus within structural-functionalism as to what are the needs of organizations, nor about whether the concept of needs or prerequisites is useful. The point for this discussion is that the utilization of such a concept is not equivalent to, and does not imply, espousal of the *status quo*.

Rationality of organization

Silverman writes: 'So we begin to distinguish "formal" from "informal" organization and to attribute rationality to the former and non-rational affectivity to the latter' (1968: 223).

In discussing the Hawthorne studies, Silverman (1968: 225) characterizes them as seeing workers' resistance to managerial objectives (maximum production under the incentive scheme) as non-rational 'sentiments'. There are discussions within the literature of organizational sociology which make such distinctions, but the question is whether this classification is central to the subject as a whole. Even the classical discussion of informal organization by Roethlisberger and Dickson (1939), central figures in the Human Relations Movement, points out that the informal practices they observed, though contrary to managements' intentions, were rational when looked at from the viewpoint of the workers practising them, given their distrust of managements' incentive scheme. (In passing, note that this is of course based on using the actor's frame of reference and this example may serve to show how the position which Silverman argues, so far from being new or radical, has a long lineage in organizational sociology, even in those works which were quite explicitly aimed at offering advice on employee relations policies to management.) Returning to the issue of rationality, systems theory does not posit that all aspects of the formal organization are rational, though they may be so intended by the managers designing them. The intentions of actual managers to be effective are often revealed by structural-functional research to be ineffective, to be less than completely rational. Organization Theory implies the intent of efficiency to formal organizations, but it does not state that all formal organizations are empirically the height of rationality. Further, structural-functionalism carried within it the argument that structures necessarily depart from that which would be expected given simple models of completely rational actions, i.e. given that action had no emotional or affectual components in terms of Weber's distinction between rational and non-rational action (Weber, 1968). Structural-functional theory directs the analyst to look for all sorts of deviations from rigidly bureaucratic norms in organizational life. Studies using such frameworks talk about rituals of integration, the necessity of socio-emotional leadership, the importance of opportunities for tension release, the existence of indulgency patterns etc. (Merton, 1949; Gouldner, 1954; Etzioni, 1975). The model of organizational life revealed by structural-functionalism is far from one of cool rationality. True that much of this takes place in the area categorized as informal organization, but structural-functionalism is not thereby seeing it as inferior or counter to organizational rationality, rather it argues that such phenomena are essential to organizational survival and adaptation.

Silverman (1968) argues that the elements he sees as implied by systems thinking, about organizations, lead the analyst to a managerial view. It becomes clear that Silverman has a particular model of managerial thinking. Managers see the workers as non-rational, believe in manipulation and dislike questions about the origins of their organization. This is a stereotype which requires reality testing.

To begin with the first issue Silverman writes: 'Above all, it seems fruitful to look for the elements of rationality in group behaviour. The Human Relations school were prevented from doing this by their vaguely social-psychological notion of group "sentiments" which fitted, only too well, into managerial conceptions of worker motivation and behaviour' (1968: 232). Yet managers and corporations continue to use wages incentive schemes which are based on a model of workers as economic men, i.e. as rational. Similarly, managers seek to control worker attendance, punctuality and work quality by systems which deploy various financial rewards and penalties. Such managers do this because they believe that workers are amenable to monetary carrots and sticks, that they make calculations and alter their behaviour accordingly. The widespread utilization and continued deployment of such schemes is testament to the very considerable degree of belief in worker rationality by modern management.

Turning to the question of the change versus functioning of systems Silverman writes: 'Similarly, it avoids managerially disturbing "why" questions, about the generation of change, and emphasizes the more "positive" question of "how" the system adjusts' (1968: 224). For Silverman, change comes about as a result of the various groups within (or around) organizations seeking to further their own ends and hence rearranging the negotiated order. Yet for many managers that is exactly how they see their work life. They are aware of differing and antithetic constituencies, shifting coalitions, various stakeholders and the constant compromises which make up organization summarized under world-weary phrases such as 'It's all politics of course.' They may not like it, and may hanker for a more settled, more unitary world, yet years of living within such situations leads to accommodation and stratagems for coping. The idea that managers leap to embrace systems and structural-functional models and eschew political-conflict models is belied by this author's experience of teaching executives.

One of Silverman's more baleful themes is that structural-functionalism leads to manipulation. The argument is that by concentrating on the needs of systems, and by stressing the necessity of member motivation towards their realization, the stage is set for the suasion of the membership: 'Moreover, because of our prior commitment to the system, we are forced to concern ourselves with how its human members can be made to adjust to its needs' (Silverman, 1968: 228).

Or again, Silverman sees in Parsons' discussion (Parsons, 1964) of the role of therapy in attaining normative integration, a direct prescription for the role of the social analyst: 'The sociologist accordingly takes as his problem the way in which people can be manipulated in order to fit impersonal ends' (Silverman, 1968: 230).

The structural-functional model explains integration of society in part by the adherence to certain norms and values of the membership, and argues that this is achieved through socialization, including indoctrination, sanctions and therapy. However, it does not follow that structural-functionalism leads proponents to actively seek to make good these processes, through social intervention. One reason that such an analyst might hold back from this mission is that structural-functionalism does not imply that all socialization and social control is functional. A uniform set of norms and values reduces the structural differentiation which structural-functionalists see as important for effective functioning and change (Lawrence and Lorsch, 1967). In the derived organizational literature, the idea that the jostling of rival departmental and occupational perspectives provides a tension which is productive is familiar, and is often caught in the term 'creative conflict'. Structural-functionalism argues only that there will be some degree of normative integration attained through some level of socialization, it does not specify that the optimum level is the maximum. An organizational analyst using the structural-functionalist model might conceivably advise greater socialization into company beliefs, but he or she might equally prescribe less. Nor is it clear that an analyst who saw the need for more socialization would necessarily accept present norms and values, nor rely on those of management. The norms and values which are most likely to be institutionalized are those which evolve out of the culture of a group of workers, or which are compatible with more fundamental elements in the culture of that group or strata or class. Moreover, efforts to alter attitudes through manipulation are likely to lead to resentment, defensiveness and resistance. The organizational behaviour literature which seeks to advise management on change is filled with cautions against manipulation, warning that it will likely backfire and increase hostility and resistance in the future (Argyris, 1964). Such writings emphasize trust-building and a key process is the way in which the parties test to see whether, by cooperating more closely with the others (such as management), they are being asked to sacrifice their interests as they see them. Modern organizational analysis of the systems type has no particular commitment to indoctrination and manipulation, either in theory or practice.

So far we have argued that Silverman confuses systems needs with systems goals, and that these are different. Earlier, a conception of systems needs was offered, but what of systems, or better, organizational goals? We have argued that they are objectives, which though originating (in the main) in the consciousness of individuals, become, through the processes of authorization and institutionalization, the attributes of the organization. But are these nevertheless the interests of the managers running the organization? The modern systems model deals in a conception of various stakeholders, each of whom gives certain inputs to the organization, but expects certain returns. The continued cooperation of the stakeholders is dependent upon the adequacy of these returns, as judged against their potential returns from other organizations. This is often referred to as the exchange-dependency model. The objectives set by management for the organization have to balance these often conflicting objectives one with another (Pfeffer and Salancik, 1978). The resulting objectives are a compromise between the differing parties' objectives reflecting their differential influence and power. One of the parties whose objectives are compromised in the formation of organizational objectives is that of the management themselves. This is integral to the stakeholder model. Hence the goals of the organization are not identical with the first preferences, the interests of the management. Management is of course interested in the organization surviving and functioning, but so are all the other parties in the exchange: the employees, the suppliers, the customers, the shareholders (if any), etc. The objectives of the organization may be described as managerialist only in the sense that they may equally well be described as 'employeeist', 'customerist', 'governmentalist', etc.

A related charge of Burrell and Morgan is that such structural studies of organization ' . . . have tended to provide explanations of social affairs which are geared to providing explanations of the *status quo*' (1979: 65). As has been shown, organization studies mainly examines differences between organizations at the same point in time. It also does examine changes in organization across time (Inkson *et al.*, 1970; Hage and Dewar, 1973; Channon, 1973; Rumelt, 1974; Dyas and Thanheiser, 1976; Dewar and Hage, 1978; Donaldson, 1980). Moreover, it has been seen that there is a very considerable interest in change, especially adaptation and differential survival. This is not an explanation of the *status quo* in the sense of saying that what is, must be. Modern contingency analysis points towards many organizations as being incongruent and therefore as needing to be changed if they are to better attain their goals (Woodward, 1965; Lawrence and Lorsch, 1967; Etzioni, 1975; Child, 1975b; Lenz, 1980; Donaldson, 1984). The method is to study extant variations, but the theory points to cases of dissonance between the potential and the actual. If by explaining the *status quo* is meant that there is little in such analysis about completely new structures and cataclysmic change towards these, then the accusation is correct. Imaginative essays of wholly novel worlds based on the principles of anarchism, socialism, behaviourism or whatever (as for example in Skinner, 1948) are not the province of organization studies. Neither social science nor historical scholarship can study phenomena which do not yet exist. Organizational enquiry can only examine variations which empirically are in occurrence. These comments apply equally to theories of societal change which concern themselves with revolutions or other discontinuities in the social order. They can only study such socialist or nationalist revolutions as have happened (Moore, 1967). For science the *status quo* is all the variation which exists to date. There are organizational studies of the comparative statistical kind which enquire into the universality of certain propositions by seeing whether they hold in socialist as well as in capitalist countries (Tannenbaum and Cooke, 1979).

Hence the scientific method does not imply an approach which neglects change and is necessarily a justification of one set of institutional arrangements out of the range of current alternatives. Social scientific analysis, including that of organizations, is concerned with explaining the *status quo*, in the sense of present variations and changes, but it is not concerned only with the issues that phrase implies, i.e. justification of certain contemporary institutions as healthy and immutable.

Conclusions

Organization Theory studies existing structures including the issue of effectiveness. Managers are concerned with efficient operation but this does not mean that the view taken by the student of organizations is identical to that of a manager of an organization. The knowledge produced in organization studies may sometimes imply that the policies and procedures employed by the management of a particular organization are ineffective. In this way the analysis constitutes a critique of current affairs. In terms of research methods, considerable attention is paid to the comparison of organizations which differ in their levels of performance. Thus researchers do not take the view that all existing organizations are perfect. Accordingly, Organization Theory does not sanctify the *status quo*. The study of organizations is empirical and intellectually open. It is neither conservative nor biased towards management.

9

Organization Theory as ideology

Accusations of managerial bias in Organization Theory are not meant to refer to technical inaccuracies, they are seen as pervasive distortions in the account given of organizational life, which makes of Organization Theory an ideology. Thus Organization Theory is useful to privileged groups within the society as a justification of their position and as a way to preserve their hegemony over the organized.

The work of Clegg and Dunkerley (1980) castigates Organization Theory as being to a large degree ideological. Moreover, it is an ideology manufactured in and for business schools. It is intended mainly for the consumption of students attending courses there, be they present, or future, managers. The idea is to produce compliant tools of the capitalist class (Clegg and Dunkerley, 1980: 538). This is done by presenting organizational analysis as being a universal phenomena divorced from an analysis of the wider political economy:

> . . . the most important aspect of the business schools, and of management education generally, is . . . their role in reproducing ideology . . . This ideology is what people do at these institutions, which is to learn the rational science and techniques of modern management, among which will be the organization theory we have criticized in this book. By providing concepts of 'the organization', for instance, which are absolutely independent of any political economy, but related only to presumed universal systems of structures of organizations, and by stressing the universal applicability of these 'rational precepts' (which on closer inspection are not always so ideologically pure as they might seem) these schools produce, on the whole, sound and reliable ruling-class functionaries who have complex rules built into them . . . (Clegg and Dunkerley, 1980: 538)

Clegg and Dunkerley continue: 'Much of the ideological work of organization theory represents such a softening, whitening, blurring and misrepresentation' (1980: 539). In particular this is done by presenting organizations as moulded by technology in a way that is inevitable, apolitical and rational. They call for more explicit treatment of the actual objectives

94

served by current organizations and the interests involved (Clegg and Dunkerley, 1980: 539).

Organization Theory is seen by Clegg and Dunkerley (1980) as an ideology, buttressing advanced capitalism and thereby aiding and abetting the exploitation of the masses. Once again this is a stereotype, not the substance of Organization Theory or the way it is taught. The reply advanced here will discuss the concept of ideology, the ideological use of Organization Theory, the neglect of the socio-economic context, the ideological nature of certain research methods and the way business schools approach the teaching of this subject.

For a neo-Marxian, the importance of using their framework in organization studies would not rest merely on its explanatory power *vis-à-vis* internal organization structure and functioning, rather the language of Marxian analysis, of exploitation, property relations, etc., has its own justification as part of an assault on the legitimacy of bourgeois thought. The use of terms such as exploitation and ownership as descriptions of organizational life contain both a reference to the macro perspective and a condemnatory evaluation. For a Marxian, any other analytic framework omits reference to the essential socio-economic and moral facts and therefore dupes the social actors concerned and is thereby doing an ideological service for the exploiters. Thus conventional Organization Theory, with its 'neutral' language of formalization, centralization, communication, decision-making and so on, is, from a Marxian standpoint, not merely technically deficient but politically and morally noxious. Even if the Marxian analysis added nothing to explaining more of organizational life the use of the newer language of class and conflict would add to the delegitimation of the existing social order and thus assist the struggle. Thus for a Marxian sociologist, any critique, be it narrowly technical or broadly sociological, of conventional Organization Theory has a certain appeal. This may go some way to explaining the animus which drives writers such as Clegg and Dunkerley (1980) to be so dissatisfied with so much of current organizational studies.

If one believes that the main moral fact of our society is class exploitation and that this is the central structuring device and motor of social change then conventional Organization Theory must seem a sham. At least this inexorable conclusion must be drawn to the extent that one sees all social analysis as politicized. If all social research is conducted within the tunnel vision of a paradigm, and if all paradigms are located in social philosophies which reflect a position in the class struggle, then all intellectual discourse about society is class conflict fought out at the symbolic level. The task of the socialist sociologist is to engage the bourgeois apologist. Yet this seems a very one-dimensional view of modern social analysis. One of the themes of this volume has been that there are areas of discourse about organizations which are not particularly politicized. Establishing empirically and theoretically that larger organizations have more specialists is surely a relatively neutral social enquiry. Again, seeking to know whether there is a causal relationship between intra-organizational communications and subsequent innovations in service is surely as much of interest to those involved in running a socialist hospital as it is to those who own and control a capitalist one.

The objection may be made that this understates the way in which the 'metaphysical' language of phrases such as 'organizational goals' can so distract attention from the underlying plurality of interest groups that it can lead certain stakeholders, such as employees, to accept objectives which give them lower returns than they would otherwise settle for. The argument is that the conceptions such as 'organizational goals' are persuasive in practice. Hence, Organization Theory is usable ideology. This raises the question: Where and when has it been used? Where are the studies documenting that the language of systems theory has in fact mystified workers or misled consumers? To describe a type of sociology as being ideology is to make an analysis in the Sociology of Knowledge. That sub-discipline relates ideas to concrete action and to social positions. Yet the critique of Clegg and Dunkerley (1980), Silverman (1968) and others, whilst laying the charge of ideology, nowhere shows that these ideas do in fact have this effect in practice, or in 'praxis'. The discussion is wholly at the level of textual material, terminating, on occasion, with a few quotations of statements which are felt to be objectionable. Proponents of this argument would be expected to be interested in studying cases of workers having been bamboozled out of their dues by systems theory, yet this literature (Clegg and Dunkerley, 1980; Silverman, 1970; Salaman, 1978) cites no such studies.

Of course it might be shown by a Marxian critic that work such as that on size-specialization has in fact been used ideologically. Suppose that it can be demonstrated that the language and results contained in writing such as Blau (1972) and Child (1973) have misled certain workers in some capitalist companies and thus assisted their exploitation. Does this mean that Organization Theory is an ideology? Marxist-Leninism is used in the Soviet bloc to justify actions by their authorities and this includes legitimating episodes of oppression. Does this mean that the social theories of Marx and Lenin are nothing but ideologies? A wide variety of theories find themselves used from time to time to justify authority and oppression, is this enough to qualify them as mere ideologies. Surely we need to distinguish between episodic use by some groups in some situations of a theory as an ideology, and that same theory as being an ideology *per se*. The latter implies that the theory is necessarily ideological, i.e. that it always functions ideologically. Moreover, to say of a social scientific theory that it is an ideology implies that there is no truth in it. Yet modern social science goes to some lengths to check on the empirical validity of theories through the use of the procedures for making inferences which are reasonably common to all contemporary sciences, and which have been formalized by philosophers of science. Thus we may concede that there may well be occasional uses of Organization Theory as an ideology without thereby reaching the conclusion that it is an ideology. A critic might reply that theories differ in the ease with which they may be used ideologically – their ideological potential – and that Organization Theory has high potential in this regard. However, is there really any evidence that the writings of Weber or Blau or Simon have been more often used ideologically than those of Marx or Lenin or Mao? In contemporary Poland we have the striking case of Marx being used by the authorities to justify their repression and by the activists to justify their dissent. Marx is invoked on both sides of the barricades: that of the Communist party and police, and that of the students and workers. One can observe this without concluding that Marxism is nothing but an ideology. This parallels the position of Organization Theory: occasional ideological use perhaps, but not an ideology.

Considering the accusation that Organization Theory de-emphasizes the political economic context, there is some truth to the statement that emphasis is given to universal aspects. This is partly because Organization Theory has come to mean those works which are general in their reference. These emphasize theoretical contributions such as those of Weber (1947) and his contemporary followers (Blau, 1972; Child, 1977; Hall, 1977), who deal in purportedly general laws such as those of bureaucratization. That such theories are taken seriously is itself defensible in view of the considerable body of empirical evidence about generalizability. For instance, the size-bureaucracy relationship has been found in studies of manufacturing firms, service firms, trade unions and educational institutions (Pugh and Hickson, 1976; Pugh and Hinings, 1976). It has been replicated in Western countries such as West Germany, Sweden and Canada and also Eastern Europe (Poland), the Middle East (Jordan), and the Far East (India and Japan) (Hickson and McMillan, 1981). The generalizability of size-bureaucracy is not simply a claim or postulate, it now has considerable empirical support. There are other relationships in the organization studies literature for which there is both a theory and evidence of generality. An example would be diversification-decentralization which has been demonstrated in business firms in Australia, France, Italy, Japan, the United Kingdom, the United States and West Germany (Chenhall, 1979; Dyas and Thanheiser, 1976; Pavan, 1976; Suzuki, 1980; Channon, 1973; Rumelt, 1974). Again there is both theory connecting routine with role formalization and considerable empirical evidence, with support for the notion that it generalizes from manufacturing to service organizations (Gerwin, 1979). Many of the phenomena dealt with in organization are generalizable to considerable portions of advanced industrial society – both capitalist and socialist. As will be discussed (Chapter 11) socio-economic-cultural factors impact on organizations but research using standardized comparative measures has helped to identify these phenomena.

Moving to the issue of ideological bias in research methods, Clegg and Dunkerley (1980) see the Aston research as exemplifying problems of ideology in organizational research:

> The research moves in an *ideological circle* from what formal theorists have argued organizations are like, or should be like, to what their students and readers have argued organizations should be like, in terms of intra-organizational formal procedures and rules. The research moves from formal theory to formal theory: the only difference is that the site of the formal theory changes from the ideological community of organization writers to the ideological community of organization executives. (1980: 226; emphasis as in original)

Clegg and Dunkerley state that in seeking to operationalize structure researchers such as those at Aston have constructed their items from formal theories of organizational management, and these prescribe what should be done (1980: 226). The researchers then collect data by enquiring of managers what they do, or should do, and the managers answer in terms of the approved practices as laid down by the theories (Clegg and Dunkerley, 1980: 226).

This implies that the items constructing the Aston scale reflect practices which are accorded the status of being what should be done. However, this is predicated upon the belief that there is some unitary formal theory of organizations which is subscribed to by all management theorists and managers. However, there is considerable dissensus within managerial theory (Hickson, 1966) between those advocating formality, tight job descriptions, clear lines of authority, detailed rules and procedures (Brown, 1960; Brech, 1957) and those advocating discretion for lower-level subordinates and reliance on informal, emergent roles (Likert, 1961; Argyris, 1960). Contemporary management writers do not seem to be in unanimity about what are the most appropriate structures.

Further, the Aston researchers in selecting questions attempted to find non-evaluative items, in order to minimize emotive or social approval biases. The items which compose the measures (see Pugh and Hickson, 1976) are fairly bland and pretty innocuous. For instance, a question about centralization of decision-making is: 'Who is the most junior person on whose decision action is normally taken about when overtime will be worked?' Again a question about Formalization (i.e. documentation) is:

'Do you have senior executive meetings? Is there a written agenda for them?' Or again, a question on the Standardization scale is: 'Is there inspection of work-in-progress?' Further, each informant typically answers a large number of such questions and this reduces the significance or drama attaching to any one of them. Some managers I have interviewed using the Aston method have expressed surprise that one wants to know about such trivia. Moreover, the items asked of a respondent may not form any particular pattern to him or her. Their significance for the research only comes into view when the replies to the various items are assembled into scales and aggregate scores calculated (Pugh *et al.*, 1968). This process is fairly opaque to the individual informant.

If the Aston scales tapped only a formal theory of 'good management' then one would expect managers to affirm all the items in the scales: 'Yes, we have all these documents.' 'Yes, we have all these specialisms.' However, for each scale organizations vary considerably in their aggregate scores, e.g. on Overall Formalization in the Aston study, the range was 4 to 49 with a mean of 27.17 (Pugh and Hickson, 1976: 73). The average respondent is saying that his or her organization does not have about half of the documents enquired after in the interview. For Overall Standardization the range is 30 to 131, with a mean of 83.88 (Pugh and Hickson, 1976: 71). Thus it is untrue to characterize respondents as claiming all the paraphernalia mentioned in modern management texts (e.g. work study, operations research, frequent stock-taking). Again, a prescription derived from classical management theory, with some currency amongst established managers, is that it is ineffective for managers to have more than six or seven direct subordinates, i.e. they will not be able to supervise them adequately. Yet the Aston researches report a range on the number of direct subordinates of the Chief Executive up to 14 (Pugh and Hickson, 1976: 75). The mean is 6.08, so that about half the organizations are over the prescribed number. Thus informants are apparently willing to avow spans in excess of what the principle prescribes.

The idea of the ideological circle is also based on a lack of understanding of the kind of prescriptions which would flow from research of the Aston type. These kinds of research produce as their output aggregate scores, e.g. this organization's Overall Formalization scale score is 23, this other organization's score is 37 on this same scale. The prescriptive implications of the Aston school of research is contained within the programmatic of the contingency approach, that the optimum structure varies depending upon the scores on the contingency variables. Child (1975) has shown that the optimum degree of Overall Standardization associated with high performance is a function of size and the degree of environmental variability. Of necessity, interviewees in studies conducted prior to the publication of Child's article (Pugh *et al.*, 1968;

Donaldson and Warner, 1974a, b), or on which Child's results were based, cannot have known the 'right answer' and so those researches cannot be contaminated in that way. A managerial informant, in a successive study, who had read Child (1975) and wanted to give the researchers the impression that the degree of Standardization in his or her organization was the most appropriate would have to know, firstly, what that was quantitatively. This would involve knowing the size of the organization and its degree of environmental variability as the research procedures would score it. He or she would then need to know the regression equations used to connect these variables. Even if the prescribed standardization score were known, the informant would then have to convincingly, selectively endorse or reject scale items in the interviews so as to produce the appropriate aggregate score. This kind of process seems pretty far-fetched. Given the nature of the sort of prescriptions which emerge from modern contingency research – quantitative, contingent, complex and technically derived – it seems that managerial informants cannot readily simply play them back to the researchers in interview.

The ideological circle critique of Clegg and Dunkerley (1980) is not viable as an objection to Aston-type research and is based on a lack of understanding of managerial theories, the thinking of practising managers, Aston research and the relationships between these elements.

Turning to the issue of politico-economic context and the supposed cloaking of vested interests served by capitalist corporations, these issues are dealt with quite explicitly both in Organization Theory (as discussed earlier) and in business school curricula. If there is a dominant paradigm in business schools, then in many of them it is economics and finance. This gives emphasis to owners' returns from corporate activity, and explicitly treats shareholders as rational economic maximizers out for pecuniary gain (Ball *et al.*, 1976). The capitalist nature of modern industrial organizations is not denied by contemporary business school curricula.

The difficulty inherent in the position taken by Clegg and Dunkerley (1980) may be seen by taking it seriously for a moment. Suppose that the managers produced by business schools have been fed, and believed, a blurred and misrepresented image of modern corporate life. As an ideology it must, by definition, be false. But how can a false view assist a manager in managing, in controlling workers or other managers to attain objectives? If the workers are on strike for more pay and the manager, deluded by behavioural science, thinks that they just need the washrooms painted pink and a counselling chat, taking these steps will still leave the manager with a strike. Again, if the manager is mystified about the nature of the interests he or she serves, how can they serve them well? If the manager has come to believe that the mission of corporations in the post-industrial society is knowledge production and so pushes up R & D expenditures to the point where there is no profit and no dividend, then the owners are unlikely to be pleased or to leave him or her in charge for very long. Real, powerful vested interests in modern industry must, by definition, make themselves felt and it is unlikely that any system of thought which sought to deny them would be believed. As we have argued, modern Organization Theory does not seek to deny the existence of interests, such as those of capital, nor to deny that they shape organizational goals and structures.

A further issue is the political neutrality, the overly bland, whitened, softened view of industry that Organization Theory supposedly contains. Many of the phenomena with which organizational sociology deals are essentially politically neutral. Some of the more significant contingencies of structure which the subject addresses – size, diversification, uncertainty – are apolitical. They have their significance for organizational structure largely irrespective of political factors which might shape other features of goals or structures. For instance, there is evidence that the size-bureaucracy phenomena occurs both in countries of the capitalist West (e.g. West Germany, UK, USA) and also in Eastern European state socialist nations, such as Poland (Hickson and McMillan, 1981). The doctrine of the politicization of everything may enjoy currency but it flies in the face of some of the facts.

In their criticisms of Organization Theory and business schools, Clegg and Dunkerley make the point that the view presented therein emphasizes rationality (1980: 537, 539), in terms of formal methods of planning, marketing, finance and the like. Yet what else would one expect curricula for business or public administration to concentrate on other than efficacious means to ends? Moreover, it is precisely by the knowledge being primarily instrumental that it can be of use to people with widely differing purposes. Information about tools can be employed to attain objectives of profitable commodity production, profitable product innovation, low-cost service, innovative service, professional standards, equality of treatment, military defence or successful trade union organization. The emphasis on means rather than ends enables individuals to draw on the body of technique and knowledge and to use them selectively to attain their desired objective. The concern with rational means rather than values is part of what makes such studies apolitical. Thus the focus on the rational, though criticized by Clegg and Dunkerley, helps avoid falling into some of the other errors of which they accuse Organization Theory and business schools.

As has been seen, Clegg and Dunkerley (1980) are critical of the role of Organization Theory as an ideology taught within business schools to practising or would-be managers. Yet it may be instructive to consider the analogy with medical schools. In the latter would-be medical practitioners are taught anatomy, physiology, the causes of disease and the uses of advanced technology for diagnosis and cure. A social critic might well point out that there is a social dimension to health: mortality rates differ by class, access to medical expertise tends to differ by class and propensity to disease is affected by differences in housing and nutrition which again are class-based. Thus in the analysis of health policy and practice a perspective from social stratification is relevant. This has led to the argument for the inclusion of socio-political and economic studies in the medical curricula. One can recognize the veracity of this argument but it does not mean that schools of medicine should not teach anatomy, physiology and so on. A perspective focusing on the structure of the human body and the functioning of the organs continues to have relevance. Thus one can appreciate the call for more material on socio-economic structures in the curricula of business and management schools without needing to deny the cogency of intra-organizational studies.

It would be difficult to see how one can intelligently discuss industrial relations, national efforts at prices and incomes policies, the reaction to the introduction of new technology at work, or relations between multi-national corporations and host countries, without recognizing that in each topic there are multiple stakeholders with distinguishable objectives and that this accounts for the conflicts therein. The argument might well be made that more such material should be in business school curricula and that certain institutions have yet to incorporate as much of this macro-scopic syllabus as a person might think appropriate. But if there were deficiencies of this kind, would Organization Theory be to blame? One might hold accountable individual organization theorists for a lack of attention to these wider issues. But this would seem to be the common problem of the blind-spots inherent in specialization, for presumably the faculty members teaching accounting or production might also lack this broader view. One might, with some justice, develop an argument about the traditional preponderance of organization theorists versus industrial relations specialists, or of psychologists over sociologists, in certain schools of business management. But it would not seem sensible to blame Organization Theory, *per se*, for having concentrated its attention on internal issues of structure and functioning such as centralization of decision-making, bureaucratic specialization, interdepartmental coordination, innovation and so on. These are issues central to organization and distinctive. That schools of business and management should include such material in their curricula is neither surprising nor does it mean that this is ideological indoctrination. Organization Theory is a specialist study focusing on those parts of the social structure which are located inside the boundaries of organizations (e.g. business firms, trade unions, protest movements, governments, international alliances, international trade agreements), as such those who manage organizations, along with other employees, find the material of some relevance.

Conclusions

The frequent criticism that Organization Theory and research is just an ideology has been examined in some detail. Contrary to the claims of its detractors there is nothing inherently ideological in such work. While the possibility of occasional ideological use exists we have noted how none of the critics document such episodes. Moreover, even if such occasional use were established this would not be sufficient grounds for classifying organizational analysis as simply an ideology. This cannot be the criteria for labelling a body of thought as an ideology for almost any system of ideas, including Marxism, would be categorized as an ideology on that test. Equally the concern in much organizational work for generalizations which hold across a range of socio-political settings has been shown to be in accord with the results of empirical studies. The concern for rationality, efficient means to ends, in schools of business and management studies has been shown to be part of an instrumental approach to administrative knowledge which allows individuals with differing values to each use it to further their own ends. Thus the subject of organization studies is not tied to the service of one particular interest group, privileged or otherwise.

A critique of alternative programmes in the study of organizations

Having considered many of the objections to orthodox Organization Theory in Part One, in Part Two attention turns to programmes which are being offered as alternatives. These are Social Action Theory, the Sociology of Organizations, Marxian Organization Theory and the Strategic Choice Thesis. These are the formulations propounded by the critics of conventional organizational studies. Each of these will be examined and shown to contain a number of difficulties and to be based on assumptions some of which are questionable.

10

Social Action Theory

Those who criticize organizational-level concepts from an individualist reductionist perspective often advocate that organization studies should adopt Social Action Theory as the theoretical framework.

The Social Action Theory is derived from Weber's (1968) interpretive sociology. The focus is on the action of the individual actor. The interpretive sociologist seeks to understand not only the behaviour of the individual but the meaning which he or she attaches to their acts. This involves trying to make sense of the world-view of the person in terms of their perceptions, beliefs and values. The action of the individual is seen as oriented towards the attainment of ends which they value, through processes of calculation and choice about efficient means to this end. This is the conception of rational action and Weber (1968) suggests that interpretive sociology should commence by attempting to understand this, rather than more emotional acts. This is to be done by gaining insights into the subjective world of actors and constructing a model of motivated actions of the typical actor in a particular social setting. Thus interpretive sociology lays stress on understanding the situation from the point of view of the actor. It thus emphasizes the subjective, the perceptual and meaning. Weber's formulation is seen as standing in a tradition of historico-cultural, qualitative analysis of the realm of the spirit and ideas. In this sense, it may be contrasted with positivistic or natural science-based approaches which deal primarily in the objectively observable and, most particularly, with behaviourism (Skinner, 1971) which entirely discounts any statements by people about their subjective experience. One of the more trenchant arguments of Social Action Theory is that, by being based on Weberian interpretive sociology, it is truly sociological, theoretically grounded, humanistic and emphasizes human volition.

However, one of the problems with Social Action Theory as currently professed in organization studies is that it is based less fully on Weber's formulation than its adherents admit.

Silverman, for instance, culminates his argument (1968, 1970) by advocating the Weberian Social Action model and quoting approvingly some examples of its use. Whilst presenting his model of the Social Action framework (Silverman, 1968: 232) as being drawn from Weber, it omits one half of that model. Weber (1968) required that the explanation offered be causally adequate at the level of meaning, and at the level of science. Adherence to the second half of this formulation requires scientific testing and the search for general causal laws. The generality of the laws may be of limited extent because of the situational specificity of the meaning for the actors. Moreover, the search for laws of causal status means that the resulting models are deterministic, though it is value and perceptual variables, rather than inanimate variables such as size or technology in positivism, which compose the explanation. This latter quality, of determinism, seems to have been overlooked by some of the champions of the Social Action approach who present it as a kind of humanistic anti-scientism (Silverman, 1968; Schreyogg, 1980). This distorts the Weberian foundation. Whilst perceptions are known not to be identical with objective social facts, it is not apparent that they are entirely unrelated, i.e. individuals' perceptions have some relationship to the objective situation as revealed by structuralist or Durkheimian analyses. Similarly, a person's values are not completely unrelated to a person's situation; both cognitive psychology and Marxism point this out. Failure to recognize the force of these observations at the theoretical level, leads to naivety in the analysis of concrete situations.

Turning to examples of the Social Action approach, Silverman (1968) quotes Cunnison's (1966) study of garment workers and Goldthorpe *et al.*'s (1968) study of car workers. Silverman reports Cunnison's finding that inplant behaviour was at least partly determined by outplant factors, such as ethnic and religious affiliations of the workers. For instance, the bargaining and conflict with supervision over work allocation reflected cleavages amongst the workers on ethnic and religious lines. This line of argument is indisputable. Indeed, whilst some early Human Relations studies may have neglected such phenomena, it has been included in even the most establishmentarian expositions such as American industrial sociology of the 1950s and early 1960s (Miller and Form, 1964). There is nothing new, or particularly radical, or related to the conscious adoption of action theory and the conscious rejection of systems theory, in this. The idea that organizational members, on the basis of ascriptive attributes, have affective solidarities which condition processes in the integrative sub-system, is not incompatible with either structural-functionalism, systems theory or organizational psychology. It is a case of an exogenous source of variation which a system will have to manage if it is to retain a satisfactory degree of integration. Thus the explanation offered in the study of Cunnison is not specific to theories of the social action type and is compatible with structural-functionalism.

Turning to the study by Goldthorpe *et al.* (1968), larger problems emerge. Silverman writes:

> Goldthorpe's study of car assembly workers similarly emphasizes the importance of analyzing the orientations which workers bring to their job and suggests the far-reaching consequences of this for the way in which we approach studies of organizational behaviour. He has demonstrated that the instrumental orientation of car-workers may be a cause of their being employed in the industry and are not a consequence of the technology with which they are engaged. If, then, we are to consider them as alienated, we can only understand this in terms of the structure of the wider society and this, clearly, calls for explanation outside of the organization. (1968: 235)

This study of workers in Luton by Goldthorpe *et al.* (1968) has become sufficient of a champion of the Social Action cause as to require comment. In this case, the rival framework which it criticizes is more that of organizational psychology rather than that of organizational sociology (hence it is not surprising that the psychologist, Argyris (1972), gave it a lengthy analysis in his critique of what he termed 'organizational sociology'). The gist of the thesis of Goldthorpe *et al.* (1968) is that these relatively affluent workers (in car, engineering and process plants) are not as 'alienated' as widely believed because of their instrumental orientation, which is that they are consciously trading-off intrinsically satisfying work against the bigger pay packets possible for less skilled workers by taking car assembly and similar, rather boring, jobs. They contrast their account, which focuses attention on individual choice processes, with that of the determinism of social psychological theories of 'response' to work. They also argue that their approach is more 'open', as it recognizes extra-plant, community factors, such as orientations to work, which precede, and indeed, lead to adopting a particular kind of employment. Further, they contrast their approach to Human Relations theory. For instance, they show that workers who have little contact with their supervisor, are not as disaffected as that theory would imply, because, as part of their instrumental orientation, the workers are quite satisfied with a lack of warm affection, or even regular interaction with, the supervisor. There are a number of problems in the study.

One obvious deficiency is that the study contains no evidence that the instrumental orientation is one that preceded current employment. The study is cross-sectional and the force of the assertion seems to rest with the fact that the sample contains some individuals, like ex-school teachers, who have left more skilled jobs of a kind which would usually be taken to be more intrinsically satisfying (Goldthorpe *et al.*, 1968). That the subjects concerned developed instrumental orientations whilst teaching (or whatever), and then left in order to attain more money, is undemonstrated.

The argument that the instrumental orientation is an outside, community factor is equally asserted rather than validated. In this case, one can enquire whether this is a sensible distinction. That people's frame of reference for thinking about their work is affected by what they hear before entering employment is highly plausible, but the content of those opinions will come from family members, neighbours and friends, whose own thinking is, at least partially, shaped by their own experience of work. Hence to term such a factor as community-based is a simplification of the criss-crossing of experience and its social formulation, back and forth between work sites and the community. A sociological perspective which was truly open would recognize this. Rather what we have is a case of an unfortunate conceptualization of a variable, confusing the identification of a complex causal process with location in a geographic sense. The subject's prior framework may shape the experience of work, but the experience of work in turn shapes mental constructs.

Part of the evidence of the study is in the form of cross-tabulations which show that differences in technology, or skill-levels of the job, are associated with differences in experienced monotony, i.e. the higher the skill-level, the less boring and the more satisfying the job (Goldthorpe *et al.*, 1968: 17, 18). This is one of the Luton study's main empirical findings. Yet it is exactly what organizational psychologists would expect from their studies (Argyris, 1964; Aldag and Brief, 1979). It is also exactly the kind of finding which has led to many organizational behaviouralists' interest in experiments to restructure jobs in order to make them less boring, and somewhat more satisfying, through techniques such as job enlargement and job enrichment (Herzberg, 1968). Despite the predictable and well-understood nature of the findings, Goldthorpe *et al.* essay a complex interpretation about the results showing the effects of prior expectations. This is no more than speculation since the authors have, as was pointed out above, no data on prior expectations and no information on the processes occurring over time. Yet this is the substance on which the major study, showing the reputed superiority of the Social Action approach, has been built.

Similarly, turning to the finding on workers' feelings about supervision, the human relations and neo-human relations theory of organizational psychology argues that employees prefer a considerate or supportive or employee-centred kind of supervision relative to the opposite, i.e. inconsiderate or authoritarian (Likert and Likert, 1976). To test such a proposition implies comparative study, yet the Luton studies contain no such comparison (Goldthorpe *et al.*, 1968). Hence they beg the question of whether the moderately satisfied workers in their sample would have been more satisfied with more considerate or supportive supervision.

Is the analysis of Goldthorpe *et al.* (1968) a sociologically adequate account? The instrumental orientation, the expectations of low intrinsic satisfaction in work, etc., may, for an individual, precede his obtaining a car-assembly job, but it is conditioned by his experience and perception of the opportunities open to him on the labour market. These are perceptions, but they are informed, to at least some degree, by the objective facts. A structuralist analysis would point out that, for people of a certain education, etc., the probability of their employment was restricted to certain places, including the Luton car-assembly plant. Any statements about the sociological significance of any trade-off such individuals may make between jobs which offer more intrinsic satisfaction and jobs which offer more money, need to be made within the framework which makes explicit these constraints. Analyses of the action type do not provide this framework because they do not make a structural analysis. Hence talk of choice processes is misleading and one-sided if it does not recognize that it occurs within an occupational structure which closely restricts the options available, and may condition individuals' expectations and work values. These are traditional and well-established themes within sociology (Parker *et al.*, 1967), yet the Social Action approach, as deployed by some of its proponents, neglects this. Accordingly, the approach must be considered sociologically inadequate. Moreover, a key notion in sociology has always been that certain aspects of the human condition are ones which people find themselves in, rather than being wholly their own creation, e.g. poverty. All such conditions may ultimately be the product of Man (in the sense of Marx's philosophical anthropology) but they are not created by each and every man, or woman, who find themselves in the given situation. Yet it is just such naive reasoning to which Social Action Theory is leading. Any branch of sociology which fails to consider the extent of social determination can claim to be humanistic only in its terminology or rhetoric.

Turning to other empirical studies utilizing the Social Action framework, one finds not only that they are localized and limited in scope, but that not much happens in them. Consider the study by Box and Ford (1967) of sixth-formers' career choices. These are shown to be a function of their values and beliefs about exam results needed for university study and their expectations about their own likely results. Note, in passing, the socially trivial nature of the object of investigation (similar remarks apply to the study of restaurant staff by Bowey (1976)), yet in terms of the Social Action Theory, as often practised currently, action is action and that which is meaningful to the actor is meaningful for the sociologist. In the absence of criteria external to the microcosm, such as is provided by the structural perspective, this is likely to be the case. The subjects choose their career paths on their perceptions, nothing else happens. But contrast this with the study of career choice by Lawler *et al.* (1975) which shows, by following up former students, that their evaluations of what they prefer change as a function of what they end up with. This is more subtle than the simplistic rationalism of Social Action Theory. It is also more dynamic. It derives from the psychological theory of the reduction of cognitive dissonance (Festinger, 1957). This goes beyond simple rationalism to show the way events and social positions influence perceptions and needs of the actor, in patterned ways, and according to laws that transcend commonsense knowledge about human action (Pfeffer and Salancik, 1978; Weick, 1969). Silverman, in collaboration with Jones (1973), has conducted field studies which describe selection interviewers adjusting their original judgements in the light of fuller information about the interviewees. Silverman and Jones miss the point that what they have demonstrated is the well-known, well-established and often-studied phenomenon of the reduction of post-decision dissonance. The opportunity to connect this field study with a rich literature was lost.

Social Action Theory tends to belie its name by producing studies in which there is little 'action' in the lay sense of the word. It employs a loose framework, rather than a developed general theory, which contains a plethora of low-level, commonsense propositions subsumed under the vague (and partial) metatheory that people's conduct is a result of their perceptions, beliefs and choice. In short, it is more an approach than a theory. Also, one would note that the model of man is extremely atomistic and deals very little with the social dimension. Hence it is neither 'social', nor much about 'action', nor a 'theory'. The name is misleading and allows it to be passed off as profoundly sociological, change-oriented and theoretically powerful. It should rather be termed the individual's frame of reference approach. Moreover, in its failure to connect work done by its proponents with other developed bodies of research, it becomes inward-looking and superficial.

Silverman concludes his article by declaring:

> However it seems both simpler and less misleading to resurrect 'Industrial Sociology' as a more analytically coherent subject which can include within its scope the systematic study of the organizations in which men work and their relationship to the social structure. (1968: 236)

Silverman's definition of Industrial Sociology is of an extremely narrow conception owing little to classical sociology. It has divested itself of the diverging theoretical themes that have made sociology intellectually lively and empirically fruitful. It claims to study organizations but in practice is confined to inter-individual and inter-group action. Most of the properties and processes distinctive of organizations, their structure and their outcomes, are not only not studied, they are denied as fit topics of sociological enquiry. Exactly similar remarks apply to social structure. What the Social Action approach leads to is a set of low-level generalizations which overstate the role of conscious choice and understate social, structural and psychological determinations.

Questions of how to make the organizations we live in better able to deliver the best quality and quantity of life for societal members are incapable of even being asked, let alone answered, in such a framework. The exploration of how best to reconcile the needs for collective organization and individual well-being is similarly neglected. This is not a humanistic sociology, it is the antithesis of such.

Conclusions

While this volume is heavily critical of Social Action Theory as *the* approach in sociology, it does not seek to deny its utility as one approach to be used together with others. For many issues in sociology and social life, explanation can be enhanced by considering the situation as it appears to the actors. In the explanation of conflict differing perceptions, beliefs, values and perceived interests are illuminating. Thus far we are 'for' Social Action Theory in principle, and indeed have applied it in practice to industrial conflict (Donaldson and Lynn, 1976). Dissent is being registered here against the programmatic that it is the only fit approach for a sociology of organization and that other systemic analyses cannot be developed. Equally, conceptions which deny the possibility of incorporating interpretive material with structural theory are rejected herein. Social Action Theory is both a worthwhile contribution yet also from the viewpoint of sociology, primitive theory, leading to low-level, unconnected, localized generalizations. This neither accords with the sociological tradition of Durkheim, Marx or Weber, nor does justice to the potential of social science.

11

Sociology of Organizations

Conventional organizational studies are criticized for neglecting the wider society and the interactions between it and the organization. This is frequently discussed in terms of insufficient attention being given to the environment in studies of organization. Some commentators have called for a broadening of enquiry into what they term the organization-in-society approach. Others champion the appellation of what they call a Sociology of Organizations. Certain writers go further and suggest that the point of departure should be the examination of society. In this chapter the merits of this movement will be addressed.

At this juncture it is as well to recall the point made earlier (Chapter 1), that the definition of organization, as used conventionally within the field, is itself flexible as to its referents. The term may be applied to a small business, a conglomerate corporation, a government or a military alliance between governments. Organization can, and has been applied at levels above that of the firm. Berry *et al.* (1974) studied national economic development councils which combine constituents from firms, trade unions and the government. Etzioni (1968) has employed Organization Theory at the level of the nation state.

Silverman (1968: 224) characterizes Organization Theory as specifying that the organization must adapt to the environment, rather than dealing with this as a two-way interrelation. Most of the earlier conventional studies have dealt with the relationship between the organization and its environment primarily in terms of the former adapting to the latter (Woodward, 1965; Lawrence and Lorsch, 1967; Blau and Schoenherr, 1977). As Child (1972) and Perrow (1972) note, the notion of the organization manipulating the environment so that it adapts to the organization has been relatively neglected. More recently, studies by Hirsch (1975b), Pfeffer and Salancik (1978) have indicated the way the organization can influence its environment through lobbying for government regulation, mergers and undertaking joint ventures. This extension of the framework of organization studies to more adequately encompass organization-environment interactions is to be welcomed. And it seems fair to attribute these moves, at least partly, to an awareness of shortcomings in the orthodox organizational literature, which has been stimulated by the critical commentaries.

Silverman (1968) also identifies a tendency for organization studies to construct general, universal theories of organization, avoiding the issue of socio-cultural settings which affect such relationships. He relates this to the practice of such latter variables being omitted from studies and only drawn upon after the fact to explain variations which are not explicable through the Organization Theory. Other contributors to the orthodox body of organization studies have concurred that there is a tendency for such wider social, economic or cultural factors to be brought in only as a residual interpretation (Child, 1981; Mansfield, 1981a; Lammers and Hickson, 1979). This is unsatisfactory from the point of methodology in that a direct test of the hypothesis is frequently not possible as the socio-cultural variable was not measured. For instance, Boseman and Jones (1974) report relationships amongst organizational behaviour variables which differ from those found in earlier work. They suggest that this may be due to their organizations being Mexican. However, the underlying variable was not specifically operationalized and tested statistically. In this and other cases the exact causal variable is left equivocal: is it need for esteem or achievement, or what? Commentators have called for the creation of theories which combine organizational variables with explicit social, economic and cultural variables (Lammers and Hickson, 1979; Mansfield and Poole, 1981). Child has exemplified this and has characterized different national settings in terms of varying socio-economig systems such as capitalism and socialism. He calls for the development of this sort of theoretical and empirical work under the title of an Organization-in-Society approach. Undoubtedly, there is a need for further enquiry along these lines and they constitute a valid broadening of traditional organization studies. In that regard, they are in response to criticisms such as that by Silverman (1968). However, many of these theoretical refinements are to broadly structural-functional, systemic models and they include concepts and variables at the organizational level (Budde *et al.*, 1982). To that extent they differ from the Social Action programme which Silverman has advocated.

Davies has gone somewhat further than Silverman and has criticized Organization Theory as failing to examine 'the conditions (social, economic and political) under which the findings obtain' (1979: 419). Davies refers to the claim by Hickson *et al.* (1974) that there are certain valid culture-free universal relationships between organizational context and structure, and describes this position ' . . . as the orthodox project of organization theory'. There is a tendency from Weber (1968) onwards to see bureaucratization in response to factors such as size as a relatively universal phenomena across different societies and institutional spheres. But not all students of organization have been willing to go as far as Hickson *et al.* (1974). Moreover, while there is interest in the research community in seeing how far these phenomena generalize (Fletcher, 1970), this has very often been seen as a set of hypotheses to be tested rather than an incontestable truth. Much of the empirical work has sought to empirically test for generalization across societies and institutions (and much of this has been done prior to the publication of this criticism by Davies in 1979). For instance, the thesis of Woodward connecting technology and organizational structure in the manufacturing industry has been tested in the UK (Child and Mansfield, 1972) and the USA (Zwerman, 1970; Blau *et al.*, 1976) and Japan (Marsh and Mannari, 1980). Studies of context and structure using the Aston scales have been made in the UK, USA, Canada, Sweden, West Germany, Poland, Jordan, India and Japan (Hickson and McMillan, 1981). They have been made across manufacturing, service, government, hospital, educational, religious and trade union organizations (Pugh and Hinings, 1976). Studies of context and structure by Blau (1972) and his colleagues in the US have been made in manufacturing, government, retail, hospital and university organizations. Studies utilizing the Perrowian concept of routineness of task and its relationship to structure have been made across manufacturing, welfare and hospital organizations in the US (Gerwin, 1979). Diversification and divisionalization have been examined in the US, Australia, France, Italy, Japan, West Germany and the UK (Rumelt, 1974; Chenhall, 1979; Dyas and Thanheiser, 1976; Pavan, 1976; Suzuki, 1980; Channon, 1973; respectively). This prodigious effort of testing replication and generalization has been spurred in part by the need to obtain empirical confirmation as to whether certain lines of theorizing, supported by factual enquiries in the USA or UK, in manufacturing or service organizations, were in fact valid for other countries and types of organization. Thus while there is curiosity about the possible wide applicability of Organization Theory this has not simply been a presumption.

Recently, there have been attempts to review a number of these strands of literature in order to see whether there is valid generalization and whether socio-economic-cultural context needs to be entered into the models as a moderator of universal relationships. Donaldson (1976) has suggested that the Woodward thesis does not replicate. However, other scholars have argued that the technology-structure relationships may generalize in modified form (Blau *et al.*, 1976; Reimann and Inzerilli, 1979; Reimann, 1980). Gerwin (1979) has indicated substantial generalizability of the Perrowian technology thesis. The relationship between size and horizontal and vertical differentiation has been shown to generalize in the US across institutional spheres (Blau and Schoenherr, 1971; Blau,

1972; Blau *et al.*, 1976). The Aston studies have indicated a fair degree of generalization of their findings as regards size and structure across societies and institutional spheres (Pugh and Hinings, 1976; Hickson and McMillan, 1981). Budde *et al.* (1982) have shown that differences in centralization between organizations in Britain and West Germany may be due to different cultural attitudes towards authority. Reviewing the cross-national studies on bureaucracy more widely conceived, Lammers and Hickson (1979) have identified a moderator variable which distinguishes between what they term as Latin and Anglo-Saxon patterns of organizational variables. The literature on diversification and divisionalization has yielded stable associations across countries and the findings may be more consistent cross-nationally than earlier reports have suggested (Donaldson, 1979b).

As discussed earlier, the identification of socio-economic-cultural variables in this literature is difficult given the *ex post facto* nature of much of this interpretation. However, research to date has enabled the tentative identification of general relationships between context and structure and preliminary exploration of societal moderator variables. This gain in knowledge about organizations has only been possible given the belief that organizations may be sufficiently alike across institutional settings and national boundaries to make such enquiry sensible, and the use of standardized variables and common measurement procedures. Refinement of means for studying socio-economic-cultural variables may reveal that they have a stronger impact on structure than certain current results suggest. However, until it is demonstrated that these societal variables so totally explain organizational structure as to deny any explanatory power to orthodox variables such as size, task and diversification, then theory and empirical work involving these relatively traditional variables will continue to be cogent. Thus a synthesis of conventional with newer approaches seems warranted, but not the eclipsing of the former by the latter.

Thus there would seem to be a tendency for organization studies to broaden its frame of reference in order to more fully study the interaction between the organization and the society. However, in advocating the 'open' systems approach Silverman goes further: 'Indeed, the logic of this approach may lead us to begin with a research problem relating to the structure of society rather than to the organization itself' (1968: 224).

This follows quite naturally from Silverman's (1968) emphasis on the need for an approach in terms of 'open' systems and 'external', as well as 'internal', factors. The implication would seem to be that the task of organization analysis is the study of society. While the study of society will potentially illuminate a number of issues in the field of organizations, the motives that led scholars to create a specialist sub-discipline of organizational sociology continue to be valid. The study of society reveals larger structures and processes of stratification, socialization, conflict and international relations, all decidedly worthy of enquiry, but already central to the programme of general sociology. A societal perspective does not pay sufficient attention to variations between and within organizations in jobs, technology, structure, communications and so on which are consequential for alienation, organizational effectiveness, public accountability and other topics with which the field has been concerned. If such studies were denied legitimacy intellectually, programmatically and sociologically, as Silverman is suggesting, then much of the knowledge accumulated in Industrial Sociology would not have come about. It would forestall the development of knowledge about how sub-systems of the society, i.e. organizations, through their structural variations, make differential contributions to the functioning of the system, i.e. society. To require that all sociological studies 'begin with a research problem relating to the structure of the society rather than to the organization itself' (Silverman, 1968: 224) is to prevent the build-up of the sort of knowledge which comes from study of 'the organization itself'. Questions about the consequences of variations in size on structure, technology on satisfaction, diversification on divisionalization, or complexity on innovation might never have been posed let alone answered if organization-level enquiries had not been pursued. Programmatics such as Silverman's have important consequences for the definition of fit subject matter in the field. If followed they would have seriously impaired the development of sociological and organizational knowledge.

Similar problems of excessively broad scope arise in the future of organization studies of health care as advocated by Davies (1979). Whilst endorsing the negotiated order critique of conventional Organization Theory, Davies (1979) sees the need to go beyond the Action approach, in order to locate intra-organizational phenomena within the wider setting of society. Davies (1979) welcomes the tendency within modern organizational analysis to move the focus of enquiry from the bounded organizational unit, such as the hospital, to the whole health system. Explanation of the latter is seen in terms of the interests and power of different social groups. The historical study of health and welfare systems is applauded by Davies when it reveals the origins and developments of those institutions in the struggle between social groupings. Davies (1979: 419) writes that: 'Some at least within organization theory are beginning to recognize that organizations are instruments of domination constructed and reconstructed by powerful interests. They are beginning to see too that this perspective opens up an exciting possibility for understanding, criticizing and transcending present social relations.' Davies culminates her article by presenting a new agenda for organizational analysis free from some of the assumptions of orthodox Organization Theory:

> One such agenda might be as follows:
> 1. What are the social constructions of individual and collective health available in a society and how are these distributed among available groups?
> 2. What is the basis on which some groups are enabled to mobilize resources for organizing health and what construction of health do they attempt to realize?
> 3. Through what specific arrangements is health organized and delivered:
>   (i) what is the division of labour in the field?
>   (ii) what is the quality of social relations in the field?
>   (iii) what are counted as viable 'products' of organized health care?
> 4. What are major complementaries and contradictions within organized health care?
> 5. What are the major complementaries and contradictions between health care and other sets of social relations in the society?
> 6. What have been the major historical transformations in the social construction of health and the organized arrangements for its provision? (1979: 419)

These are clearly large questions, at the level of the entire health care system or beyond.

It becomes reasonable to ask whether the issues being canvassed for study by those who reject conventional Organization Theory, are, really, organizational ones. Organization Theory seems to be distinguishable as a body of thought by a concern for internal characteristics such as differentiation, specialization, standardization, integration, coordination, centralization and the like. These are not only traditional aspects of attention, they are recognizably organizational phenomena. Theories of organization are frameworks for explaining the interrelation of such variables. Often these are related, via theories of the structural-functional type, to systems outcomes such as production, efficiency, or rates of innovation. It seems to this author both conventional and sensible to refer to such frameworks as Organization Theory. Many of the phenomena to which Davies refers, different social and occupational groupings, have conventionally been studied within general sociology, i.e. the analysis of societies. The very language which Davies uses is precisely the language of sociological theory: 'the social and political structure', 'struggle between classes', 'different clientele', 'upper class' (all in 1979: 418). This is not an exercise in broadening Organization Theory, it is supplanting it by the framework of sociological theory. There are issues and problems appropriate to Organization Theory, and there are concerns and concepts appropriate to societal analysis. But in moving from one to the other, it is misleading to describe this as if it is a widening of Organization Theory, when it is an abandonment, not only of the framework, but of the objects of study of that theory. Davies is asking for issues such as the growth and support of national medical systems (what sort of services, which clients to be treated, how many hospitals, etc.) to be given priority. This seems perfectly reasonable as a research agenda for part of medical sociology. Yet to couch this in terms of the resolution of the supposed inadequacies of Organization Theory is strange. Organization Theory could, it would seem, make a contribution to such issues. But it would be a limited contribution. Issues such as the appropriate degree and form of specialization and integration at the level of the system as a whole, and of the internal structure of differentiated units (hospitals, mobile blood donation teams) appropriate for optimum output (efficiency, innovation, patient friendliness and so on) could be tackled. But other issues to do with the different social groups, their perception of their self interest, their mobilization and manoeuvrings for power – these are conventionally the province of the general sociologist, the political sociologist, or the political scientist. The organization theorist lays no claim to expertise in the study of such phenomena. Those sociologists who wish to study such societal issues, and who very naturally adopt a macro framework, are, whatever their previous origins and interests, no longer acting as organization theorists. To describe such people and their activities as within Organization Theory stretches the meaning of the term beyond any real utility.

Yet it is a common fallacy. The gambit of delineating phenomena which Organization Theory cannot handle, and then using this to 'prove' the 'inadequacy' of the 'approach', is both widespread and invalid. Part of the reason for the credibility of what is, when examined, clearly a false move, stems from the ambiguity of the term 'organization' (Pugh, 1973; Urwick, 1973). As has been noted, it is used to mean both the arrangement and delineating of roles in a bounded corporate group, but also the entire goings-on within the envelope: the people, the machines, the buildings and so on. This wider use of the word encompasses friendship groupings of employees, the language used by members, dissatisfactions with pay and so on. These phenomena, as sociologists rightly point out, are influenced by factors in the wider society. They are part of what may be termed organizational life, in the sense of life within organizations, but Organization Theory does not thereby lay claim to an exclusive understanding of such phenomena. Organization Theory, in the structural form, is mainly about the analysis of different designs, and their contingencies and their outcomes. In terms of the paradigm of March and Simon (1958) it is about the structure and processes of decision-making. But even this paradigm does not claim to explain the content of every decision made by every member. Its focus is on collectively salient decision issues such as production levels, the individual's decision to participate, or innovation. The distinction between genuine organizational phenomena and all the things which go on within organizations needs to be kept clear. Otherwise Organization Theory can easily be shown to fail by setting for it a standard which it has never claimed to attain – the task of explaining all organizational goings-on.

Similar remarks apply to the study of the manipulation of the environment. The organizational literature now contains a number of attempts to articulate the structures and processes employed by organizations to influence governments, competitors and other external parties (Hirsch, 1975b; Pfeffer and Salancik, 1978). This is a valuable development in organizational sociology. However, the study in detail of much of this might gain from the sort of enquiries conducted within political science, economics, consumer behaviour and legal studies. Specialists with disciplinary backgrounds other than sociology or organization studies have much to contribute here. Much of this work is conducted outside of the boundaries of organizational sociology. While there is much to commend in scholars drawing upon the work of colleagues from other disciplines there would seem little merit in organization theorists attempting to duplicate the work of others who have distinctive competence. A sounder approach would be for organizational students to pursue enquiries based upon their special expertise and which draw upon their particular frameworks. The way forward for research in organizational behaviour may well include a fuller study of the environment but it would seem sensible to retain as a central reference point the organization within that environing field.

Conclusions

The field of organization studies needs to study more fully the interaction of the organization with its environment. The influence of culture and socio-economic system upon organizational behaviour, structure and goals deserves to be understood more fully. Likewise, the impact of the organization on society in terms of perpetuation, change, social stratification, innovation and other outcomes, and the mechanisms by which these are attained require further investigation. This will no doubt lead to an enhancement of the current theoretical framework in organization studies. However, some continued differentiation between organization studies and the rest of the social sciences seems prudent. Complete assimilation into more general or more macroscopic-societal schema to the point that phenomena such as organizational structure, which are distinctive of organizations and which traditionally form core elements in the subject area, are no longer studied, is to be avoided. Considerations of the academic specialization of labour suggest that this would be unwise.

Moreover, the success of organizational research to date in contributing to the knowledge about organizations and to sociology either as a sub-discipline or as an autonomous field suggest the prospects for continued fruitful work by organization studies. More particularly the subject so far has produced, by its pursuit of general theories and standard operational definitions, indications as to both the universality and to the localization of organizational phenomena. Moves to widen conventional frameworks are to be applauded, moves to eradicate traditional concepts and objects of study are to be resisted.

12

Marxian Organization Theory

Perhaps the most dramatic alternative to the orthodoxy is provided by the suggestion that the field should adopt a Marxian Organization Theory. The need for a dialectical view has been argued as has the imperative of recognizing that under capitalism, organizational control is in order to maximize the extraction of surplus from employees. Our discussion suggests that recognizing this may be less of a revolution in organization studies than certain commentators believe. Further, the idea of a specifically Marxian Organization Theory is shown to be a contradiction.

Benson has contributed a critical discussion of conventional Organization Theory and offers instead a 'dialectical view' based on Marxism (1977: 2). This seeks to incorporate mainstream positivistic and other positions but within a more general 'critical emancipatory' position (Benson, 1977: 19). Liberation is offered through recognition of the arbitrary and conditional nature of present structures and the existence of rival alternatives. Benson affirms the commitment of the dialectician to practical action. A task of such analysis is to dereify current organization structures and theories, through a more penetrating analysis of their bases in power and ideology. This enterprise is to be furthered through deploying Marxian concepts such as totality and contradiction. Goldman and Van Houten (1977) and Clegg and Dunkerley (1980) propose that organizations be treated as instruments of class oppression. And Heydebrand (1977) provides an initial outline of a Marxian Organization Theory.

An initial problem with this approach is that of the level of analysis. Marx's theory is principally concerned with explaining the rise and transformation of capitalism, i.e. it is societal and world-historical. Organizations are more circumscribed, relatively micro, phenomena. Benson contends that underlying Marx's discussion of capitalism there is a more 'general perspective' (1977: 2), and this is the framework which he seeks to use to illuminate organizations. Some of the general concepts are given specifically organizational-level reference, as in the notion of intra-organizational contradictions (Benson, 1977: 5). However, this sits uncomfortably with another precept, which is that all phenomena are to be understood as part of the totality, that is all the organizational and societal relations and their interconnections (Benson, 1977: 4). The problem here is that a basically societal-level theory, Marxism, is being made to do work for which it was not devised, that is the explanation of organizations. The resultant concept, organizational contradiction, displays these difficulties. These contradictions refer to inconsistencies and incompatibilities between structural sub-units such as divisions or hierarchical levels. The dialectical concept consists then of dysfunctions and conflicts between organizational sub-units, reflecting their partial autonomy. These are the phenomena dealt with in work on differentiation and integration (Lawrence and Lorsch, 1967; Lorsch and Allen, 1973; Khandwalla, 1973). Thus the concrete meaning of the new dialectical concept of intra-organizational contradictions is that which has been studied in conventional organizational sociology. Again, a further source of such contradictions is seen by Benson (1977: 15) to lie in multiple, inconsistent goals, as in rehabilitation and custodial objectives for prisons. Those structural tensions have been recognized in mainstream organizational sociology (Etzioni, 1975). This reflects the dilemma of Marxian Organization Theory. It can be new and authentically Marxian by analysing societal issues in which case it is not an Organization Theory, or it can be genuinely organizational, in which case the novel elements are mainly semantic.

For Benson intra-organizational contradictions may have their source also in the environment of the organization. To the extent that changes within organizations can be explained with reference to extra-organizational, societal phenomena, such as the Marxist contradictions in capitalism, then the exercise becomes one of societal theory. Organizations are the mere arenas in which these world-historical contradictions between the classes, or between the forces and means of production, are played out. There is nothing specifically organizational about such theorizing. The referent is not spans of control or hierarchic authority or interdepartmental coordination or any of the other phenomena which are distinctive of organizations. These are what have conventionally composed the subject matter, and made sensible terms such as Organization Theory or organizational sociology. By contrast, the notion of totality is a reference to everything – nothing is excluded. The whole of economics, sociology, anthropology, psychology, political science and so on, fall under its orbit. Such a conception is not surprising in a theory, such as that of Marx, which defines its subject matter as global systems over substantial historical periods. But by the same token, it cannot stand for a body of enquiry which takes as its topic issues of structure and coordination in goal-oriented instrumentalities. Thus the not insubstantial intellectual ambitions of studying the totality must, to the extent that they are realized, turn the enquiry from Organization Theory into a theory of society.

A further source of organizational contradictions is seen in the interaction of the structure, or morphology as Benson (1977: 15) terms it, with the sub-structure, the underlying interest groups with their varying power. These are exemplified by class or racial groups. Benson (1977: 15) further notes the heightening of contradictions when cleavages of the sub-structure, such as class, reinforce those due to the organization structure, such as hierarchical level. The identification of class or ethnic or educational lines of demarcation between organizational members has been made within organizational sociology (Crozier, 1964) and is not precluded by conventional Organization Theory. And the notion that multiple overlapping lines of conflict produce more disharmony than lines of conflict which are cross-cutting is recognized within conflict theory, including those of a non-Marxian or pluralistic kind (Galtung, 1965). Once more, the concrete referents of Benson's dialectical innovation are familiar and not incompatible with mainstream analysis.

Benson (1977: 4) describes current organizational studies as abstract and calls for the examination of the concrete totality. Yet all academic enquiry proceeds through the use of concepts which are, by definition, abstract. Theories are bodies of propositions which render our experience more coherent. Concepts do not stand for concrete things in a one-to-one correspondence between the symbolic and the real worlds (Toulmin, 1962). Clearly contradiction, social construction and production, interests, power and other terms which Benson (1977) employs are abstract concepts. Moreover, all social scientific enquiry works through the postulation of simplifying 'as if' models. The call to study the totality in some direct way unmediated by concepts is naive, and an impossible programme. Inevitably, social theorists, if they be Marxians, will study actual society through abstract simplifications such as class, capitalism and so on. They may claim the ontological status of the real and historical for their subject matter. But in practice limited amounts of quantitative and qualitative data will be assembled according to the underlying premises of their theory. This is equally true of any social scientific investigation be it structural-functional or social action or whatever. In setting up a contradistinction between abstract organizational science and concrete, historical Marxism, Benson is creating a false antithesis, and making a critique which is philosophically groundless.

Heydebrand (1977) has offered a preliminary statement of a Marxian theory of organizations. His contribution is of considerable importance to the present discussion because here we see an explicitly Marxian approach being offered. More particularly, Heydebrand sets out to construct a Marxian theory not of society but of organizations. By so doing this constitutes a more serious challenge to the domain of conventional organization studies, than have those approaches from Marx which are fundamentally concerned with societal analysis. However, in the case of writing in the Heydebrand (1977) mould, the object of study, i.e. the organization, is much more nearly the same, between Marxian and conventional approaches, and thus the claim to explanation does constitute the assertion of a theory to rival the present frameworks.

Heydebrand (1977) begins with an exposition of Marx's theory and then applies this to the courts of law in the contemporary USA. In particular, the Marxian concepts are used to analyse certain conflicts therein in terms of contradictions. In the exposition of theory, emphasis is laid by Heydebrand on the focus in Marx's intellectual system on historically, concrete dialectical forces unfolding within the totality.

In analysing the tensions and processes of change in the US courts of law Heydebrand writes of the conflicts between the judiciary and the higher administration of the legal system, between professional autonomy and bureaucratic hierarchy and between concern for quality of professional work and cost:

> One important example is the contradiction between established 'professional' authority whose dominance is partly the result of previous successful application of 'technique', on the one hand, and further rationalization of work, usually by the bureaucratic-administrative forces in organizations on the other. (1977: 97)

> The absence of fiscal autonomy for courts and the external control, manipulation and restriction of resources set up a certain degree of competition and conflict among them and accentuates the contradiction within them. This contradiction may initially be one between stated goals and the adequacy of resources necessary for implementation, but it will tend to manifest itself structurally as a conflict between groups (e.g., between quality-oriented professionals and efficiency-oriented managers) and ultimately as a conflict between ideological and political positions. This process appears as a conflict between judges and administrators, defense counsel and prosecutors, the due-process oriented legal elite and the case-management-oriented legal-bureaucratic rationalizers . . . and ultimately between the proponents of such legal-political positions as 'judicial activism' and 'judicial restraint', frequently ascribed in recent times to Chief Justices Earl Warren and Warren Burger, respectively. (1977: 99)

> The universalism of cost-effectiveness under the ideology of scarce resources, comes into contradiction with the universalism of formal rationality and equality before the law. (1977: 103)

Much of this is the neo-Weberian analysis of organization, particularly the trend towards rationalization, and the existence of professional-bureaucratic conflict. These have been staple elements in the orthodox discussions of organizations (Blau and Scott, 1963; Hall, 1972). There is nothing new or radical or Marxian about these conceptualizations of contemporary events in public administration. It is noticeable that Heydebrand accompanies the substantive material on law courts by explicit exegesis of Weber (1977: 94, 97).

Linkage back to Marx is provided in two ways, through concepts such as the contradiction between established institutions and productive forces, and through placing the conflicts in the judicial system within the context of pressures introduced by the macro-system, the society.

Heydebrand repeatedly uses the imagery of the world which has been created coming into conflict with the world which is being now constructed through the activity of the ongoing forces of production (1977: 87). This idea is used both in the exposition of Marxian theory (1977: 87) and in the discussion of the law courts. To give one example:

> Very simply put, the forces of production (productivity measures, new technologies, rationalization of procedures) are encountering the increasing resistance of the relations of production (i.e. the accumulated legal apparatus and status system of the judiciary). (Heydebrand, 1977: 100)

There is a problem in this kind of use of Marx's concepts of the forces and relations of production. As noted earlier, Heydebrand, in his exposition of the theory of Marx, emphasizes that such elements are historically situated and concrete. Heydebrand (1977: 88) is critical of those social theorists who transmute Marxian tools into ahistorical or ideational constructs. Yet it must be asked whether this is not what Heydebrand has done. As he points out Marx's own work was centred on the 'development of industrial capitalism' (1977: 88). The productive forces are distinctly economic. By contrast the concepts deployed by Heydebrand are so abstracted that they include the rise of due process in Western law, and, more generally, Weberian formal rationality. Such an exercise in abstraction is perhaps inevitable in an enquiry which seeks to explain internal organizational happenings in one branch of public administration. As Heydebrand (1977) notes much of Marxian concern has been with the relationship between government and the administrative apparatus in general. This more traditional Marxian focus is part of the concern for the role of bureaucracy and state within the ongoing class struggle in the society as a whole. Thus the problem for Heydebrand (1977) is how to turn a set of concepts which are inherently societal into tools for internal organizational analysis. Given the inherently macroscopic and world-historical nature of Marx's terms, they can be transmogrified into the latter only through rendering them no longer Marxian. Marxism is a theory of society therefore it cannot be a theory of organization. An

Organization Theory can claim to be Marxian only if that derivation is so attenuated as to become meaningless.

If the Marxian identity of the conceptual armoury is problematic, there is also the issue of more substantive linkages in the way organizations are affected by their wider society. Heydebrand (1977: 98) writes of the contradictions in the courts of law having as some part of their cause the fiscal crisis based on the gap between state revenues and expenditures occasioned by the private appropriation of societal surplus in capitalist economies. In this way societal-level analysis can enter the picture by explaining the environmental origins of certain pressures which operate inside the organization, in this case the court system. Such explanations are in principle, unexceptionable. Nor would there be anything strange about the theories being used to illuminate such societal phenomena being different from those used to elucidate intra-organizational phenomena. For instance, capitalism causes fiscal pressures on public administration (societal theory); in the court system this leads to conflict between the professional judiciary and the administrators (Organization Theory – professionals *v.* bureaucracy). While the societal theory adds to the explanation it does not become the organizational theory. Societal theories may complement organizational ones, yet each can retain their own domain, in the sense of what they directly explain. Marxian theorizing may contribute to the explanation of societal-level events, such as fiscal crises. In so doing Marxian theory is playing the traditional role, and the one for which it was created, the explanation of macroscopic social change. It is a Marxian theory of society and it can be called a theory of organization only by stretching the use of that phrase beyond the point where it retains any utility.

The Marxian theory of organization offered by Heydebrand (1977) is a contradiction in terms. It becomes a theory of organization only by so divorcing itself from its Marxian roots as to be no longer recognizable as such and to become, in this case, indistinguishable from conventional Weberian organizational sociology. To maintain the coherency of a position which is genuinely Marxian involves restricting its application to the world-historical, societal level, in which case it has consequences for organizations, but it is not a theory of organization. In making explicit what would be involved in attempting to produce a Marxian theory of organization, Heydebrand (1977) has brought into the open the difficulties inherent in such an exercise. In so doing Heydebrand (1977) lays open to scrutiny what is, when made plain, a self-contradictory theory.

Of the neo-Marxian writings considered herein perhaps the most explicitly and traditionally Marxian is that by Goldman and Van Houten (1977). After noting the relative neglect of bureaucracy within Marxism, they state the need for an understanding of bureaucratic administration as a means of furthering the interests of the owning, capitalist class. In particular they are concerned to show that bureaucratic rationality in private industry is oriented towards profit maximization. Clegg and Dunkerley (1980) also make this point.

Goldman and Van Houten (1977) point out the way in which management seeks to minimize cost through reducing the returns to employees. In this way the interests of owners are realized against those of the working class. Much of management strategy is shown to be an attempt to keep control over workers in order to give effect to this object. This is related to the increasing concentration of capital, neo-imperialism (Baran and Sweezy, 1968) and the historical class struggle.

Much of this is, once again, a respecification of behaviour which is situated in and around organizations into societal terms. Moreover the model of society used is the Marxian one: classes in conflict with increasing contradictions which lead to wide-scale socio-economic change. For others the societal significance of this organization behaviour would be seen differently reflecting a differing societal theory. A liberal economist might speak of enhanced labour productivity leading to surplus which is reinvested within an internationally competitive environment producing a long-run growth in national wealth that benefits all classes. Whether the Marxian or the liberal view is more correct is an issue of intense current debate and one which is beyond the scope of this volume. But in transliterating organization behaviour into the language of class, conflict and contradiction, Marxists are attending to the wider societal picture, but doing so selectively, for there are other views. That Marxism should structure the perceptions of its adherents is in no way surprising, this is one of the functions of any theory, and liberal economics is no less paradigmatic. The point is that those who adopt the Marxist approach are moving away from not only organization theoretic concerns towards the societal but also towards a very particular view of world history. Those who choose to stay, for at least some of their research, at the organizational level may do so for reasons of research focus rather than the absence of understanding of societal matters. And if they decline to adopt a Marxian view it may be due to an awareness of its limitations *vis-à-vis* other socio-economic perspectives.

Goldman and Van Houten develop their theme with reference to a number of supposed inadequacies of conventional organizational sociology, especially in its Weberian form. For instance, they write that: 'For the bourgeois sociologist, formalization represents order, for Marxists power' (1977: 119).

This kind of juxtaposition is echoed by other neo-Marxians such as Clegg and Dunkerley (1980) who reiterate as a theme of their volume that organization is control. Yet in Weber (1968) the bureaucratic order is a control system most especially of those lower down the hierarchy to those at the top. Neo-Weberian organization theorists have retained this explicitly in their writing. For Etzioni (1975) the principal dimension in his comparative analysis of organizations is compliance. Child (1972b) writes of impersonal structure and personal decision-making by higher levels as alternative strategies of control. Blau and Schoenherr (1971) note that formalization and professionalization are each means of attaining control over bureaucratic employees. That bureaucratic order involves the subjugation of one section of the members to others is not denied or evaded in conventional organizational sociology. Since this order is created and maintained for the purposes of goal-attainment and, since in most privately owned economic enterprises their objective sets give emphasis to profit maximization, it necessarily follows that a neo-Weberian analysis of such firms would include the fact that control is exercised for profit realization. This is made explicit in those studies that relate structure to organizational performance, which is assessed by indicators that encompass measures of profit such as return on investment or returns to shareholders (Woodward, 1965; Lawrence and Lorsch, 1967; Rumelt, 1974; Child, 1975; Lenz, 1980).

Clegg and Dunkerley have jointly contributed a volume *Organization Class and Control* (1980). This represents a joint venture between a British sociologist and a colleague who now works in Australia. The volume is a textbook which reviews much of the material of organizational sociology and places it within the context of sociological theory and social change. Moreover, its perspective on society and organizations is broadly Marxian. Clegg and Dunkerley argue forcefully for the need to approach organization studies from within a neo-Marxian framework. Accordingly, they give considerable emphasis to class, conflict, systems contradictions, workers struggles and movements towards socialism. In many ways it is a revisiting of conventional organizational studies from the world-view of the New Left. Using the terms of Burrell and Morgan (1979), the predominant paradigm is radical structuralism. Given this, and the length and scope of the volume, *Organization Class and Control* constitutes the major statement of radical structuralism considered in the present book. That this more recent of critiques should so unequivocally adopt a Marxian historical structuralist approach, seems both a culmination and a confirmation, of the trend which has been noted in the present work, for critics of organizational sociology to display some shift from radical humanism to radical structuralism, over the decade of the 1970s.

Clegg and Dunkerley (1980) offer, in their exegesis, a large number of purportedly damaging criticisms against orthodox organizational sociology and go on to sketch the outlines of an alternative neo-Marxian approach. The present discussion will consider some of the criticisms while others were answered in other chapters (5 and 9). This line of enquiry leads to the view that neo-Weberian and neo-Marxian sociologies may be somewhat less antagonistic than Clegg and Dunkerley (1980) imply. This prompts consideration of the possibility that there may be more complementarity between conventional organizational sociology and Marxian societal analysis than they state. However, there remain differences in levels of analysis between Marxian and organization theories, which preclude assimilation. Moreover, the Marxian world-view is only one of a number of perspectives on society and Organization Theory should be pursued without confining itself to any one of these.

Clegg and Dunkerley (1980: 251) are critical of studies such as those of the Aston school (Pugh *et al.*, 1969; Child, 1973) which postulate that bureaucracy is determined by context factors such as size. They counterpose the explanation of the growth of bureaucracy with size as being due to systems needs for coordination, with the explanation that bureaucracy is instituted by management in the interests of their domination (Clegg and Dunkerley, 1980: 253). They go on to comment of the increasing use of 'impersonal control' that it could be 'deliberate invention, rather than determined functional necessity' (Clegg and Dunkerley, 1980: 256). In so doing, Clegg and Dunkerley are contrasting structural-functional with conflict theory formulations. However, such an opposition may be unhelpful and unnecessary. Elites wishing to attain goals such as profitability will have to ensure that the organization is properly organized, that coordination between parts is adequate and that members are sufficiently clear and motivated about their duties. In the language of structural-functionalism, the systems requisites for integration, pattern maintenance and so on will need to be met. Thus the management attain control through ensuring adequate coordination. The structural-functional and conflict theory-derived explanations are not mutually exclusive, they are compatible. Similarly, impersonal controls can be functionally necessary means of coordination for organizations larger than a certain size, and therefore determined by size and the requirement for adequate functioning, and also can be deliberately invented. The impersonal controls, such as accounting systems, job descriptions and the like, are constructed and introduced by managerial actors in the organization. Thus the functional adjustments to structure in response to size happen through the acts of human agents. Child (1973) presents a formal causal model of how size leads to the proliferation of administrative specialists who develop the impersonal controls. This is supported by empirical evidence (Child, 1973). The size-bureaucracy nexus is compatible both with structural-functional and with conflict theories. Indeed the size-bureaucracy postulate is reconcilable to a Marxian view of organizations:

in small firms capital controls through direct decision-making; in large firms capital controls through indirect, impersonal webs of bureaucratic structure. Such a formulation seems quite compatible with Marxism. There is no necessary antipathy between certain discoveries in organizational sociology, such as the size-bureaucracy nexus, and the fundamental world-view of Marx.

Clegg and Dunkerley (1980), discussing the technology-structure, job redesign or intra-organizational power literatures, are highly critical and purport to find damaging objections to existing lines of work. Yet is this really all so incompatible with a Marxian perspective on organizations? Clegg and Dunkerley (1980) describe the tendency of capitalist firms through the competitive struggle to arrive at few large corporations dominating in many industries. This phenomena of monopoly capitalism is a standard argument in contemporary Marxism (Baran and Sweezy, 1966). There is thus a tendency towards increased company size. Moreover, many contemporary Marxists, socialist radicals and union organizers recognize that workers in those factories are subject to impersonal, bureaucratic control systems. Further yet the idea that mass production encourage technologies and control system which lead to degradation of the worker is a commonplace observation. Marx (1968) gave emphasis to the idea that technology influences the social organization of society and its component parts: the means of production determine the relations of production. And Clegg and Dunkerley follow this view at the societal level and, in places, in terms of factory organization. For instance, they write in their case study of workers' control at the *Scottish Daily News* that: 'The technology of newspaper production enables little variation in work design . . . ' (Clegg and Dunkerley, 1980: 521). Again, Clegg and Dunkerley comment in their discussion of the People's Republic of China: 'If Western technology is adopted, one wonders at the extent to which the adoption of Western work design and organization can be avoided' (1980: 530). For Marxians there would appear to be no particular problem in accepting that the development of capitalism leads to an increasing number of large, highly bureaucratic organizations and that capital investment in machinery leads to the adoption of work practices with determinate consequences for the interpersonal relationships and well-being of the work-force. Thus the idea that there are connections between context and organization structure, or between task and individual job satisfaction, is not inconsistent with a Marxian view of society.

Clegg and Dunkerley (1980: 348) follow Fox (1974) in arguing a relationship between the amount of discretion given to employees and their class and status. Those of higher social background may be viewed by management as more trustworthy and this may explain the association between higher social economic standing of incumbents and more autonomous jobs. Much literature in Organization Theory has explained degree of job autonomy and lack of subjection to bureaucratic controls of certain roles primarily in terms of the amount of uncertainty in the task (see Gerwin, 1979 for a review). Yet it is noticeable that high discretion jobs in one of these studies (Hage and Aiken, 1967) tend to be held by more professionally qualified persons. This is compatible with the argument from uncertainty as professional training equips the employee to deal with relatively novel, nonroutine problems (Hage and Aiken, 1967; Blau and Schoenherr, 1971). However, professional employment tends to be attained by those from higher social class backgrounds and is itself an attainment of social status for the occupant (Blau and Duncan, 1967; Hall and Jones, 1950; Kelsall *et al.*, 1972). Thus there is a prima facie case that certain results in the conventional organizational sociology literature are explicable in terms of class theory.

Reference to social class involves factors other than those which have been most central to orthodox Organization Theory, such as size, technology or task. However, class and status are sociological concepts which are not restricted to neo-Marxism. They figure prominently in the writings of Weber (1968) and also in theories of social stratification of a structural-functionalist variety (Barber, 1957). Thus if variables such as class and status are shown to add to the explanation of organizational phenomena offered by size, task uncertainty and so on, this does not constitute, in itself, evidence for, or adoption of, a neo-Marxian framework in Organization Theory. Crozier's classic study (1964) explains barriers to vertical communication in French bureaucracy partly in terms of the different social and educational backgrounds of officials at various levels in the hierarchy. Yet this is not a work of neo-Marxism. The addition of variables of social stratification to explanatory models of organizational behaviour, would be part of the Organization-in-Society programme (Chapter 11), rather than necessarily being the fulfilment of a Marxian Organization Theory.

To qualify as distinctly neo-Marxian one would need to show the connection between work life in the organization and change at the societal level. In Marxism the exploitation and brutalism in the capitalist factory leads to increasing social tension and eventual revolution. Thus the significance of organizational-level phenomena such as individual remuneration, job satisfaction and intra-organizational stratification would have to be established with respect to the wider socio-political class struggle. This would involve considerable focus on the societal level of analysis, Once again, a Marxian approach requires that the primary focus be macroscopic. Organizations would be studied only as sites at which the wider contradiction and class struggle were played out. Studies which restricted themselves to the organizational level could not be neo-

Marxian. Organization studies might be drawn upon by neo-Marxians to understand the detailed factory-level working of the contradictions and conflict. But this would require connecting organizational phenomena such as individual job dissatisfaction to societal phenomena such as class consciousness and political revolution. Thus much would need to be added to turn the results of organizational enquiry into neo-Marxism, and this would involve the taking of a more macroscopic perspective. Once more, the adoption of a Marxian approach to organizations would involve the complete subsumption of organizational enquiry into a theory of society.

Conclusions

Since Marxian sociology and Organization Theory are not mutually exclusive as intellectual systems it is not necessary for Goldman and Van Houten (1977) and Clegg and Dunkerley (1980) to attack the latter in order to propound the former.

However, the focus of analysis of Marxism and Organization Theory is distinct in terms of being primarily concerned with the society and the organization, respectively. Attempts such as those by Benson (1977) and Heydebrand (1977) to construct a Marxian Organization Theory are therefore beset with difficulties at the outset. As we have seen, much of the content of their work turns out to be conventional organizational or sociological work, often of a neo-Weberian kind.

13

The Strategic Choice Thesis

So far in this volume attention has been focused, in the main, on those who have criticized the practice of organizational sociology from the outside, in that most of the authors concerned have not been contributors to the body of research which they have taken to task. In this chapter the discussion turns to one of the central figures within the orthodox, quantitative, analytic, structuralist approach to the study of organizations.

Child has contributed significantly to the corpus of empirical research within this tradition, in particular through his massive study of 82 business organizations in six industries in England and Wales. The National Study, as it has been called, is a major replication of the original Aston study. Moreover, in his presentation of the results of this survey Child has, through a series of articles, offered a theoretical interpretation of the National and earlier findings (Child, 1972a, 1972b, 1973a, 1975). Much of the credit for showing that such quantitative, 'objectivist' investigation need not be atheoretical must go, in the case of the Aston programme, to Child. The explanations offered in this work include some of a decidedly structural-functionalist kind, as in the argument that centralized, personal decision-making and impersonal regulation by bureaucratic rules and role definitions are alternative structural means for ensuring control over organizational members (Child, 1972b). Further a concern for organizational design issues has been manifest by Child (for example, 1973b, 1975, 1977a and 1977b).

Nevertheless other writings by Child make explicit considerable concurrence with doctrines of the critical camp, in particular with that of Silverman. As was noted in Chapter 1, Child, in a review of the field, cited Silverman approvingly and referred to the notion of supra-individual goals and processes as 'reification' and as 'quasi-metaphysical manoeuvres' (1969: 27). The implications of an approach to the study of organizations which draws more directly on the Social Action Theory was worked through and presented by Child in an article which has been widely received as seminal: 'Organization Structure, Environment and Performance: The Role of Strategic Choice' (1972a). In this Child depicts a number of weaknesses in organizational sociology and argues for recognition of ' . . . the role of strategic choice as a necessary element in any adequate theory of organizational structure . . . ' (1972a: 17). This is discussed in terms of a model of political action. In particular it explicates the role in decision-making of the powerful actors, the dominant coalition, and in this way eschews the metaphysical elements of supra-individual constructs to which Silverman objects:

> The dominant coalition concept draws attention to the question of who is making the choice. It thus provides a useful antidote to the sociologically unsatisfactory notion that a given organizational structure can be understood in relation to the functional imperative of 'system needs' which somehow transcend the objectives of any group of organizational members. In this way the analytical contribution of a functional interpretation of organizational behaviour referring to system maintenance in response to contextual constraints, is supplemented by a political interpretation which does not regard such constraints as necessarily acute or immutable, and which highlights the role of choice. In shifting attention towards the role of choice, we are led to account for organizational variation directly through reference to its sources rather than indirectly through reference to its supposed consequences. This shift of emphasis meets one of the major criticisms that Silverman (1970) has raised against much contemporary organization theory. (Child, 1972a: 14)

Thus through the Strategic Choice model there is a major attempt by one of the practitioners of analytic structuralism to reconcile that approach to certain lines of criticism, and with the social action framework. The thesis of this volume is that many such criticisms are, at bottom, confused or else based on preferences about topics of investigation which are extrasociological. Accordingly, attempts at accommodation, such as the Strategic Choice formulation, should be approached with caution. As will be seen, the thesis of Child makes a number of observations about contingency work which require qualification and suggest a programme which would be counter-productive of further contingency research, and which would vitiate the objectives which Child sets for it.

An overview of difficulties in the Strategic Choice Thesis

Child's attempt at the reconciliation of the perspective of those such as Silverman with mainstream organization studies leads to an eclectic combination which is in some respects a progression, yet in other ways is retrogressive. By drawing attention to the role played by individuals, especially powerful ones, in creating and modifying structures an enhanced framework for the explanation of structure is offered. This usefully supplements the systemic approach by adding concepts for analysing the internal micro-processes, such as politics and negotiation, which mediate the relationship between context, structure and performance. The action perspective with its concepts of individual values and personal stratagems provides a valuable set of additional concepts for the fuller understanding of how particular structures come about. However, the mission of this research programme is to explain structure. This in itself cannot answer the question of which structure is more appropriate in terms of leading to goal-attainment for given contingencies. Yet this is the issue confronting anyone who wishes to know what design an organiz-ation should adopt if it is to attain certain objectives. This is the sort of knowledge which several earlier studies of organizations (e.g. Wood-ward, 1965; Lawrence and Lorsch, 1967) have sought to produce, that is they have been concerned with design rather than simply explaining the status quo. One of the problems of the Strategic Choice Thesis is that it also embraces this as the goal yet outlines a programme which cannot pro-duce knowledge of organizational design. This is one of the pitfalls from seeking to adopt too uncritically an approach which gives primacy to causes rather than to consequences. Since design knowledge is necessary if those influencing organizations are going to be able to attain certain goals and not others, the programmatic outlined by Child will not assist the build-up of a capacity for informed choice in organizational affairs.

A second problem is the real significance of the concept of choice in the Strategic Choice Thesis. Much of the attribution of humanism to Social Action Theory, in contradistinction to systems theories, rests on the emphasis given in the former to the individual choosing between alterna-tives according to their values. This emphasis on human agency as opposed to systems imperatives is part of the reason that such frame-works are presented as humanistic. Yet, as will be seen, while individual choice features in the analytic foreground, in the intellectual background there is a deterministic model of society. The interaction of these two themes produces a position for which Strategic Choice is a misnomer. The received version of the thesis, that it draws attention to the role of managerial choice in the formation of structure, sits uncomfortably with this second wider-ranging programmatic whose interest is in showing that organizations are shaped by, and form part of, the social stratification sys-tem of society.

Other commentators on the thesis of Child have argued that he over-states the degree of choice, and they have reasserted that environment and context shape structure fairly closely (Aldrich, 1979; Hage, 1980). The present remarks are not concerned with debating the degree of choice that is open to the dominant coalition, nor to denying a role for choice, rather the interest is to take issue with certain programmatic and analytic points about the nature of contemporary organization studies which are raised by Child in making his argument.

In the following discussion the Strategic Choice Thesis will be first outlined, then the issue of structural determination will be examined. This will involve a contrast with an organization design approach, and the problems of attaining the objective set by Child by means of his programmatic will also be explicated. Next, shortcoming in contingency analysis to which Child refers in advancing his thesis is dealt with. Latterly, the limitations introduced by nascent determinism are considered. Finally, the discussion turns briefly to a related issue in the writings of Child, a sequel to Strategic Choice, but a continuation of the themes of correcting what are seen as inadequacies in the contingency approach, the idea of an alternative class of consistency theories.

The Strategic Choice Thesis

Child makes a critique of organizational sociology as being too deterministic, giving insufficient role to choice and argues that ' . . . many available explanations over-emphasize constraints upon that choice' (1972a: 19). This is developed by showing a number of shortcomings in contemporary explanations and showing how the imperatives of the contingencies are weak, in fact. The constraints are loose in a number of regards: design does not have a great impact on performance (Child, 1972a: 12), sub-optimal performance is acceptable under certain conditions (1972a: 4, 15 and 16) and multiple contingencies may have conflicting structural implications (1972a: 17). An alternative framework is presented which features the dominant coalition and other parties exercising their preferences over the structure of organizations (Child, 1972a: 13). The call is made for ' . . . research into organizations of a processual and change-oriented type . . . ' (1972a: 2) utilizing a framework of political action. Only by such means can the fatalism borne of determinism regarding structure be replaced by hope derived from the possibilities of purposeful choice. Current approaches over-emphasize constraint:

> In so doing they draw our attention away from the possibilities first of choosing structural arrangements that will better satisfy the priorities of those in charge of organizations, or indeed of any interested party; and secondly away from the exploration of organizational design as a means of reconciling more successfully economic and social criteria of performance. Until we revise these theoretical perspectives, we shall fail to shake off the 'metaphysical pathos of much of the modern theory of group organization . . . that of pessimism and fatalism' which Gouldner noted fifteen years ago. (Child, 1972a: 19)

Once again, rumours of liberation are in the air. And again the path is seen to lie away from structural-functionalism. And yet again, the explanatory process gives prominence to power and ideology:

> In short, when incorporating strategic choice in a theory of organization, one is recognizing the operation of an essentially political process in which constraints and opportunities are functions of the power exercised by decision-makers in the light of ideological values. A consideration of these values has been outside the scope of this paper, but their existence implies that the degree of association which different contextual factors have with structural variables will not conform to any stable mathematical function. Only when these political factors can be adequately measured is greater predictive certainty likely to be achieved. (Child, 1972a: 16)

The discussion will now turn to a more detailed examination of components of the Strategic Choice Thesis.

The explanation of structure

The view of Child on the nature of previous work in organization studies is shown in his opening passage:

> Systematic comparative investigation of the relationships between organizational structure and situational variables has been the guiding principle for major research programmes both in the United States, under Blau, Hage and Aiken, Hall, Lawrence and Lorsch, and in Britain under Pugh and Woodward. In their work . . . these researchers have attempted to discover the degree of empirical variations in organizational structures and to establish the conditions of such variation. Their findings, together with those from other less extensive studies, provide the material from which models of structural determination have been constructed. (Child, 1972a: 1)

Thus the research tradition is characterized as structural determination, not as structural design.

Child goes on to argue, as in the passage quoted earlier, that greater ability to predict structure will be attained only when political factors are incorporated into the analysis along with the contextual variables (1972a: 16). Thus the research question being posed is the more complete explanation of structure, not the issue of organizational design. The latter would be concerned with the question of which structure is most appropriate for high performance.

While the work of Blau (such as 1972) and that under Pugh (Pugh *et al.*, 1963, 1968, 1969a) has been mainly concerned with the relationship between context and structure, the work of Woodward (1965) and Lawrence and Lorsch (1967) has been concerned with the relationship between context, structure and business performance. The study of Hage and Aiken (1967, 1970) has also included concern with the relationship of structure to aspects of performance, particularly innovation. Thus design issues have been prominent within this literature and to characterize the body of work as simply structural determination sets the terms of the discussion, at the outset, too narrowly.

The distinction between structural determination and organizational design programmes involves certain technical differences in analysis. In the former programme, each structural variable (e.g. functional specialization) is accounted for in statistical analyses by showing associations with contextual variables (e.g. size, technology, size of owning group, etc.) (Child, 1973a). A frequently used procedure is to demonstrate that a large multiple correlation can be obtained between the structural variable and the context variables (Pugh *et al.*, 1969a; Child, 1973a). Contextual determinism would hold that if enough salient aspects of context can be identified and entered into the analysis then all the variations in the structural variable will be explained (i.e. the multiple correlation coefficient = 1.0). This is the programmatic goal of contextual determinism.

The organizational design approach posits that the fit (or otherwise) of context and structure affects performance. For each structural variable and each salient contextual variable there is a line or curve of best fit between them. High-performing organizations lie on that line, low-performing organizations are scattered off this line or curve. For example, Woodward shows that there is a ˆ-shaped curvilinear relationship between operations technology (a contingency) and the span of control of the first-line supervisor (a structural variable) for companies with high performance (1965: 69). For companies with low performance they form a broad ˆ-shaped band scattered either side of this curve (Woodward, 1965: 69). This means that the association between the contingent and structural variables (i.e. between operations technology and the span of control of the first-line supervisor) is higher for the high-performing companies than for the low-performing ones. Khandwalla (1973) also demonstrates this difference between high- and low-performing organizations in degree of association between contingencies and structure. Design studies require three-way analyses: context, structure and performance variables considered simultaneously. Moreover, performance moderates the relationship between contingency and structure. The complete explanation of structure (i.e. multiple correlation between a structural variable and the set of all salient contingency variables = 1.0) is possible only for organizations which are high in performance. For samples which contain organizations that vary in performance the maximum value of the multiple correlation between any structural variable and its contingencies will be less than unity ($R < 1.0$) because of the scatter introduced by the lower-performing organizations. Therefore, unless performance controls are introduced into the analysis, the goal of the organizational design programme is less than complete explanation of structure by contingencies.

Moreover, the low-performing organizations are scattered around the curve of best fit. For the same contingency value they may have a low or high value of structure relative to the optimum, that is be above or below the curve (see Woodward, 1965: 69). The design tradition is not necessarily concerned with explaining why some poor performers are above and others below the curve (Woodward, 1965; Khandwalla, 1973). However, a theory of structural determination of the kind which Child proposes would be.

Thus while design models have affinities with models of structural determination, in that both are interested in broad relationships between contingencies and structure, they are distinct. Moreover, design work seeks an exhaustive specification of the appropriate structure for all the differing values of the contingencies, for given performance variables. It is the absolute values of the appropriate, not the actual, structural scores which design-orientated research seeks to know with exactitude.

Thus the programmatic intent of the theory of organization structure which Child propounds is at odds with preceding organizational enquiry on fundamental grounds. Woodward (1965) and Lawrence and Lorsch (1967) treat their subject matter within a design framework. Both studies report organizations whose structures are mismatched to their contingencies and which display poor performance. Both studies interpret poorer performance in terms of lack of fit of structure to contingencies. Neither study takes as its goal the exact explanation of structure: their interest is in the elaboration of rules for good design.

Moreover, the adjustment of fit is presumed to be at least partly amenable to managerial control, that is the *raison d'être* for producing and teaching such knowledge, and is the reason for the term 'design' which implies conscious choice. Recall Woodward's request in her 1965 volume for findings such as her own to be the subject matter of management education. Again, Lawrence and Lorsch (1967) see the appropriate levels of differentiation and integration as set by the environment as being brought about, at least in part, by management decision. They discuss the level of resource expenditure by management, which is necessary in order to coordinate the organization effectively. Thus managerial choice is an integral component of classic studies within the design literature.

An illustration of the tendency by Child to blur the distinction between structural explication and design-oriented studies is contained in his argument that the dominant coalition may seek to satisfy their own preference for certain structural arrangements at the expense of maintaining a mismatch (1972a: 11). Taking this into account will enable better explanations of the actual structure, but will not help in discerning the appropriate structure. From the viewpoint of the rationalist design perspective, discovering such tendencies towards sub-optimization simply catalogues the forms of irrationality. Again, it becomes apparent that the programmatic of Child is the explanation of structure and not the construction of a theory of organizational design.

Paradoxically, it is only in a world where performance consequences are completely constraining, so that fit is always maintained and adjustments are instantaneous, that there is no structural deviation from the optima, and hence that a theory of organization design would be identical to a theory of organizational structure. In that case, the actual structure will always also be that which is the best design.

A theory of organization structure of the kind proposed by Child would explain extant structures and changes in them. Moreover, his thesis offers propositions about when change will be towards better fit (1972a: 11). However, in avoiding the whole notion of design-oriented studies in organization research, the programmatic of Child leaves such adjustments underspecified in important ways. Where ineffective structures are leading to performance problems the nature of the structural mismatch is only identifiable through design research. When the dominant coalition adjusts the structure towards better fit, what actually constitutes better fit will remain shadowy, without substance, in the absence of design knowledge. The concept of structural change as adjustment, that is as intentional improvement, as opposed to just a structural alteration, is predicated upon some model of organization design. Nevertheless, as a framework for the explanation of structure, and of changes in structure, Child's model possesses much that is useful, i.e. the political model of several parties each pursuing their ends by means of their differential power.

Applications of organizational research

Child concludes his Strategic Choice article by seeing in his newer approach an antidote to the metaphysical pathos, the pessimism and fatalism which Gouldner (1955) has ascribed to Organization Theory. In particular, Child (1972a: 19) writes of his choice-based perspective as directing attention towards the selection of structures which will accord better with the preferences of those in charge of organizations, or of other interest groups. Further, this facilitates organizational design as a way of 'reconciling more successfully economic and social criteria of performance' (Child, 1972a: 19).

Talk of metaphysical pathos refers to Organization Theory as positing the inevitable tendency towards certain structures, such as bureaucracy, which are felt to be objectionable. In identifying a role for choice, Child is arguing that such structures are not inevitable and that at least some actors can exercise a conscious choice towards other forms, which are more consonant with their preferences. However, the design tradition also posits some indeterminacy between context and structure, and a role for choice. Thus inevitability of structure, given context or environment, is not necessarily implied in conventional studies of organization.

In order to make informed choices *vis-à-vis* structures in instrumental terms, those choosing will need the kind of knowledge which is the product of design research, i.e. that certain outcomes come from one set of conjunctions of contingencies and structures and others from another, specified set. Yet, as has been seen, the programme advocated by Child will not realize this knowledge for it omits a design orientation in favour of the explanation of structure.

Turning to the final objective advanced by Child, similar remarks apply. Conventional studies of organization take as their performance criteria economic indicators such as profit, growth in sales and the like (Woodward, 1965; Lawrence and Lorsch, 1967; Rumelt, 1974; Child, 1975). Social concern revolves around other issues such as the results of organizational activity in terms of employment security, employment equality, pollution, safety, product quality, employee satisfaction and so on. To inform choice with respect to these, design research would need to broaden the current sets of performance measures to include this second list. Resultant knowledge would enable those choosing to more accurately assess the social and economic consequences of their structural options. Once again this requires that the design programme be prosecuted, and in this case extended in a non-trivial way. Simply recording the preferences of the various interested parties in and around the organization will not aid their selection of designs. Noting their differential power will assist prediction of which structure will be implemented, but, this, in itself, will contribute little towards the reconciliation of social and economic criteria of performance.

The structural explanation approach for which Child argues would not meet the objectives which he has laid down for organizational enquiry. These would be attained only through the design approach.

The problem of multiple contingencies

An area of difficulty for contingency analysis is seen by Child in multiple contingencies. He notes that modern contingency research reveals more than one factor which may need to be taken into account by those designing organizations, and that this creates an opportunity for the exercise of choice. Child writes that:

> Other variables which have often been regarded as independent deter-
> minants of organizational structures are, within this perspective, seen to
> be linked together as multiple points of reference for the process of
> strategic decision-making. (1972a: 15)

This is exemplified by the way in which uncertainty and technology conjointly determine effective designs, as do technology and size (Child,
1972a: 15). Later Child develops this point in his conclusion:

> . . . constraints upon structural choice are weakened in effect to the
> extent that: . . . Organizational decision-makers perceive that the nature
> of contextual constraints pose conflicting implications for structural
> design – this could, for example, be the case with a combination of large
> size and location within a variable environment. Conflicting impli-
> cations derived from contextual combinations of this kind themselves
> impose some degree of structural choice. (1972a: 16)

The idea is that conflicting contingencies create a grey area for designers
and generate room within which choice may be exercised. Yet the concept
of conflicting contingencies is a curious one. Mintzberg deploys the same
notion in his discussion of what he terms 'contradictory contingency factors' (1979: 474), which lead to dysfunctional structures. Both Child and
Mintzberg refer to the problem of one contingency factor requiring one
sort of structure, say decentralization, while the other contingency factor
has a value for that organization, which requires centralization. The
notion is that this forces a trade-off so each contingency is limited by the
other. Yet if we go back to the basic conception of a contingency this is
illogical.

A contingency is a variable which specifies what structures are appropriate in order to realize high performance. If there is more than one contingency variable which affects a given structural variable then one cannot
unambiguously specify the right structure for high performance on that
single variable in isolation. The appropriate structure can only be
specified by combinations of the two (or more) variables. The resultant
centralization level may be less than that which one contingency in
isolation would suggest, but this is not a deviation away from high performance, it is the realization that the centralization level prescribed by
that single contingency was actually too high for the most effective performance. Thus, contingencies cannot be contradictory, and multiple
contingencies are not causes of dysfunctional forms.

Thus there is nothing in the idea of multiple contingencies which
interact to set the optimum level of a structural variable which implies a
zone of choice. Multiple contingencies interacting conjointly are the
logical fulfilment of the contingency approach recognizing the complexity
of organizations and their situations. Choice brought about by lack of

constraint is implied in contingency models where there is equifinality. When the same functional outcomes can be attained by a range of alternative structures for the same contingencies, then there is a lack of constraint on the judgement. Decision-makers may choose in such a situation with no performance penalty. Within the logic of Child's argument, that choice occurs when constraint is diminished, and it is the possibility of the optimum as a range rather than a singular value which constitutes a zone of discretion; but the existence of multiple contingencies of a structural variable does not necessarily imply equifinality.

Choice or determinism

Having criticized contextual determinism, Child launches the field towards Social Action Theory. But what are we to make of the Social Action Theory-based programme as proposed by Child?

Child (1972a) argues for a political model in which the differing parties weigh their options according to their values and ideology, and the structural outcome reflects their differing power. In this way, the emphasis is upon the frame of reference of the individual and the way in which he or she chooses options according to their perceptions and values (Rex, 1961; Silverman, 1968, 1970). Yet power is to at least some degree determined by the organization structure, the hierarchy of authority, the distribution of expertise and the control over critical uncertainties (Hickson *et al.*, 1971; Blau, 1973; Weber, 1968). Similarly ideology, in Marxian theory, is traditionally seen as reflecting social position, of which owner, chief executive, worker and so on would be important examples. Within the Weberian schema (1968) there are ideal as well as material interests and sociological theory usually treats ideology as somewhat less completely determined by economic factors than does Marxism. Nevertheless it would be extremely unusual for a sociologist deploying that term to believe that there are no structural determinants. And in other work by Child (1969), managerial ideology is seen as a way of legitimating the exercise of hierarchic authority. Hence in presenting the political process as characterized by the play of power and ideology Child is introducing a further set of determinants into the analysis. Therefore to speak of all this as introducing a role for choice is quixotic. For the element of choice, of volition, and of shaping destiny by human intervention, is no sooner posited than it is rendered determinate through the concepts of power and ideology.

The thesis of Child is determinism at one remove. Pre-existing states of the organizational and social structure determine the present organizational structure. There is nothing incompatible with sociological theory in such an idea. But it rests uneasily with the espousal of Social Action

Theory as giving a non-trivial role to choice, and as being humanistic in a way that contextual determinism, say, is not.

A reply might be that, stripped of its voluntaristic trappings, Child has contributed an approach which allows organizations to be seen as they often are: the projects of the powerful. While they undoubtedly are that, to at least some degree, this is only once more to avow a programme whose interest is to explain the actual structures of organization – to account for the *status quo*. The design literature has been interested in another issue, to divine the most appropriate form, given situational variables. In so far as the aim is the explanation of structure and of organizational change then power, ideology and politics may contribute to the explanation. Such factors set important limits to which designs are feasible.

Ideology or lay theory

While choice is integral to both the Social Action Theory and to a design orientation there are differences in what are regarded as the cognitive processes involved. Where ideology is seen as operative, the outcomes of the decision process are depicted as being determined by organizational and social position (Willer, 1971). In the design orientation choice is seen as dependent upon a number of ideas and feelings of the individual, among which is the Organization Theory to which he or she subscribes. Lay beliefs about structure vary from explicit, codified and consistent theories, to assortments of odd propositions, departmental cultures and psychodynamic thoughts of a defensive kind. For many individuals their thinking may be a mixture of these. Education seeks to alter these thoughts through lectures, reading and so on, as well as through processes which aim at having the individual externalize his or her beliefs, such as by case discussion. The term 'management theory' implies beliefs which are capable of rational formulation, discussion and some modification in the light of evidence. The use of such a term in connection with organizational design as a topic taught in education is part of the rationale for teaching such a subject. The presumption is that managerial actions, and hence organization structure and contingencies, can be affected, to at least some degree, by changing the theories to which managers subscribe, through education. Thus a concern for implementing design knowledge leads to a wish to understand management theory, to inquire how far it is potent in structuring organization (Argyris and Schon, 1978), and to seek to learn how it can be changed. Thus attention turns to the cognitive processes of managers and other individuals. These are modelled, at least *a priori*, as involving choice and management theory. This lay thinking is to be seen as a product of a rational, scientific-like process and also a sociological and psychological determination through ideology, social position, personality and other factors. Thus a causal role for ideology and social position is not denied. However they are only one strand in a more complex web of causation. Study of individuals' decision-making needs to take the larger causal map sketched here, in which management theory, reasoning and education play a role. If it does not then the field of organization studies would be perverse, for it would study organization design yet subscribe to a model which denied that such knowledge could ever affect organizations. To cast the role for choice in the narrow terms of ideology runs the risk of encouraging neglect of these other processes in the study of lay thought and organizational change. This would reduce our understanding of how most usefully to feedback the results of design research.

Paradoxically, such a model of choice based on rational reflection upon information and structured by particular concepts is consonant with the Social Action Theory in its original Weberian form (Weber, 1968). This illustrates the extent to which this volume is not a rejection of Social Action Theory, *per se*, as an approach to be used selectively alongside others such as structural and systematic frameworks. The concern here is only to combat arguments which seek to attack these other frameworks and to replace them in the study of organizations.

Summary of problems in the Strategic Choice Thesis

In formulating a model in which organizational structure is explained in terms of the action of political actors Child has shifted attention from consequences to causes and kept faith with the call of Silverman. But this approach is incapable of answering the questions which many, including Child, have asked of organization studies and to which that intellectual tradition has offered illumination. Study of effective structures requires concern for functional imperatives or systems needs. This does not imply that they work in some metaphysical way. The political actors through their acts alter the structures and consequent functioning, and do so wittingly or unwittingly, and with a variety of purposes in mind. For those actors to better realize their purposes, and for them to make better informed and more conscious choices, a necessary prerequisite is the development of the sort of design knowledge which can only be created through a continuation of what has been here identified as the design orientation in organizational research. While Child has written of his aims in terms of supplementing structural-functional-type models by those of political action, his thesis has in fact eclipsed the contribution of the former position behind a critique of contextual determinism. In this way the thesis of Child chimes with the damning criticisms of organizational sociology by those such as Silverman's.

The Strategic Choice argument, though containing much that is laudable, is in many respects curious. It argues cogently for a role for choice and does this by making a critique of contextual determinism. While Child is right to point out inadequacies in that approach, he canvasses as the alternative a form of structural determinism. This does a disservice to organization studies by distracting attention away from a third possibility, the programme of organizational design, which is consonant with structural-functionalism, socially applicable and represents the most accurate depiction of mainstream organization studies. Moreover Child's thesis, on this occasion, contains several omissions in regards to the working through of the logical implications of contingency-design approaches. They suggest an intellectual development which reflects the influence of sociological metatheory inimical to Organization Theory. Child seeks a role for choice in answer to the charges of Silverman. However having embraced radical humanism, nascent determinism is imported through the concepts of power and ideology, and the thesis becomes sociological determinism. Further, the programme proposed is incapable of offering useful advice about structural forms and their consequences either to the dominant coalition or any other interested party, and this is true whether they are interested in maximizing profits or in ensuring employment security, or safety.

In short the Strategic Choice Thesis, as it stands, is problematic as a way forward for organizational sociology and it illustrates the difficulties introduced when attempts are made to accommodate within that field, critical counter-perspectives of the social action or neo-Marxian kinds.

Consistency or contingency approaches

The foregoing discussion has been of the lack of attention to design within a metatheoretical and programmatic statement, the Strategic Choice article. However, as noted earlier, Child has made several substantial contributions to the design literature. A number of pieces of work subsequent to the Strategic Choice article use a contingency-design framework (e.g. Child, 1973b, 1975). Nevertheless, counter-orthodox tendencies are again manifest by Child in later writings (1977a, 1977b) where he deals with design in a new approach which he sees as going 'beyond' contingency theory (1977a: 169). The argument is that consistency of one structural feature with another is important for design, as is fit of structure to contingency, and that simultaneously optimising both sets of matches may be difficult with 'some conflict' between these two considerations (Child, 1977b: 170). Further, '[t]he benefits of retaining consistency between the elements of an organizational design may indeed prove to be considerable in their own right' (Child, 1977b: 173). In adopting this position Child has moved away from the mainstream framework of organization studies, yet in a different way from that in the 'Strategic Choice' thesis. By so doing, Child has once more manifest a tendency to discount the contingency perspective, and has advocated a new departure which seems questionable. Once again there are signs that this disavowal of the contingency approach is premature, being based on reasoning which reflects a lack of working through of the contingency logic. Moreover continuities with earlier positions are visible in that what have been identified, in previous writings by Child (1972a), as shortcomings in organizational studies, are drawn upon once more.

Child notes difficulties in attempts to establish a contingency-based theory of organizational design. Included in these problems are that 'multiple contingencies' pose 'conflicting design implications' (Child, 1977b: 173). However, while reasserting the difficulties which multiple, conflicting contingencies create for contingency-design prescriptions (1977a: 181), Child offers an example of how the joint implications of multiple contingencies can produce coherent advice through multivariate modelling (1977a: 176). In this case, analysis is of how the contingencies of size and environmental variability, interact to effect the most appropriate levels of structuring and delegating (see also Child, 1975).

As an alternative to contingency theory Child (1977b) offers consistency theory as a fruitful approach to organizational design. The case for consistency theory in opposition to contingency rests on showing that the range of optimum structural forms is unconstrained by contextual factors.

The study by Child, which he uses to illustrate his argument for consistency theory and against contingency theory, is of four airlines. These each operate with similar technology in a similar market, but two have high economic performance (Child, 1977b: 171) and two have low performance. Of the former, one is divisionalized, and the other is functionally organized. The argument for consistency arises from the fact that both structures provide adequate functioning despite being different, yet with only one of them, the divisional structure, being in Child's account, that which contingency theory would see as appropriate.

Of the two successful airlines one has a centralized system, the other a divisionalized one. Both are described as facing similar contingencies and the success of their contrasted structures is ascribed to each being internally consistent. Leaving aside whether there were differences in other contingencies not mentioned in the case, whether the divisional structure is the appropriate one and whether the structures really operated in so different a way, contingency analysis may yet illuminate this seemingly inexplicable pair.

Child notes that in the first airline the structure was relatively central-ized, with little autonomy to operating units. However, conflict was low and communications were fostered and disagreements resolved infor-mally. Child relates these features to the 'very long service management' (1977b: 171). The other organization used regional delegation and long-range planning, and conflicts were settled through the 'formal decision process' (1977b: 171). It seems that part of the answer is that in the first company the informal system handled problems dealt with through the formal system in the latter. Structural analysis has long emphasized that informal systems may substitute for the formal organization (Miller and Form, 1964). In this case, this seems to be built on the *contingency* of the long-service management who had come to trust each other.

The two poor performers had instituted a divisionalized system yet had not delegated decision-making as would have been consistent. But on the case descriptions given by Child this seems explicable in contingency terms: In one of them, staff gave as the reason for the lack of decentraliz-ation the 'poor quality divisional level management . . . ' (Child, 1977b: 172). It is recognized that a prerequisite of decentralization and del-egation is that the abilities of the lower levels must be commensurate with their new authority, and that for decentralization to occur higher levels have to perceive them as able and trustworthy (Handy, 1976). Hence the delegation did not 'happen' in this case because one of the *contingencies* for effective decentralization was violated. In the case of the other airline, it was publicly accountable. The Aston studies have demonstrated that public accountability is associated with greater centralization of decision-making (Pugh *et al.*, 1969a and b; Donaldson and Warner, 1974b). Hence the problems at this airline may well stem from their trying to implement a structure which does not give sufficient attention to the public account-ability *contingency*. These are both *prima facie* cases of the new structure not being the requisite structure which results from considering all of the contingencies mentioned.

In sum, the airline study of Child (1977b) may be interpreted in a way which makes it compatible with a contingency approach. Given the limited facts presented the exercise herein must be viewed as extremely tentative. However, it does serve to suggest that even Child's example of consistency analysis may be placed within a contingency framework.

The point of concern here is that Child (1977b) has chosen to shift from a contingency to a consistency approach in modelling this empirical material without apparently exhausting the potentialities of the former framework. This speaks of a less than firm conviction for the contingency paradigm.

These remarks are not meant to imply that consistency theory, distinct from contingency theory, may not add to the explanatory power of organization studies at some point. However, a proper appreciation of the merits of these two approaches can only be based on a full prosecution of the two frameworks in their ability to interpret empirical evidence.

Once again there is manifest a tendency to distance from the contingency approach. The origins of this lie at least partly in a concern over certain perceived 'difficulties' in contingency analysis. Yet many of these problems seem resolvable if the logic of contingency approach is pursued more fully. The 'problem' of conflicting contingencies may represent the shortcoming of certain earlier studies, but as an awareness of multiple contingencies grows so too does the use of techniques for dealing with this complexity such as multivariate analysis (Pugh *et al.*, 1969a; Child, 1975).

The apparent readiness to see in relatively technical 'hitches' fundamental inadequacies in the paradigm is often symptomatic of having become converted to another paradigm, or at least of having limited commitment to the former paradigm. Kuhn writes of this gestalt switch in which material is perceived in a very different way (1970; 1977). If one were to internalize the criticisms of systems and structural-functional perspectives made by those such as Silverman (1968, 1970), then one's whole frame of reference towards contingency work would be that it is problematic. Difficulties encountered in its pursuit would, within such a world-view, be quite expected and would support prior reservations about the paradigm.

The consistency argument de-emphasizes the idea that there are contingencies, environmental or contextual factors, which determine the structures which are effective in each situation. This down-plays the notion that there are positivistic factors such as size or product diversity or market conditions which constitute imperatives for effective structures. In this way the critical position which seeks to denigrate the contributions from positivism is given fulfilment in the field of organizations – an objective highly compatible with the programmatic of writers such as Silverman.

Conclusions

While Child has made considerable empirical and theoretical contributions to organizational sociology his later programmatic writings, and indeed elements of his later empirical investigations, are only partially helpful as guides for future organization studies. They contain a number of rather uncertain conceptual and theoretical points which do not constitute the best working through of the organization studies framework. Child has made an important contribution in reaffirming a role for choice and in indicating the complex characteristic of adaption processes. But this has been done through a contrast with contextual determinism. Such a duality detracts attention from the more fruitful framework for organization studies – the contingency-design approach. The writings of Child discussed here reveal the extent to which the attack on organizational sociology has been interjected into members of the mainstream research community, and the deleterious consequences.

PART THREE

Implications of contingency research for organization design

14

The design of organizations

Thus far in this volume the emphasis has been on defending organization studies as an intellectually legitimate field of endeavour with an orientation towards practical problems. Hopefully enough has been said thus far to provide an appreciation of the coherency and scientific merits of the enterprise. The book has not set out to be a text guide to the literature and there are several excellent works currently available (Hage and Azumi, 1972; Khandwalla, 1977; Mintzberg, 1979; Kotter *et al.*, 1979; Hage, 1980; Child, 1977b). Moreover, the rationale for continued research in this field need not predicate that all is known in this area nor that all questions are answered. It is precisely a sense of the problematics – of the gaps in knowledge – which provides justification and stimulus for further enquiry. However if Organization Theory is offered as a promising line of enquiry, then it behoves the adherents to at least indicate some of the achievements in understanding which have flowed from research to date. Accordingly, this chapter will offer a brief guide to some of the major points to emerge from comparative studies of organization and their implications for design. What follows is not exhaustive but merely illustrative. In order to make the discussion more accessible many of the technical niceties will be passed over.

The modern approach to prescription about how best to organize asserts that there is no single form which will be equally effective under all circumstances – no one best way. Organization structure is conceived of as being made up of several different facets. Some of these are characteristics of the organization chart, such as the number of persons reporting to the Chief Executive (the span of control of the Chief Executive). Another such aspect is the way responsibilities are divided up amongst the subordinates of the Chief Executive. Are they specialized by function, in which case their titles may be heads of Marketing, Production, Research and so on. Alternatively, they may be specialized by products such as Domestic Appliances, Computers or Radar. Function, product, geographic area and the like are bases of differentiation. They vary across organizations. Also they may often vary within an organization being,

155

say, by product at the first level (below the Chief Executive) and by function at the next tier down, the second level of differentiation. A further aspect of the organization chart is the number of levels in the hierarchy, the length of the chain of command.

A second way of talking about differences is more abstract. The organization is considered to be a system of interlocking roles. An organizational role is defined as a set of expectations focusing on a particular position. Roles differ one from another in how far their job content is organizationally laid down in precise task prescriptions and written instructions, how much autonomy or discretion they can exercise in the decisions involved in doing their job, how much role-holders participate in discussions about wider issues such as organizational policy. One can compare across different sections or different departments in how far the jobs are codified, formalized, autonomous and participatory. At a more macro level one can compare across organizations. What degree of specialization by function exists? Are there distinct roles such as accountants, market research and statistician in a company, or is all this book-keeping and correspondence, in as far as it is done, done by the Chief Executive and his or her secretary, in which case functional specialization on such matters is virtually absent? Does an organization possess a great many rules, regulations and standard procedures? Are there manuals of procedures, forms, written records and files? An organization which has much of this is said to be highly formalized. A further variable which may be used to compare across organizations is centralization of decision-making authority. In some organizations decisions are almost all taken at the top. In others authority on issues such as deciding which make of machine to purchase or who is to be appointed as foreperson is delegated down to middle or junior levels of management. These abstract properties of role formalization or organizational centralization are measured on scales. Thus one can construct a profile of a particular organization on the variables of function specialization, formalization and centralization and compare this with another organization. Similarly, there can be a comparison of roles.

Thus a variety of aspects of an organization may be catalogued as either discrete categorizations, for example the first-level basis of differentiation is either by function or product, or as variables, for example, the functional specialization score is 11 out of a maximum possible 16.

The intention of this classificatory and measurement exercise is to provide a value-neutral way of describing an organization. There is no implication that having a low score on say formalization is either ineffective or morally wrong. Indeed the modern contingency view has to a degree arisen as a rejection of the classical management theories which tended to equate sound administration with a very high degree of organizational policy specification by the centre, formalization and centralization (Brech, 1957). As will be seen, research provides little support for this notion. Rather it appears that different situations require different sorts of organization for peak effectiveness.

Thus alongside of the various facets of structure modern research elucidates a number of aspects of situation or context. Some of the more important of these are size, diversification, public accountability and task uncertainty. Each organization aspect under study is influenced by one or more of these contingency factors, in that the level of the latter which are present in a particular situation leads to a specific value of the structural variable being required for effective performance. Research seeks to identify and verify the exact form of such relationships. From this kind of research a model may be constructed as follows. In the exposition the initial focus will be on the more overall aspects of organization structure and then interest will switch to the more specific and localized character-istics of the structure around the apex.

As a beginning, consider the issue of the degree to which an organiz-ation approximates to a bureaucracy. Leading aspects of bureaucratiz-ation are a high degree of function specialization and a high degree of formalization (documents, etc.). Both of these aspects are highly corre-lated with each other and so will be treated together for present purposes. A major factor contributing to the growth in hierarchy is an increase in size such as by having many employees. Organizations of large size go further than smaller ones in specializing functions, prescribing conduct through regulations, using written documents and so on. Once a pro-cedure is established such as a standard start time for factory employees it can be applied across a large number of individual cases. This reduces information processing, time, administrative effort and uncertainty in dealing with this issue. Thus, given routine, recurring activities, bureauc-ratization results in reduced operating expenses. Similarly specialization by function enhances effectiveness through facilitating the development of skills and expertise in incumbents. Part of this cost saving is through the creation of routine jobs which require less education for their perform-ance and which can be filled with employees on lower wages (Blau, 1972). Many of the new systems and procedures of accounting, personnel and the like are promoted by administrative experts who grow in number as one component of the increasing specialization by function which size advances (Child, 1973a). There is some evidence that companies with greater levels of bureaucracy for their given size, at higher size levels, tend to have higher financial performance (Child, 1975). This finding is compatible with the notion that a certain increase in bureaucratization is required as an organization grows, and that failure to develop more specialized and formalized administration leads to reduced effectiveness.

A further context factor which impinges on bureaucratization is that of group size. If the organization under study is enmeshed in a larger owning group, for example, if it is the subsidiary of a multi-national corporation, then group size is the total employees of the latter world-wide. Group size raises the level of specialization and formalization. The parent company requires the subsidiary to have additional procedures, documents and specialists over that which would result from the size of the subsidiary alone (Pugh *et al.*, 1969a; Child, 1973a). These extra components are necessary for the subsidiary to synchronize with the parent in the sense of providing detailed financial and other reports in order to be consistent with global corporate control systems and policies.

A second aspect of bureaucratic structure is the number of levels in the hierarchy. This also increases with size of the organization (Pugh *et al.*, 1969a; Pugh and Hinings, 1976). As an organization grows from one superordinate plus several direct subordinates to there being, say, twenty subordinates, there comes a point at which the boss can no longer immediately supervise all these subordinates. A couple of subordinates will have to be nominated as supervisors and the rest of the employees split among them into two or more sections. Thus a new intermediary level of supervision is introduced. In this way the hierarchy increases with growth in size, due to limitations on the optimum span of control, that is the number of subordinates who can be managed effectively by any one supervisor.

A third aspect is the decentralization of authority to take decisions. With growth in size the range of activities grows in an organization. For example, in a large factory there are many employees and many different types of machines. Issues of scheduling work between work stations arise and take on a complexity greater than that known in a small organization. Thus decisions are more complex. Moreover, in a large organization, information is dispersed across and down the hierarchy. Expertise about the machinery in a particular workshop is usually greatest in and around that shop. Centralization of decision-making on such matters would involve retrieving information through several levels of the hierarchy and then synthesizing it by people who lack real understanding. Moreover the range of such issues to be decided would strain and overload a central decision-maker. Thus extreme centralization of decision-making is neither feasible nor effective in large organizations. Hence growth in size leads to decentralization of decision-making (Pugh *et al.*, 1969a; Child, 1973a; Pugh and Hinings, 1976). The larger organization possesses a longer hierarchy with more levels of middle management, and delegates more authority down to them in comparison with a smaller unit.

A further contingency of centralization of authority resides in, once again, the presence or absence of some superordinate organization. If the focal organization is a subsidiary of a parent company there will be decisions which require authorization by the parent. Thus the autonomy of the focal organization is reduced, whereas an independent company would make such decisions internally (Pugh *et al.*, 1969a).

A third situational factor relating to centralization has been termed public accountability. Is the ownership of a company closely held as in a private family company, or are the shares quoted on the stock exchange requiring disclosure of information and the vesting of authority in non-executive board members? Companies which tend towards the latter tend to be more centralized in their decision-making, as more decisions require board approval (Pugh *et al.*, 1969a). Likewise, nationalized companies tend to be more centralized than private ones (Pugh *et al.*, 1969a).

Public accountability tends also to raise the level of bureaucratic documentation, partly as a reflection of the written reports to board members and the like to enable them to vet and scrutinize (Pugh *et al.*, 1969a).

Some organizations deliberately seek to be democratic in their operations, to remove themselves from the oligarchy and elite control that they see in traditional bureaucracies. What sort of structure do they implement? Do they mark radically different kinds of structure than the ones discussed so far? The author and his colleague, Malcolm Warner, investigated structures in British trade unions, as examples of non-capitalist organizations largely run by and for the working class. One of the primary mechanisms for assuring member control over the administrative apparatus is a top representative body, an Annual Conference or the like at which delegates exercise a review of union affairs and determine policy. A sub-set of this group meets more frequently as a National Executive Committee (or similar title) to provide a more immediate supervision of operations and of the full-time administrative staff. This is a function quite analogous to that of a Board of Directors in a public company or a council in a nationalized industry. Every union in the sample had such an arrangement, and they displayed greater centralization of authority (Donaldson and Warner, 1974b). Thus representative institutions which take the form of agents of the members positioned at the apex of the administrative hierarchy lead to centralization of decision-making authority.

An implication of the foregoing is that if there were to be an increase in industrial democracy or workers' control throughout countries such as Australia, Britain, France or the USA then enterprises would become more centralized in their decision-making authority. The doctrine that asserts the desirability of democratization and the imperative to seiz power by taking over the command posts of management entails a diminution in decision-making authority at lower organizational levels.

A further institutional manifestation of the impulse to democracy is in the way persons with managerial authority gain and retain such posts. The bureaucratic means is by appointment from hierarchic superiors (Weber, 1968). A democratic alternative is through elections by the membership. Unions differ in how far they utilize such electoral control over officials and this has been measured (Donaldson and Warner, 1974a). This scale draws a negative correlation with other bureaucratic aspects such as formalization (Donaldson and Warner, 1974a). Elections and the need to win popular support introduce an element of unpredictability into administration, forestalling attempts to extend bureaucratization. The architects of bureaucracy are permanent officials developing long-term plans. The time horizon of politicians is the next election. Thus the electoral control of officials works to reduce bureaucratization somewhat.

Thus the impact of democracy on structure is two-fold. Representative institutions at the apex lead to greater centralization of decision-making authority. Having elected, or representative, officials inside the administrative hierarchy reduces the degree of formalization.

Thus the overall structure of an organization in aspects such as functional specialization, formalization, number of hierarchic levels, centralization of decision-making and electoral control over officials is dependent upon the variables of size, group size, public accountability and the degree to which there are democratic intentions. This is a model of some degree of complexity, but it is not confused or confusing for the relationships are specified between particular variables. A summary is given in Figure 1.

A more specific facet of structure is the organization of senior management. More particularly the managers who report directly to the Chief Executive Officer may be arranged in several ways. Duties may be divided among them by functions (e.g. marketing, production, research, etc.). Or the work of the company may be split into divisions, either by products (e.g. steel, chemicals, fast food, etc.) or by areas (e.g. Europe, North America, Pacific, etc.). Or again the top of the firm may be structured as a matrix. The characteristics of each of these structures will be outlined together with the situation in which each is most appropriate.

The functional form is relatively centralized in decision-making. Each function (production, marketing, etc.) is interdependent upon the others (Kotter *et al.*, 1979; Mintzberg, 1979). For instance, marketing sells what production makes. Therefore production needs to be given sales orders and information on changing customer tastes, customer assessment of product quality, etc. Equally, marketing is dependent for the manufac-

ture and supply of products to the customers on the Production Department. Where problems or issues of coordination between departments
cannot be solved by direct interaction between the two or more units concerned, the matter has to go to their immediate superior for resolution.
This means that the attention of the Chief Executive is required. The
profitability of operations in total is computed for the whole enterprise.
Each of the departments is judged against sub-objectives for their function. For example, the Production Department is assessed against the
cost of producing products, their quality and the timeliness of their manufacture. While a company produces a single product the activities are
highly interdependent and a functional structure is appropriate. However, as the range of products increases this organization becomes less
suitable. With multiple products the range of issues which the Chief
Executive is required to grasp and adjudicate on increases. The coordination of the production and marketing of a single product has to travel
up the hierarchy to the departmental chiefs and, on occasions, to the
Chief Executive Officer for decision. This consumes time and communication is liable to be poor.

In order to avoid such difficulties multi-product and multi-area firms
often employ a multi-divisional structure (for examples see Figure 2). The
interdependent activities such as those involved in designing-making-
selling a single product are grouped together organizationally, separate
from the other clusters of interdependency around each of the other
products. Each product is then made into a division with its own

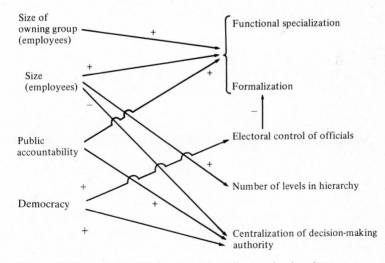

Figure 1. The relationship between overall organizational structure
and contingency factors.

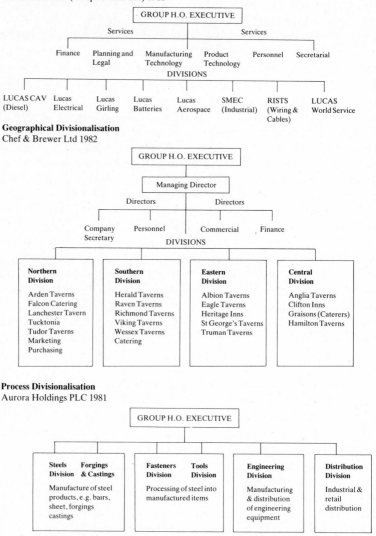

Bases of Multi-divisional Structures

- Organisations may be divisionalised on different bases, amongst which are included product market, geography and processes.

Product Market Divisionalisation
Lucas Industries (Joseph Lucas Ltd) 1982

Geographical Divisionalisation
Chef & Brewer Ltd 1982

Process Divisionalisation
Aurora Holdings PLC 1981

Source: Gerry Johnson and Kevin Scholes, *Exploring Corporate Strategy* (London, Prentice-Hall International, 1984), p. 273, from company annual reports.

Figure 2. Examples of three bases of first-level differentiation in divisionalization.

resources, functional specialists in production, marketing, etc. and headed by a general manager (Chandler, 1962; Rumelt, 1974; Dyas and Thanheiser, 1976). The division is given autonomy over operating matters such as the volume of production, the price to be charged for the products, etc. Thus the divisional system is more decentralized in decision-making than the functional form (Chenhall, 1979). Divisional management is granted more discretion over means but is monitored over ends in the sense of contribution to corporate financial performance (Chandler, 1962; Mintzberg, 1979). The profitability of divisions is calculated in terms such as return on assets and a comparison is made across divisions. Such data are drawn upon by corporate management in making decisions on resource allocation, divestment and rewards for general managers. The Chief Executive Officer is relieved of much involvement in day-to-day operating decisions. This leaves more time for strategic issues such as divisional performance review, acquisitions and longer-term planning as well as matters such as those relating to the financial community, the government and other external bodies.

Where the company diversifies primarily in terms of extension into new geographical areas with different culture, customer taste and regulations, etc., the appropriate form of organization would be the area division. Companies in the food or beverage industry, such as Chef and Brewer Ltd or Bass Charrington, often use this form as the low-value, high-weight nature of the product makes shipment between areas uneconomic (Channon, 1973). Therefore they tend to create self-sufficient areas each organized as a division. This holds also for products such as concrete as in Ready Mix Concrete (Channon, 1973).

Returning to the product division form this is seen in its purest form in the case of the conglomerate corporation, that is a company such as Ling-Temco-Vought, which produces several products each of which is unrelated to the others: stereos, meat packing, aircraft and car rentals (Rumelt, 1974). At the other end of the continuum of relatedness, one has the highly related one-product company manifesting high interdependency between all core activities and using a functional structure. In between these two extremes are a variety of structural forms which mix divisional and functional elements (see Table 1). The unrelated case will often have a sparse corporate office consisting of the CEO deputies, assistants to, secretarial staff and a small number of specialist advisers in roles such as legal, finance, personnel and public relations (Pitts, 1976). The next less divisionalized case is the related product company, where there are several products but they share a common technology of product design, e.g. electronics in an electrical goods company or pharmaceuticals in a pharmaceutical company (Pitts, 1976). Such companies often organize each product as a product division in order to stimulate

Table 1. *Relationship between degree of product diversification and high-level organizational structure*

Degree of product diversification

Number of products

| Organizational characteristics | Single | More than one | | Unrelated |
| | | Related | | |
		Vertical integration	Common product design technology	
Structure	Functional	Product Division	Product Division	Product Division
Sub-units	Functions	Product Divisions	Product Divisions	Product Divisions
Interdependencies	High	Medium	Limited	Low
Self-sufficiency of sub-units	Nil	Limited	Substantial	High
Autonomy of sub-units	Low	Medium	Substantial	High
Central functions	Full range of functions report directly to CEO	Finance Legal Corporate Planning Public Relations Production Planning Transport Planning	Finance Legal Corporate Planning Public Relations R & D	Finance Legal Corporate Planning Public Relations
Central influence over sub-units	High	Interdivisional transactions: volume, time and price	New product investment, development and allocation	Low
Sub-unit objectives	Functional e.g. cost centre, volume	Profit with arms-length transfer prices or profit for down-stream units and upstream units as cost centres	Profit moderated by product development factor	Profit

innovation (for reasons to be given below); however, the common research effort of the company may be centralized in a large Research and Development laboratory at the corporate level. This adds appreciably to the corporate overhead charged to divisions. The corporate management is involved in decisions such as the level and direction of R & D and which division is to receive the new products from the laboratory. This reduces somewhat divisional autonomy and reduces their direct control over their own profitability (Pitts, 1976).

A type of company in which there is even more relationship between products is where they are vertically integrated. Here the output of one product provides the input for the next product in a chain. Products may also be sold to the outside market at each point in the chain. For instance, Alcoa mines bauxite, refines it into primary aluminium and then fabricates it into cookware, window frames, automobile parts and other goods (Rumelt, 1974). Some of the primary aluminium is also sold to the market direct (Rumelt, 1974). Each product process stage may be designated as a division often with its own marketing as well as production function. In such a company the products have a serial interdependence (Thompson, 1967), in that the output of one sub-unit is the input of the next sub-unit. In Alcoa the amount of bauxite mined has to be sufficient to keep up with the demand for primary aluminium, and the refinery capacity has to be sufficient to meet the needs of the fabrication plants. Thus there is a need for coordination on issues such as production and inventory levels and transportation. This involves the divisions in participating in interdivisional planning and this is often facilitated by the presence of specialists in production and transport in the corporate headquarters staff (Lorsch and Allen, 1973).

The profitability of a division in such a vertical chain is positively affected if they can charge, for their output, a high price to the downstream division. In such transactions the supplying division has an incentive to maximize the sales price and the recipient division has an incentive to minimize the price paid. This produces an in-built zero-sum conflict which gives rise to resentment and lack of cooperation (Kotter *et al.*, 1979). Some amelioration may be possible in certain circumstances by the use of an arms-length price for the transaction based on that prevailing in the open market. However, vertical integration is often associated with imperfect competition such that the company does not simply take a market determined price. Further in some multinational corporations international transactions prices are subject to manipulation in order to yield taxation benefits. Thus transfer pricing is a sufficiently sensitive issue to lead either to the assessment of divisional profitability being highly modified by subjective judgements by corporate management of real contribution or its partial abandonment. In some successful vertically integrated companies the downstream divisions, those at the end of the chains, are assessed in terms of profitability, whereas the upstream divisions are assessed in terms of volume and cost objectives. In the forest products industry, this means that the mill which converts logs to paper and board, is treated, is terms of objectives, as like a Production Department subject to functional criteria of performance. By contrast the separate product divisions, one each for packaging and containers (the former produces differentiated products to customer specification involving artwork, the latter produces undifferentiated cardboard boxes and the like) which draw on the mill for materials supply are each treated as a profit centre (Lorsch and Allen, 1973). Thus the vertically integrated company requires a structure which is a combination of the divisional and functional types. The process stages are each designated as divisions but there is less autonomy and more coordination than in the pure divisional type. Similarly, both profit and functional criteria may be used to monitor divisional performance.

As has been indicated the relationship between the corporate centre and the divisions varies according to the degree of relatedness of products and hence of interdependence. In the unrelated or conglomerate situations the divisions are strong and they include the full range of functions (Lorsch and Allen, 1973; Cassano, 1983). Headquarters and divisions spend relatively little time in dealing with one another (Lorsch and Allen, 1973). In the more vertically integrated or related product company the headquarters is more powerful and intrusive *vis-à-vis* the divisions which are less likely to have the full range of functions (Lorsch and Allen, 1973). Further corporate-divisional relationships consume more of the time of both parties. There is evidence that the more companies conform to these patterns the higher is their performance (Lorsch and Allen, 1973; Cassano, 1983). However, at the intermediary level of product diversity, where a company has several related products either a functional or product divisional structure may be selected (Donaldson, 1985), if cost economies are sought then the simple, unified functional structure will be preferred. However, if product innovation is the priority then the product divisional system will be more advantageous.

For example, a large Japanese producer of synthetic textiles had up till 1970 a functional structure (Donaldson, 1979a). The company produced three main products: synthetic textiles, plastics and industrial chemicals. The textiles and plastics came from a vertically integrated production process and the chemicals were a by-product. In the search for enhanced growth and product innovation the company made each of these into a product division. As the seventies progressed the economic climate deteriorated with increasing prices of raw materials and enhanced foreign competition. The company sought to gain cost economies through reorganizing all the manufacturing plants under the control of a central production department. The functional elements of marketing and research were likewise dispersed from the disbanded divisions back into central functions and the general managers left the company. Financial and personnel matters were re-centralized in the functions. This renewed centralization was sought in part to facilitate resource allocation into new products outside of the mainstream, such as computer-systems. Hence the selection of structure at intermediary level of diversification is affected by the priority being given to innovation or to cost control.

Product innovation in a company may be facilitated through the use of project teams. These bring together the diverse specialists needed to cope

with the uncertainty of new product research, development and commer-
cialization. Placing them in one team fosters interaction. The leadership
by a project officer charged with this as a sole responsibility promotes a
drive to timely completion. Project teams may be appended to an organization structure at many places, reporting to the Chief Executive Officer
or the divisional general manager or at other levels. For a multi-product
company the product divisional system offers more product focus than
does a functional system. As has been seen, the choice between product
division and functional structure is largely determined by the degree of
product diversification.

The remaining major distinct form of structure at the apex of the
company is the matrix. Matrices arise where a corporation needs one
form of differentiation, say, by area and also another, say, by product
(Davis and Lawrence, 1977). The essential part is that neither is satisfactory on its own, so a multidivisional form of structure is needed. The
underlying situational factor is that the interdependence between
activities is of a medium level. There is neither the low interdependence
of the highly diversified case, nor the high interdependence of the single-
product company. Instead there will be some degree of diversity in either
product or area, or both, which forces a multi-product or multi-area
organizational form. If there is diversity of both product and area then a
product-area matrix will be appropriate. If the diversity is just on product
then a product-functional matrix will be called for. Again, if the diversity
is on area then an area-functional matrix is needed.

Whatever the nature of the dimensions all two-dimensional matrices
have the following characteristics. Managers at the level below the two
arms of the matrix report to two bosses: one on each arm (e.g. in a
product-area matrix to a product and area head). This has potential for
conflict (Knight, 1976) and any such which cannot be resolved between
the two bosses will need to go to their boss (who in this discussion would
be the CEO) for resolution. Since there are many possible combinations
of the matrix managers taken pairwise (e.g. if there are five product heads
and five area heads there may be 25 subordinates each with a unique pair
of bosses), if conflicts constantly rise to the overall superordinate for
settlement he or she will quickly become overloaded. Some amelioration
of this potential for conflict can be attained by two practices. First by
clarifying the respective role and authority of each boss over the subordinate and second by developing a culture of open communication and
problem-solving (Davis and Lawrence, 1977).

An example of matrix management is the project-functional matrix
used in the Gelac division of Lockheed-Georgia (Corey and Star, 1971).
The heads of each of the projects (different types of aircraft designed and
manufactured by the division) had responsibilities for the completion of

Table 2. *Forms of high-level structure and their relationship to diversity of product and area*

		Diversity of product		
		Low	Medium	High
Diversity of area	Low	Functional	Product/Functional Matrix	Product Divisions
	Medium	Area/Functional Matrix	Product/Area Matrix	Product Divisions divided into areas
	High	Area Divisions	Area Divisions divided into products	Product or Area Divisions

the project on time, to specification (weight, speed, range, etc.) and profitably. To do this they had day-to-day control over the personnel assigned to their project. They would make appraisals of these staff to the heads of functions and could negotiate on which personnel would be available for their project and when. By contrast the heads of functions were in charge of resources such as assembly halls, machining rooms, wind tunnels and engineering personnel. They had responsibilities for the selection, development, utilization and replacement of these material and human resources. They had ultimate line authority over these in the matrix. They were charged with maintaining cost-efficient utilization of resources. This involved planning the aggregate demand by the various projects on resources over time achieved through negotiation with the project heads.

Commentators have noted that in practice the two-boss system produces conflict despite attempts to ameliorate it. There is very likely some inescapable cost of this kind to be borne in employing matrix structures. A company only need utilize such a complex organizational form where there is no alternative. When the underlying interdependencies require simultaneous dual focus a matrix is seemingly at present the only option.

Thus the structural form taken at the apex of an organization reflects the interdependencies of the activities to be managed. Table 2 summarizes this showing the circumstances under which each structure is appropriate: Functional, Divisional or Matrix of varying types.

Adjusting the organization structure to fit the degree of diversification which the corporation has attained in its operations appears to have important consequences for performance. There are four degrees of product diversification: Single, Dominant, Related and Unrelated, which are progressively higher levels of diversity. There are also four different ways of structuring the organization at the apex: Functional, Functional-

Table 3. *Congruent and incongruent combinations of strategy and structure*

Structure	Strategy			
	Single business	Dominant business	Related businesses	Unrelated businesses
Functional	c	i	i	i
Functional-with-Subsidiaries	c	c	i	i
Product Divisional	i	c	c	c
Holding Company	i	i	i	i

c = Congruent = Matched = Fit
i = Incongruent = Mismatched = Misfit

with-Subsidiaries, Holding Company and Product Divisional. The first and last of these have been defined above. Functional-with-Subsidiaries is an arrangement whereby the core of the company is organized functionally and there are also subsidiary companies whose Chief Executive Officer reports to the CEO of the parent company. The Holding Company form of organization has each operating unit as a subsidiary reporting to a parent company that is non-operating, which has a small staff and allows the subsidiaries more autonomy than is found in divisions in a divisional system (Rumelt, 1974; Dyas and Thanheiser, 1976). For each particular degree of diversification, certain organization structures correspond as appropriate and constitute a match while others are a mismatch. The four strategy categories and four structure categories yield sixteen different combinations, which of these is a match and which a mismatch is indicated in Table 3.

For a Single business, which is defined as deriving 95 per cent or more of total sale revenues from a single product (Rumelt, 1974), the simple, unified Functional structure is appropriate. The Functional-with-Subsidiaries structure would also be appropriate for those companies which derive up to five per cent of their total sales from an unrelated product which could sensibly be organized as a subsidiary. For a Dominant Company, one with between 70 and 94 per cent of its sales revenue from a single product, there is a significant degree of pluralism in the product lines, and this requires a structure attuned to diversity. Either the Functional-with-Subsidiaries or the Product Division structure can provide this. By contrast, the Functional structure would be overwhelmed by attempting to deal with this degree of diversification. The Related company achieves less than 70 per cent of its sales revenues from a single product and yet attains more than 70 per cent of revenue from a related group of products. Usually a Product Divisional structure will be the one required and functionally based structures will be overloaded. Finally, the Unrelated structure is one which receives less than 70 per cent of revenue from one set of related products. This is the most diversified company and a Product Divisional structure is appropriate. Functionally based structures would be ineffectual. The Holding Company structure is not appropriate for any level of diversification and seems in practice to be often a transitional form.

Being in match between strategy and structure rather than mismatch is associated with increasing financial performance. Corporations which are in fit have higher rates of growth in profits (Donaldson, 1985c). This is related to the improving ability of the matched corporations to yield profits from sales and also from invested capital. Shareholders benefit from match through growing earnings per share. Both match and performance are measured over the same ten year period, and hence there is the possibility of an affect of performance on match. However, the fact that performance shows an increase after match has been established is consistent with the interpretation that match causes performance.

Given the importance of strategy-structure match for performance a company in mismatch would be well advised to adjust as soon as possible. In so far as a reason for not making the adjustment is a failure to recognize that the company is mismatched, or the consequences thereon, or what a more appropriate structure would be, then there is a need to bring this information to the attention of those managing such organizations. Thus managers, directors, shareholders, union officials and governments need to have this knowledge if they are seeking to boost the performance of the corporations with which they are involved.

To help guide selection of an appropriate design among the varying forms of higher-level structure which have been discussed (Functional, Divisional and Matrix), these structural options are presented together with the contingency factors in Figure 3. This arranges the preceding theoretical argument into a decision tree. Thus for any particular organization there are four key questions:

a. What is the degree of diversity by geographic area?
b. What is the degree of diversity by products?
c. If there are several related products, what is the nature of the relationship?
d. And if there are several products related through the manufacturing resources utilized, what is the degree of product innovation required?

The answers to each of these questions takes one down a particular branch to the next question and so on to the structure which current research suggests would be most fitting. Thus, in this way, the possibility of algorithms to guide decision-making on organizational design for the apex structure come into view (for a decision-tree model of overall struc-

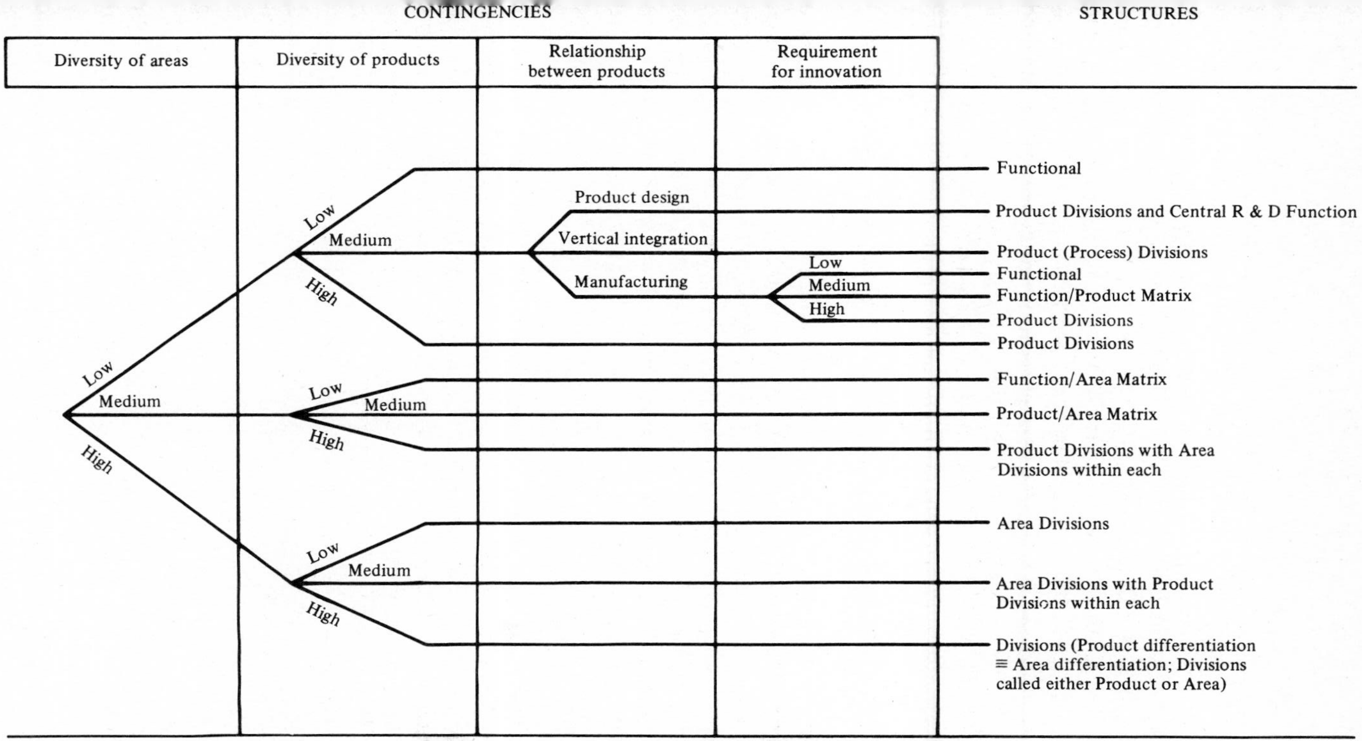

CONTINGENCIES
STRUCTURES
Diversity of areas
Diversity of products
Relationship between products
Requirement for innovation
Low
Medium
High
Low
Medium
High
Product design
Vertical integration
Manufacturing
Low
Medium
High
Functional
Product Divisions and Central R & D Function
Product (Process) Divisions
Functional
Function/Product Matrix
Product Divisions
Product Divisions
Low
Medium
High
Function/Area Matrix
Product/Area Matrix
Product Divisions with Area Divisions within each
Low
Medium
High
Area Divisions
Area Divisions with Product Divisions within each
Divisions (Product differentiation ≡ Area differentiation; Divisions called either Product or Area)

Figure 3. Decision tree for selecting organizational design of higher-level structures for each situation.

ture see Duncan, 1979). These prescriptive devices already exist in fields of micro-organizational behaviour such as leadership style (Vroom and Yetton, 1973).

Summary

The structure which is most appropriate for an organization depends on the situational contingencies. Larger organizations require more bureaucratic structure, taller hierarchies and more decentralization of decision-making. Sub-units of larger organizations will have additional bureaucratic elements. Public accountability requires more centralization of decision-making and somewhat more documentation. Democratization which takes the form of electing officials leads to a lesser degree of bureaucratization. Democracy manifested in a top representative body centralizes authority.

The structure at the apex varies from Functional to Divisional according to the degree of interdependency based on diversity of either product or area. Organizations would be advised to adopt divisional structures as they diversify. The purest form of diversification however is appropriate in the highly diversified case only. Lesser degrees of diversification merit less fully divisionalized structures in the forms outlined. Where substantial interdependencies exist between activities, but there is sufficient diversity and of a kind to warrant dual focus, then a matrix is the appropriate design.

Conclusion

As indicated at the start of this chapter, the foregoing is not meant to be exhaustive of the topic of organization design. The emphasis has been on showing how, within certain sections of the organizational literature, meaningful, consistent models can be constructed. Much work remains to be done on the validation and generalization of these organization design ideas. The point of the exercise has been to suggest that a potentially fruitful framework can be abstracted from the research to date. Given that there is both intellectual coherency and some evidence of practical significance discernible within the approach, continuation of enquiry of this type would seem to be justified, and, indeed, worthwhile.

15

Conclusions

The theses against organization studies have been advanced at many levels: philosophical, logical, theoretical, methodological and empirical. Of most concern in this volume have been those of the former kind – philosophical, logical and theoretical objections – mounted in conjunction with advocacy of rival metatheories and 'alternative' methods. For those seeking to censure organization studies these are the best forms of criticism, for they purport to strike at fundamental assumptions and to sweep away the whole edifice. Yet as has been shown in this volume, when these criticisms are examined carefully, one by one, it is possible to provide an answer to them. Many of them turn out to be a misappreciation of the philosophy of science. Others reflect a misunderstanding of sociological theory. Yet others criticize established methods based upon a caricature of them. This often fails to record the extent to which present studies are modest steps in a wider programme of enquiry. There are, however, numerous unresolved issues in theory and methods in organizational sociology. Many points require continuing critical scrutiny and refinement. Yet this will only be fruitful if conducted within a framework which utilizes a model of the organization as a purposeful structure functioning in an environment.

The rival metatheories and their attendant, implicit or explicit, research programmes espoused by critics of the established approach, be they Social Action Theory, Radical Structuralism or 'Strategic Choice', have each been shown to be deficient as agendas for organization studies. Social Action Theory is naive sociologically as it dispenses with the whole structural approach which has proved useful in organizational and societal explanation. Radical Structuralism is a package of theories and value positions which may be of considerable interest in sociology or political studies or political economy or Marxism. However, this can contribute little to the study of organizations when, under certain programmatics, they are denied therein as fit objects of enquiry. The neo-Marxian position by explicating linkages between organizations and socioeconomic structures may prove fruitful for organizational sociology. But many may see the Marxian theory of society as questionable and to be best drawn upon selectively. The 'Strategic Choice' position is a programme of the sociological explanation of extant structures rather than of developing design knowledge which can help change structures to better serve human purposes.

Organization sociology is neither the study of the whole world nor of the entirety of sociology. It is a modest enquiry into organizations which is slowly enabling people to better understand how their aims may be helped or hindered through certain collective arrangements. As such the results of these enquiries make a contribution to social discourse, widely valued by different members of society. They also provide the sociologist interested in societal analysis with useful materials on the functioning of component parts, organizations. The sub-discipline is coherent internally, cogent as a field of enquiry and of social value. Organizational sociology should continue its development untrammelled by these attacks.

Bibliography

Abegglen, James C. (1973) *Management and Worker: The Japanese Solution*, Tokyo: Sophia University

Abell, Peter (1971) *Model Building in Sociology*, London: Weidenfeld and Nicolson

(1975) (ed.) *Organizations as Bargaining and Influence Systems*, London: Heinemann

(1981) A Note on the Theory of Democratic Organization, *Sociology*, 15, No. 2 (May, 1981), pp. 262–4

Abell, Peter and Mathews, D. (1973) The Task Analysis Framework in Organizational Analysis, in Malcolm Warner (ed.), *The Sociology of the Workplace*, London: George Allen and Unwin

Aguilar, Francis J. (1967) *Scanning the Business Environment*, New York: Macmillan

Albrow, Martin (1970) *Bureaucracy*, London: Macmillan

Aldag, Ramon J. and Brief, Arthur P. (1979) *Task Design and Employee Motivation*, Glenview, Illinois: Scott, Foresman and Company

Aldrich, Howard E. (1972) Technology and Organizational Structure: A Reexamination of the Findings of the Aston Group, *Administrative Science Quarterly*, 17 (1972), pp. 26–43

(1975) Reactions to Donaldson's Note, *Administrative Science Quarterly* (September, 1975), pp. 457–9

(1977) Organization-sets, Action-sets and Networks: Making the Most of Simplicity, in Paul Nystrom and William Starbuck (eds.), *Handbook of Organizational Design*, Amsterdam: Elsevier

(1979) *Organization and Environments*, Englewood Cliffs, New Jersey: Prentice-Hall

Alker, Hayward Jr (1965) *Mathematics and Politics*, New York: Macmillan

Allen, Stephen A. (1978) Organizational Choices and General Management Influence Networks in Divisionalized Companies, *Academy of Management Journal*, 21 (1978), pp. 341–65

Andreatta, Helen and Rumbold, Bronwen (1974) *Organizational Development in Action*, Melbourne: Productivity Promotion Council of Australia

Ansoff, H. Igor (1965) *Corporate Strategy: An Analytic Approach to Business Policy for Growth and Expansion*, New York: McGraw-Hill

Argenti, John (1976) *Corporate Collapse: The Causes and Symptoms*, London and New York: McGraw-Hill

Argyris, Chris (1960) *Understanding Organizational Behavior*, London: Tavistock

(1964) *Integrating the Individual and the Organization*, New York: Wiley

175

(1972) *The Applicability of Organizational Sociology*, Cambridge University Press

Argyris, Chris and Schon, Donald (1978) *Organizational Learning: A Theory in Action Perspective*, Reading, Mass.: Addison-Wesley

Austin, J. L. (1970) *Philosophical Papers*, Oxford University Press

Bachrach, P. and Baratz, M. S. (1962) The Two Faces of Power, *American Political Science Review*, 56 (1962), pp. 947–52

Bain, George Sayers (1972) *The Growth of White Collar Unionism*, Oxford University Press

Ball, R., Brown, P. and Officer, R. R. (1976) Risk and Return in the Share Market, Part I: Theories and Evidence, *The Australian Accountant*, 46, No. 2 (March, 1976), pp. 68–75

Banfield, Edward C. and Wilson, James Q. (1963) *City Politics*, Boston: Harvard University Press and MIT Press

Baran, P. and Sweezy, P. (1968) *Monopoly Capital*, Harmondsworth: Penguin

Barber, B. (1957) *Social Stratification: A Comparative Analysis of Structure and Process*, New York: Harcourt, Brace and World

Barnard, Chester I. (1938) *The Functions of the Executive*, Cambridge, Mass.: Harvard University Press

Beer, Michael and Davis, Stanley M. (1979) Creating a Global Organization: Failures Along the Way, Chapter 3 in Stanley M. Davis (ed.), *Managing and Organizing Multinational Corporations*, New York: Pergamon Press, pp. 212–30

Bell, Gerald D. (1968) Variety in Work, *Sociology and Social Research*, 50, No. 1 (January, 1968), pp. 160–72

Benguigui, Georges (1970) L'evaluation de la bureaucratisation des enterprises, *Sociologie du Travail*, pp. 140–51

Benson, J. Kenneth (1977) Innovation and Crisis in Organizational Analysis, in J. Kenneth Benson (ed.), *Organizational Analysis: Critique and Innovation*, Sage Contemporary Social Science Issues 37, Beverly Hills: Sage Publications, pp. 5–18

(1977a) Organisations: A Dialectical View, *Administrative Science Quarterly*, 22, No. 1 (March, 1977), pp. 1–21

Berger, Peter L. (1973) *Invitation to Sociology: A Humanistic Perspective*, Woodstock, New York: Overlook Press

Berger, P. L. and Luckmann, T. (1966) *The Social Construction of Reality*, Garden City, New York: Doubleday

Berger, P. L. and Pullberg, S. (1966) Reification and the Sociological Critique of Consciousness, *New Left Review*, 35 (1966), pp. 56–71

Berry, Dean F., Metcalf, Les and McQuillan, Will (1974) 'NEDDY' – An Organizational Metamorphosis, *Journal of Management Studies*, 11, No. 1 (1974), pp. 1–20

Blackburn, Richard S. (1982) Dimensions of Structure: A Review and Reappraisal, *Academy of Management Review*, 7, No. 1 (1982), pp. 59–66

Blackler, F. H. M. and Brown, C. A. (1980) *Whatever Happened to Shell's New Philosophy of Management: Lessons for the 1980s from a Major Socio-Technical Intervention of the 1960s*, Westmead, Farnborough, Hants.: Teakfield Ltd

Blalock, Hubert M. Jr (1961) *Causal Inferences in Nonexperimental Research*, Chapel Hill: University of North Carolina Press

(1972) *Social Statistics*, 2nd edn, New York: McGraw-Hill
Blau, Peter M. (1970) A Formal Theory of Organization, *American Sociological Review*, 35 (1970), pp. 210–18
   (1972) Interdependence and Hierarchy in Organizations, *Social Science Research*, 1, No. 1 (April, 1972), pp. 1–24
   (1973) *The Dynamics of Bureaucracy*, 2nd revised edn, University of Chicago Press
Blau, Peter M., Falbe, Cecilia McHugh, McKinley, William and Phelps, K. Tracy (1976) Technology and Organization in Manufacturing, *Administrative Science Quarterly*, 21, No. 1 (March, 1976), pp. 20–40
Blau, Peter M. and Duncan, Otis Dudley (1967) *The American Occupational Structure*, New York: Wiley
Blau, Peter M. and Meyer, Marshall W. (1971) *Bureaucracy in Modern Society*, Second Edition, New York: Random House
Blau, Peter M. and Schoenherr, P. A. (1971) *The Structure of Organizations*, New York: Basic Books
Blau, Peter M. and Scott, W. Richard (1963) *Formal Organizations: A Comparative Approach*, London: Routledge and Kegan Paul
Blauner, R. (1964) *Alienation and Freedom: The Factory Worker and His Industry*, University of Chicago Press
Boseman, F. G. and Jones, R. E. (1974) Market Conditions, Decentralization and Organizational Effectiveness, *Human Relations*, 27, No. 7 (1974), pp. 665–76
Boudon, Raymond (1971) *The Uses of Structuralism*, London: Heinemann
Bower, Joseph L. (1970) *Managing the Resource Allocation Process*, Cambridge, Mass.: Division of Research, Graduate School of Business Administration, Harvard University
Bowey, Angela (1976) *The Sociology of Organizations*, London: Hodder and Stoughton
Bowey, Angela and Lupton, Tom (eds.) (1975) *Handbook of Salary and Wage Systems*, Epping, Essex: Gower Press
Box, Steven and Cotgrove, Stephen (1968) The Productivity of Scientists and Industrial Research Laboratories, *Sociology*, 2 (1968), pp. 163–72
Box, S. and Ford, J. (1967) Commitment to Science: a Solution to Student Marginality, *Sociology*, 1, No. 3 (September, 1967), pp. 225–38
Bradley, David A. and Wilkie, Roy (1980) Radical Organization Theory – A Critical Comment, *British Journal of Sociology*, 31, No. 4 (December, 1980), pp. 574–9
Brech, E. F. L. (1957) *Organization: the Framework of Management*, London: Longman Green
Brown, W. (1960) *Exploration in Management*, London: Heinemann
Buckingham, G. L., Jeffrey, R. G. and Thorn, B. A. (1975) *Job Enrichment and Organizational Change – A Study in Participation at Gallaher Ltd*, Epping, Essex: Gower Press
Budde, Andreas, Child, John, Francis, Arthur and Kieser, Alfred (1982) Corporate Goals, Managerial Objectives and Organizational Structures in British and West German Companies, *Organization Studies*, 3, No. 1 (1982), pp. 1–32
Burns, Thomas and Stalker, G. M. (1961) *The Management of Innovation*, London: Tavistock
Burns, Tom (1967) The Comparative Study of Organizations, in Victor Vroom

(ed.), *Methods of Organizational Research*, University of Pittsburgh Press, pp. 113–70

Burrell, Gibson (1979) Radical Organization Theory, in David Dunkerley and Graeme Salaman (eds.), *The International Yearbook of Organization Studies*, London: Routledge and Kegan Paul

Burrell, Gibson and Morgan, Gareth (1979) *Sociological Paradigms and Organizational Analysis: Elements of the Sociology of Corporate Life*, London: Heinemann

Byrt, William J. (1980) *The Human Variable: Text and Cases in Organisational Behaviour*, Sydney: McGraw-Hill Book Company

(1981) *The Australian Company: Studies in Strategy and Structure*, London: Croom-Helm

Carby, Keith (1976) *Job Redesign in Practice*, London: Institute of Personnel Management

Cassano, James S. (1983) Making Strategy Work – Links between Corporate Strategy, Structure and Performance, Presentation to Strategic Management Society, Paris, November 1983

Caves, Richard E. (1980) Industrial Organization, Corporate and Structure, *Journal of Economic Literature*, 18 (March, 1980), pp. 64–92

Chandler, Alfred D. Jr (1962) *Strategy and Structure: Chapters in the History of American Industrial Enterprise*, Cambridge, Mass.: MIT Press

Channon, Derek F. (1973) *The Strategy and Structure of British Enterprise*, Boston: Division of Research, Graduate School of Business Administration, Harvard University

Chenhall, Robert H. (1979) Some Elements of Organizational Control in Australian Divisionalized Firms, *Australian Journal of Management*, Supplement to 4, No. 1 (April, 1979), pp. 1–36

Child, John (1969a) *British Management Thought: A Critical Analysis*, London: Allen and Unwin

(1969b) *The Business Enterprise in Modern Industrial Society*, London: Collier-Macmillan

(1972a) Organizational Structure, Environment and Performance: The Role of Strategic Choice, *Sociology*, 6, No. 1 (January, 1972), pp. 1–22

(1972b) Organization Structure and Strategies of Control: A Replication of the Aston Study, *Administrative Science Quarterly*, 17, No. 2 (June, 1972), pp. 163–77

(1973a) Predicting and Understanding Organization Structure, *Administrative Science Quarterly*, 18, No. 2 (June, 1973), pp. 168–85

(1973b) Parkinson's Progress: Accounting for the Number of Specialists in Organizations, *Administrative Science Quarterly*, 18, No. 3 (September, 1972), pp. 328–48

(1974) Managerial and Organizational Factors Associated with Company Performance, Part 1, *Journal of Management Studies*, 11 (October, 1974), pp. 175–89

(1975a) Managerial and Organizational Factors Associated with Company Performance, Part 2: A Contingency Analysis, *Journal of Management Studies*, 12 (February, 1975), pp. 12–27

(1975b) Comments on Donaldson's Note, *Administrative Science Quarterly*, 20 (September, 1975), p. 456

(1977a) Organizational Design and Performance: Contingency Theory and Beyond, *Organisation and Administrative Science*, 8, No. 2 (1977), pp. 169–83

(1977b) *Organizations: A Guide to Problems and Practice*, London: Harper and Row

(1981) Culture, Contingency and Capitalism in the Cross-National Study of Organizations, in L. L. Cummings and B. M. Staw (eds.), *Research in Organizational Behaviour*, vol. 2, Greenwood, Conn.: JAI Press, pp. 303–56

Child, John and Mansfield, Roger (1972) Technology, Size and Organization Structure, *Sociology*, 6, No. 3 (September, 1972), pp. 369–93

Child, John and Kieser, Alfred (1979) Organization and Managerial Roles in British and West German Companies – An Examination of the Culture-Free Hypothesis, in C. J. Lammers and D. J. Hickson (eds.), *Organizations Alike and Unlike*, London: Routledge and Kegan Paul

Child, John and Fulk, J. (1982) Maintenance of Occupational Control: the Case of Professions, *Work and Occupations*, 9 (1982), pp. 155–92

Chomsky, Noam (1969) *American Power and the New Mandarins*, Harmondsworth: Penguin, pp. 50–1

Christensen, C. Roland, Andrews, Kenneth R. and Bower, Joseph L. (1978) *Business Policy: Text and Cases*, 4th edn, Homewood, Illinois: Richard D. Irwin, Inc.

Clegg, Stewart (1981) Organization and Control, *Administrative Science Quartrly*, 26 (1981), pp. 545–62

Clegg, Stewart and Dunkerley, David (1977) *Critical Issues in Organizations*, London: Routledge and Kegan Paul

(1980) *Organization, Class and Control*, London: Routledge and Kegan Paul

Corey, Raymond and Star, Steven H. (1971) *Organization Strategy: A Marketing Approach*, Boston: Division of Research, Graduate School of Business Administration, Harvard University

Crozier, Michel (1964) *The Bureaucratic Phenomenon*, University of Chicago Press

Cunnison, Sheila (1966) *Wages and Work Allocation*, London: Tavistock

Cyert, R. M. and March, J. G. (1963) *A Behavioural Theory of the Firm*, Englewood Cliffs, New Jersey: Prentice-Hall

Daft, Richard L. (1980) The Evolution of Organizational Analysis in *ASQ*, 1959–1979, *Administrative Science Quarterly*, (1980), pp. 623–4

Dahrendorf, Ralf (1959) *Class and Class Conflict in Industrial Society*, Stanford University Press

Dalton, Melville (1959) *Men Who Manage*, New York: Wiley

Davies, C. (1979) Organization Theory and the Organization of Health Care: a Comment on the Literature, *Social Science and Medicine*, 13A, No. 4 (June, 1979), pp. 413–22

Davis, Stanley M. (1972) Basic Structures of Multinational Corporations and Trends in the Organization of Multinational Corporations, in Stanley M. Davis (ed.), *Managing and Organizing Multi-national Corporations*, New York: Pergamon Press

Davis, Stanley M. and Lawrence, Paul R. (1977) *Matrix*, Reading, Mass.: Addison-Wesley

Dewar, Robert and Hage, Jerald (1978) Size, Technology, Complexity and Structural Differentiation: Toward a Theoretical Synthesis, *Administrative Science Quarterly*, 23, No. 1 (March, 1978), pp. 111–36

Donaldson, Lex (1975a) Job Enlargement: A Multidimensional Process, *Human Relations*, 28, No. 7 (September, 1975), pp. 593–610

(1975b) Organizational Status and the Measurement of Centralization, *Administrative Science Quarterly*, 20 (September, 1975), pp. 453–6

(1975c) *Policy and the Polytechnics: Pluralistic Drift in Higher Education*, Farnborough, Hants.: Saxon House, D. C. Heath Ltd

(1976) Woodward, Technology, Organizational Structure and Performance – a Critique of the Universal Generalization, *Journal of Management Studies*, 13 (October, 1976), pp. 255–73. Also in Harold Koontz, Cyril O'Donnell and Heinz Weihrich (eds.), *Management: A Book of Readings*, 5th edn, New York: McGraw-Hill, 1980, pp. 369–80

(1979a) Regaining Control at Nipont, *Journal of General Management*, 4, No. 4 (Summer, 1979), pp. 14–30

(1979b) The Transition from Functional System to Multidivisional Structure: A Critical Analysis, in Ray McLennan, David Smith, Kerr Inkson and Nick Marsh (eds.), *People in Organizations: Studies in Australia and New Zealand*, Department of Business Administration, Victoria University of Wellington, Wellington, New Zealand, pp. 311–31

(1982a) Comments on Contingency and Choice in Organization Theory, *Organization Studies*, 3, No. 1 (1982), pp. 65–72

(1982b) Divisionalization and Size: A Theoretical and Empirical Critique, *Organization Studies*, 3, No. 4 (1982), pp. 321–37

(1982c) Divisionalization and Diversification: A Longitudinal Study, *Academy of Management Journal*, 25, No. 4 (1982), pp. 909–14

(1983a) Organizational Growth, the M-Form and Performance: A Critique of the Thesis of Williamson, Working Paper, Australian Graduate School of Management

(1985a) The Interaction of Size and Divisionalization: Grinyer Revisited, *Organization Studies* (forthcoming)

(1985b) Organization Design and the Life-Cycles of Products, *Journal of Management Studies*, 22, No. 1 (January, 1985), pp. 25–37

(1985c) Strategy, Structure-Fit and Financial Performance: Further Validation of a General Model, Working Paper, Australian Graduate School of Management

Donaldson, Lex and Lynn, R. (1976) The Conflict Resolution Process: The Two Factor Theory and an Industrial Case, *Personnel Review*, 5, No. 2 (Spring, 1976), pp. 21–8

Donaldson, Lex and Warner, Malcolm (1974a) Bureaucratic and Electoral Control in Occupational Interest Associations, *Sociology*, 8, No. 1 (1974), pp. 47–57

(1974b) Structure of Organizations in Occupational Interest Associations, *Human Relations*, 27, No. 8 (October, 1974), pp. 721–38

Duncan, O. D. (1966) Path Analysis: Sociological Examples, *American Journal of Sociology*, 72 (1966), pp. 1–16

Duncan, Robert (1979) What is the Right Organization Structure? Decision Tree Analysis Provides the Answer, *Organizational Dynamics* (Winter, 1979), pp. 59–80

Dunkerley, David, Spybey, Tony and Thrasher, Michael (1981) Interorganization Networks: A Case Study of Industrial Location, *Organization Studies*, 2, No. 3 (1981), pp. 229–47

Dunphy, Dexter C., Andreatta, H. and Timms, L. (1976) Redesigning the Work Organization at Philips, *Work and People*, 2, No. 1 (Autumn, 1976), pp. 3–11

Dunphy, Dexter C. (1981) *Organizational Change by Choice*, Sydney: McGraw-Hill Book Company

Durkheim, Emile (1938) *The Rules of Sociological Method*, Glencoe, Ill.: Free Press
(1951) *Suicide*, trans. J. A. Spaulding and George Simpson, Glencoe, Ill.: Free Press
(1964) *The Division of Labour in Society*, trans. G. Simpson, New York: Free Press
Dyas, Gareth P. and Thanheiser, Heinz T. (1976) *The Emerging European Enterprise – Strategy and Structure in French and German Industry*, London: Macmillan
Egelhoff, William G. (1980) Structure and Strategy in Multinational Corporations: A Re-examination of the Stopford and Wells Model, *Proceedings of the Academy of Management* (1980), pp. 231–5
Eilon, S. (1977) Editorial: Structural Determinism, *Omega, The International Journal of Management*, 5, No. 5 (1977), pp. 499–504
Emery, F. E. and Phillips, C. (1976) *Living at Work*, Canberra: Australian Government Publishing Service
Etzioni, Amitai (1961) *Modern Organizations*, New Jersey: Prentice-Hall
(1968) *The Active Society: A Theory of Societal and Political Processes*, London: Collier-Macmillan; New York: Free Press
(1975) *A Comparative Analysis of Complex Organizations*, 1st edn, 1961; revised and enlarged edn, New York: Free Press
Festinger, L. A. (1957) *A Theory of Cognitive Dissonance*, Stanford University Press
Flanders, Allan David, Pomeranz, Ruth and Woodward, Joan (1968) *Experiments in Industrial Democracy: A Study of the John Lewis Partnership*, London: Faber
Fletcher, Colin (1969) Correspondence: Silverman on Organizations: A Further Comment, *Sociology*, 3, No. 1 (January, 1969), pp. 113–14
(1970) On Replication: Notes on the Notion of a Replicability Quotient and a Generalizability Quotient, *Sociology*, 4 (January, 1970), pp. 51–69
Ford, Jeffrey D. and Slocum, John W. Jr (1977) Size, Technology, Environment and the Structure of Organizations, *Academy of Management Review*, 2, No. 4 (October, 1977), pp. 561–75
Fox, A. (1974) *Beyond Contract: Work, Power and Trust Relations*, London: Faber and Faber
Franko, Lawrence G. (1974) The Move Toward a Multidivisional Structure in European Organizations, *Administrative Science Quarterly*, 19, No. 4 (December, 1974), pp. 493–506
(1976) *The European Multinationals – A Renewed Challenge to American and British Big Business*, London: Harper and Row
Freeman, John Henry and Kronenfeld, Jerrold E. (1973) Problems of Definitional Dependency: The Case of Administrative Intensity, *Social Forces*, 52 (September, 1973), pp. 108–21
French, J. R. P. and Raven, B. (1960) The bases of social power, in D. Cartwright and A. Zander (eds.), *Group Dynamics: Research and Theory*, London: Tavistock, pp. 607–23
Fullan, Michael (1970) Industrial Technology and Worker Integration in the Organization, *American Sociological Review*, 35 (December, 1970), pp. 1028–39
Galbraith, J. K. (1967) *The New Industrial State*, Boston: Houghton Mifflin
Galbraith, Jay R. (1973) *Designing Organizations*, Reading, Mass.: Addison-Wesley

Galtung, Johan (1965) Institutionalized Conflict Resolution – A Theoretical Paradigm, *Journal of Peace Research*, 2, No. 4 (1965), pp. 348–96
   (1967) *Theory and Methods of Social Research*, London: George Allen and Unwin
Gerwin, Donald (1979) Relationships between Structure and Technology at the Organizational and Job Levels, *Journal of Management Studies*, 16, No. 1 (February, 1979), pp. 70–9
Goldman, Paul and Van Houten, Donald R. (1977) Managerial Strategies and the Worker: A Marxist Analysis of Bureaucracy, in J. Kenneth Benson (ed.), *Organizational Analysis: Critique and Innovation*, Sage Contemporary Social Science Issues, 37, Beverly Hills: Sage Publications, pp. 110–27
Goldthorpe, John H., Lockwood, David, Bechhofer, Frank and Platt, Jennifer (1968) *The Affluent Worker: Industrial Attitudes and Behaviour*, Cambridge University Press
Gouldner, Alvin (1954) *Patterns of Industrial Bureaucracy*, Glencoe, Ill.: Free Press
Gouldner, A. W. (1955) Metaphysical Pathos and the Theory of Bureaucracy, *American Political Science Review*, 49 (1955), pp. 496–507
Gilbert, Michael (ed.) (1972) *The Modern Business Enterprise*, Harmondsworth: Penguin
Greiner, Larry E. (1967) Patterns of Organization Change, *Harvard Business Review*, 45 (May–June, 1967), pp. 119–30
   (1972) Evolution and Revolution as Organizations Grow, *Harvard Business Review*, 50, No. 4 (1972), pp. 37–46
Grinyer, Peter H., Yasai-Ardekani, Masoud and Al-Bazzaz, Shawki (1980) Strategy and Structure, the Environment and Financial Performance in 48 United Kingdom Companies, *Academy of Management Journal*, 23 (1980), pp. 193–220
Grinyer, Peter H. and Yasai-Ardekani, Masoud (1980) Dimensions of Organizational Structure: A Critical Replication, *Academy of Management Journal*, 23 (1980), pp. 405–21
   (1981a) Research Note: Some Problems with Measurement of Macro-Organizational Structure, *Organization Studies*, 2, No. 3 (1981), pp. 287–96
   (1981b) Strategy, Structure, Size and Bureaucracy, *Academy of Management Journal*, 24, No. 3 (1981), pp. 471–86
Guest, Robert H. (1962) *Organizational Change: The Effect of Successful Leadership*, London: Tavistock
Hage, Jerald (1965) An Axiomatic Theory of Organisations, *Administrative Science Quarterly*, 10, No. 4 (December, 1965), pp. 289–320
   (1974) *Communications and Organizational Control: Cybernetics in Health and Welfare Settings*, New York: Wiley Inter Science
   (1980) *Theories of Organization: Form, Process and Transformation*, New York: Wiley
Hage, Jerald and Aiken, Michael (1967) Program Change and Organizational Properties: A Comparative Analysis, *American Journal of Sociology*, 72 (March, 1967), pp. 503–19
   (1970) *Social Change in Complex Organizations*, New York: Random House
Hage, Jerald and Azumi, K. (1972) *Organizational Systems: a Text Reader in the Sociology of Organizations*, Lexington, Mass.: D. C. Heath
Hage, Jerald and Dewar, Robert (1973) Elite Values versus Organizational

Structure in Predicting Innovation, *Administrative Science Quarterly*, 18, No. 3 (September, 1973), pp. 279–90

Hall, J. and Caradog Jones, D. (1950) The Social Grading of Occupations, *British Journal of Sociology*, 1, No. 1 (1950), pp. 31–55

Hall, Richard H. (1963) The Concept of Bureaucracy: An Empirical Assessment, *American Journal of Sociology*, 69 (July 1963), pp. 32–40

(1977) *Organizations Structure and Process*, 1st edn, 1972; 2nd edn, Englewood Cliffs, New Jersey: Prentice-Hall

Hambrick, Donald C. (1981) Environment, Strategy, and Power within Top Management Teams, *Administrative Science Quarterly*, 26, No. 2 (June, 1981), pp. 253–75

Handy, Charles (1976) *Understanding Organizations*, Harmondsworth, Penguin

Heller, Frank A. (1971) *Managerial Decision-Making: A Study of Leadership Styles and Power-Sharing among Senior Managers*, London: Tavistock

Herzberg, F. (1968) One More Time: How Do You Motivate Employees?, *Harvard Business Review*, 46 (January–February, 1968), pp. 53–62. Reprinted in Louis E. Davis and James C. Taylor (eds.), *Design of Jobs*, Harmondsworth: Penguin, 1972

Heydebrand, W. (1977) Organizational Contradiction in Public Bureaucracies: Toward a Marxian Theory of Organizations, in J. Kenneth Benson (ed.), *Organizational Analysis: Critique and Innovation*, Sage Contemporary Social Science Issues 37, Beverly Hills: Sage Publications, pp. 85–109

Hickson, David J. (1966) A Convergence in Organization Theory, *Administrative Science Quarterly*, 11 (1966), pp. 225–37

Hickson, David J., Pugh, D. S. and Pheysey, D. G. (1969) Operations Technology and Organization Structure: An Empirical Reappraisal, *Administrative Science Quarterly*, 14, No. 3 (September, 1969), pp. 378–97

Hickson, David J., Hinings, C. R., Lee, C. A., Schneck, R. E. and Pennings, J. M. (1971) A Strategic Contingencies Theory of Intraorganizational Power, *Administrative Science Quarterly*, 16, No. 2 (1971), pp. 216–29

Hickson, David J. and McMillan, Charles J. (eds.) (1981) *Organization and Nation: the Aston Programme IV*, Farnborough, Hants.: Gower Press

Hickson, David J., Hinings, C. R., McMillan, C. J. and Schwitter, J. P. (1964) The Culture-free Context of Organization Structure: a Trinational Comparison, *Sociology*, 8, No. 1 (1974), pp. 59–80

Hickson, David J., Donaldson, Lex, Chapman, John B., Sayles, Leonard, Baker, Charles, Donaldson, John and Reeves, Tom Kynaston (1978) Feedback-Structural Determinism, *Omega, The International Journal of Management*, 6, No. 2 (1978), pp. 109–15

Hinings, C. R., Hickson, D. J., Pennings, J. M. and Schneck, R. E. (1974) Structural Conditions of Intraorganisational Power, *Administrative Science Quarterly*, 19 (1974), pp. 22–44

Hinings, C. R. and Lee, Gloria (1971) Dimensions of Organization Structure and their Context: A Replication, *Sociology*, 5 (1971), pp. 83–93

Hirsch, Paul (1975a) Organizational Analysis and Industrial Sociology: An Instance of Cultural Lag, *The American Sociologist*, 10 (February, 1975), pp. 3–12

(1975b) Organizational Effectiveness and the Institutional Environment, *Administrative Science Quarterly*, 20, No. 3 (September, 1975, pp. 327–44

Hunt, J. W. (1972) *The Restless Organization*, Sydney: Wiley

Ingham, Geoffrey K. (1974) *Strikes and Industrial Conflict: Britain and Scandinavia*, London: Macmillan

Inkson, J. H. K., Pugh, D. S. and Hickson, D. J. (1970) Organization Context and Structure: An Abbreviated Replication, *Administrative Science Quarterly*, 15, No. 3 (September, 1970), pp. 318–29

International Management (1974) Switching Off the Assembly Line (December, 1974), pp. 61–7

(1976) Volkswagen Steers its Dealers towards Job Enrichment (September, 1976), pp. 54–6

Jelinek, Mariann, Litterer, Joseph A. and Miles, Raymond (1981) *Organization by Design: Theory and Practice*, Plano, Texas: Business Publications, Inc.

Johnson, Gerry and Scholes, Kevan (1984) *Exploring Corporate Strategy*, London: Prentice-Hall International Inc.

Kelsall, R. K., Poole, Anne and Kuhn, Annette (1984) *Graduates: The Sociology of an Elite*, London: Methuen

Kenny, Graham K. and Palmer, Ian (1980) Individual Power Bases in Organization: A Case Study, *Management Forum*, 6, No. 4 (December, 1980), pp. 227–31

Kenny, Graham K. and Wilson, David C. (1984) The Interdepartmental Influence of Managers: Individual Sub-Unit Perspectives, *Journal of Management Studies*, 21 (1984), pp. 409–27

Khandwalla, Pradip N. (1973) Viable and Effective Organizational Design of Firms, *Academy of Management Journal*, 16, No. 3 (September, 1973), pp. 481–95

(1974) Mass Output Orientation of Operations Technology and Organizational Structure, *Administrative Science Quarterly*, 19, No. 1 (March, 1974), pp. 74–97

(1977) *The Design of Organizations*, New York: Harcourt Brace Janovich

Kingdon, D. R. (1973) *Matrix Organization*, London: Tavistock

Kmetz, John L. (1980) A Preliminary Test of Relationships Between Organization Slack and Theoretically Related Variables, *Proceedings of the Academy of Management* (1980), pp. 246–50

Knight, Kenneth (1976) Matrix Organization: A Review, *Journal of Management Studies*, 13, No. 2 (May, 1976), pp. 111–30

Kotter, John P., Schlesinger, Leonard A. and Sathe, Vijay (1979) *Organizations: Texts, cases and readings on the management of organizational design and change*, Homewood, Illinois: Richard D. Irwin, Inc.

Kuhn, Thomas S. (1970) *The Structure of Scientific Revolutions*, 2nd enlarged edn, University of Chicago Press

(1971) *The Essential Tension: Selected Studies in Scientific Tradition and Change*, University of Chicago Press

Lammers, Cornelis J. (1981a) Contributions of Organizational Sociology: Part 1: Contributions to Sociology – A Liberal View, *Organization Studies*, 2, No. 3 (1981), pp. 267–86

(1981b) Contributions of Organizational Sociology: Part II: Contributions to Organizational Theory and Practice – A Liberal View, *Organization Studies*, 2, No. 4 (1981), pp. 361–76

Lammers, C. J. and Hickson, D. J. (eds.) (1979) *Organizations Alike and Unlike*, London: Routledge

Lansbury, Russell D. (1977) *Organization: An Australian Perspective*, Melbourne: Longman Cheshire Pty Ltd

Lansley, Peter, Sadler, Philip and Webb, Terry (1974) Organization Structure, Management Style and Company Performance, *Omega, The International Journal of Management Science*, 2, No. 4 (August, 1974), pp. 467–85

Lawler, Edward E. III, *et al.* (1975) Job Choice and Post Decision Dissonance, *Organizational Behaviour and Human Performance*, 13 (1975), pp. 133–45

(1976) Control Systems in Organizations, Chapter 29 of Marvin D. Dunnette (ed.), *Handbook of Industrial and Organizational Psychology*, Chicago: Rand McNally College Publishing Company, pp. 1247–91

Lawrence, Paul R. and Lorsch, Jay W. (1967) *Organization and Environment: Managing Differentiation and Integration*, Boston: Division of Research, Graduate School of Business Administration, Harvard University

Lenz, R. T. (1980) Environment, Strategy, Organization Structure and Performance: Patterns in One Industry, *Strategic Management Journal*, 1 (1980), pp. 209–26

Levine, Joel H. (1972) The Sphere of Influence, *American Sociological Review*, 37, No. 1 (February, 1972), pp. 14–27

Likert, K. (1961) *New Patterns of Management*, New York: McGraw-Hill

Likert, R. and Likert, J. G. (1976) *New Ways of Managing Conflict*, New York: McGraw-Hill

Lockwood, D. (1964) Social Integration and System Integration, in George K. Zollschan and Walter Hirsch (eds.), *Exploration in Social Change*, London: Routledge and Kegan Paul, pp. 244–57

Lorange, Peter and Vancil, Richard F. (eds.) (1977) *Strategic Planning Systems*, Englewood Cliffs, New Jersey: Prentice-Hall

Lorsch, Jay W. and Lawrence, Paul R. (eds.) (1972a) *Organization Planning: Cases and Concepts*, Homewood, Illinois: Richard D. Irwin Inc. and the Dorsey Press

Lorsch, Jay W. and Lawrence, Paul R. (1972b) Environmental Factors and Organizational Integration, in J. W. Lorsch and P. R. Lawrence (eds.), *Organization Planning: Cases and Concepts*, Homewood, Illinois: Richard D. Irwin Inc. and the Dorsey Press, pp. 38–48

Lorsch, Jay W. and Allen, Stephen A. (1973) *Managing Diversity and Interdependence: An Organizational Study of Multidivisional Firms*, Boston: Division of Research, Graduate School of Administration, Harvard University

Lupton, T. (1963) *On the Shop Floor*, Oxford: Pergamon

Mannheim, Karl (1936) *Ideology and Utopia*, London: Kegan Paul

Mansfield, Roger (1973) Bureaucracy and Centralization: An Examination of Organizational Structure, *Administrative Science Quarterly*, 18 (1973), pp. 477–88

(1981a) Developing a cross-national perspective, Chapter 1 in Roger Mansfield and Michael Poole, *International Perspectives on Management and Organization*, Aldershot, Hampshire: Gower Press

(1981b) The international study of organizational structure, Chapter 2 in Roger Mansfield and Michael Poole, *International Perspectives on Management and Organization*, Aldershot, Hampshire: Gower Press

Mansfield, Roger and Poole, Michael (1981) *International Perspectives on Management and Organization*, Aldershot, Hampshire: Gower Press

March, J. G. and Simon, H. A. (1958) *Organizations*, New York, Wiley

Marsh, Robert M. and Mannari, Hiroshi (1976) *Modernization and the Japanese Factory*, Princeton University Press
    (1980) Technology Implications Theory: A Japanese Test, *Organization Studies*, 1 (1980), pp. 161–83
    (1981)Technology and Size as Determinants of the Organizational Structure of Japanese Factories, *Administrative Science Quarterly*, 26, No. 1 (1981), pp. 33–57
Marx, K. (1969) The Eighteenth Brumaire of Louis Bonaparte, in L. S. Feuer (ed.), *Marx and Engels: Basic Writings of Politics and Philosophy*, London: Fontana
    (1954) *Capital*, Moscow: Progress Pubs., vol. 1
    (1973) *Economic and Philosophical Manuscripts of 1844*, edited with an introduction by Dirk J. Struik, translated by M. Milligan, London: Lawrence and Wishart
Marx, K. and Engels, F. (1968) *Selected Works*, London: Lawrence and Wishart Ltd
Mayhew, Bruce H., Levinger, Roger L., Miller, J., Macpherson and James (1972) System Size and Structural Differentiation in Formal Organizations: A Baseline Generator for Two Major Theoretical Propositions, *American Sociological Review*, 37 (1972), pp. 629–33
Merton, R. K. (1949) *Social Theory and Social Structure*, Chicago, Illinois: Free Press
    (1975) Structural analysis in sociology, in P. M. Blau (ed.), *Approaches to the Study of Social Structures*, New York: Free Press
Miles, Raymond E. and Snow, Charles C. (1978) *Organizational Strategy, Structure and Process*, Tokyo: McGraw-Hill, Kogakusha Ltd
Millar, J. A. (1978) Contingency Theory, Values and Change, *Human Relations*, 31, No. 10 (1979), pp. 885–904
Miller, D. C. and Form, W. H. (1964) *Industrial Sociology*, 2nd edn, New York: Harper and Row
Miller, E. J. and Rice, A. K. (1967) *Systems of Organization: The Control of Task and Sentient Boundaries*, London: Tavistock
Mintzberg, H. (1979) *The Structuring of Organizations: A Synthesis of the Research*, Englewood Cliffs, New Jersey: Prentice-Hall
Mintzberg, Henry, Raisinghani, Duru and Theoret, Andre (1976) The Structure of Unstructured Decision Processes, *Administrative Science Quarterly*, 21, No. 2 (June, 1976), pp. 246–75
Mohr, L. (1971) Organizational Technology and Organizational Structure, *Administrative Science Quarterly*, 16 (1971), pp. 444–59
Moore, Barrington Jr (1967) *Social Origins of Dictatorship and Democracy: Lord and Peasant in the Making of the Modern World*, London: Allen Lane, The Penguin Press
Morgan, Gareth (1980) Paradigms, Metaphors, and Puzzle Solving in Organization Theory, *Administrative Science Quarterly*, 25, No. 4 (1980), pp. 605–22
    (1981) The Schismatic Metaphor and its Implications for Organizational Analysis, *Organization Studies*, 2, No. 1 (1981), pp. 23–44
Mouzelis, Nicos P. (1969) Correspondence: Silverman on Organizations, *Sociology*, 3, No. 1 (January, 1969), pp. 111–12
Mumford, E. and Pettigrew, A. (1975) *Implementing Strategic Decisions*, London: Longman

McKelvey, B. (1975) Guidelines for the Empirical Classification of Organizations, *Administrative Science Quarterly*, 20 (1975), pp. 509–25

Nakane, Chie (1970) *Japanese Society*, University of California Press

Negandhi, A. R. and Reimann, B. (1972) A Contingency Theory of Organizations Re-examined in the Context of a Developing Country, *Academy of Management Journal*, 15 (1972), pp. 137–46

Nichols, Theo (1970) *Ownership, Control and Ideology*, London: George Allen and Unwin

Parker, S. R., Brown, R. K., Child J. and Smith, M. A. (1967) *The Sociology of Industry*, London: George Allen and Unwin

Parsons, T. (1951) *The Social System*, Chicago, Illinois: Free Press
  (1964) Suggestions for a Sociological Approach to the Theory of Organizations, in Amitai Etzioni (ed.), *Complex Organizations: A Sociological Reader*, New York: Holt

Patchen, M. (1974) The Locus and Basis of Influence on Organisational Decisions, *Organisational Behaviour and Human Performance*, 11 (1974), pp. 195–221

Paul, William J., Robertson, Keith B. and Herzberg, Frederick (1969) Job Enrichment Pays Off, *Harvard Business Review*, 47 (1969), pp. 61–78

Paulson, Steven K. (1980) Organizational Size, Technology and Structure: Replication of a Study of Social Service Agencies Among Small Retail Firms, *Academy of Management Journal*, 23, No. 2 (1980), pp. 341–7

Pavan, R. J. (1976) Strategy and Structure – Italian Experience, *Journal of Economics and Business*, 28, No. 3 (1976), pp. 254–60

Payne, R. L. and Mansfield, R. (1973) Relationships of Perceptions of Organizational Climate to Organizational Structure, Context and Hierarchical Position, *Administrative Science Quarterly*, 18 (1973), pp. 515–26
  (1978) Correlates on Individual Perceptions of Organizational Climate, *Journal of Occupational Psychology*, 51 (1978), pp. 209–18

Payne, R. L. and Pheysey, D. C. (1971) G. G. Stern's Organization Climate Index: a Reconceptualization and Application to Business Organization, *Organizational Behaviour and Human Performance*, 9 (1971), pp. 110–19

Pennings, J. M. (1975) The Relevance of the Structural Contingency Model of Organizational Effectiveness, *Administrative Science Quarterly*, 20 (1975), pp. 393–410

Perrow, Charles (1967) A Framework for the Comparative Analysis of Organizations, *American Sociological Review*, 32 (April, 1967), pp. 194–208
  (1979) *Complex Organizations: A Critical Essay*, 1st edn, 1972; 2nd edn, Glenview, Illinois: Scott, Foresman and Company

Pettigrew, Andrew M. (1972) Information Control as a Power Resource, *Sociology*, 6 (1972), pp. 187–204
  (1973) *The Politics of Organizational Decision-Making*, London: Tavistock
  (1977) Strategy Formulation as a Political Process, *International Studies of Management and Organization*, 7, No. 2 (Summer, 1977), pp. 78–87
  (1979) On Studying Organizational Cultures, *Administrative Science Quarterly*, 24, No. 4 (December, 1979), pp. 570–81

Pfeffer, Jeffrey and Salancik, Gerald R. (1978) *The External Control of Organizations: A Resource Dependence Perspective*, New York: Harper and Row

Pitts, Robert A. (1974) Incentive Compensation and Organization Design, *Personnel Journal*, 53, No. 5 (May, 1974), pp. 338–44
  (1976) Diversification Strategies and Organizational Policies of Large

Diversified Firms, *Journal of Economics and Business*, 28, No. 3 (Spring/ Summer, 1976), pp. 181–8

(1977) Strategies and Structures for Diversification, *Academy of Management Journal*, 20, No. 2 (1977), pp. 197–208

Poensgen, Otto H. (1974) Organizational Structure, Context and Performance, European Institute for Advanced Studies in Management, Working Paper, 1974, pp. 47–74

Popper, K. R. (1945) *The Open Society and Its Enemies, Volume 2, The High Tide of Prophecy: Hegel, Marx and the Aftermath*, London: Routledge and Kegan Paul

Pugh, D. S. (1966) Modern Organization Theory: A Psychological and Sociological Study, *Psychological Bulletin*, 66, No. 4 (October, 1966), pp. 235–51

(1973) Colonel Urwick and 'Organization', *Omega, The International Journal of Management Science*, 1, No. 3 (1973), pp. 347–52

(1981) The Aston Program of Research: Retrospect and Prospect, in The Aston Program Perspective, Chapter 4 of A. Van de Ven and W. Joyce, *Perspectives on Organization Design and Behavior*, New York, Wiley

Pugh, D. S., Hickson, D. J., Hinings, C. R., MacDonald, K. M., Turner, C. and Lupton, T. (1963) A Conceptual Scheme for Organizational Analysis, *Administrative Science Quarterly*, 8, No. 3 (December, 1963), pp. 289–315

Pugh, D. S., Hickson, D. J., Hinings, C. R. and Turner, C. (1968) Dimensions of Organization Structure, *Administrative Science Quarterly*, 13, No. 1 (June, 1968), pp. 65–105

(1969a) The Context of Organization Structures, *Administrative Science Quarterly*, 14, No. 1 (March, 1969), pp. 91–114

(1969b) An Empirical Taxonomy of Structures of Work Organization, *Administrative Science Quarterly*, 14, No. 1 (March, 1969), pp. 115–26

Pugh, D. S. and Hickson, D. J. (1972) Causal Inference and the Aston Studies, *Administrative Science Quarterly*, 17, No. 2 (June, 1972), pp. 273–6

(1976) *Organizational Structure in its Context: The Aston Programme I*, Farnborough, Hants.: Saxon House

Pugh, D. S. and Hinings, C. R. (eds.) (1976) *Organizational Structure: Extensions and Replications: The Aston Programme II*, Farnborough, Hants.: Saxon House

Pugh, D. S. and Payne, R. L. (eds.) (1977) *Organizational Behaviour in its Context: The Aston Programme III*, Farnborough, Hants.: Saxon House

Ranson, Stewart, Hinings, Bob and Greenwood, Royston (1980) The Structuring of Organizational Structures, *Administrative Science Quarterly*, 25, No. 7 (March, 1980), pp. 1–17

Reeves, Kynaston T. and Turner, Barry A. (1972) A Theory of Organization and Behaviour in Batch Production Factories, *Administrative Science Quarterly*, 17, No. 1 (March, 1972), pp. 81–98

Reimann, Bernard C. (1974) Dimensions of Structure in Effective Organizations: Some Empirical Evidence, *Academy of Management Journal*, 17 (1974), pp. 693–708

(1977) Dimensions of Organizational Technology and Structure: An Exploratory Study, *Human Relations*, 30, No. 6 (1977), pp. 545–66

(1980) Organization Structure and Technology in Manufacturing: System Versus Work Flow Level Perspectives, *Academy of Management Journal*, 23, No. 1 (1980), pp. 61–77

Reimann, Bernard C. and Inzerilli, Giorgio (1979) A Comparative Analysis of

Empirical Research on Technology and Structure, *Journal of Management*, 5, No. 2 (1979), pp. 167–92

Rex, John (1961) *Key Problems of Sociological Theory*, London: Routledge and Kegan Paul

Ritzer, G. (1975) Sociology: A Multiple Paradigm Science, *American Sociologist*, 10, No. 3 (1975), pp. 156–67

Roberts, K. (1970) On Looking at an Elephant: An Evaluation of Cross-cultural Research Related to Organizations, *Psychological Bulletin*, 74 (1970), pp. 327–50

Roethlisberger, Fritz J. and Dickson, William J. (1939) *Management and the Worker*, Cambridge, Mass.: Harvard University Press

Roy, Donald (1954) Efficiency and the Fix, *American Journal of Sociology*, 60 (1954), pp. 255–66

Rumelt, R. P. (1974) *Strategy, Structure and Economic Performance*, Boston: Division of Research, Graduate School of Business Administration, Harvard University

Rushing, William A. (1968) Hardness of Material as Related to Division of Labour in Manufacturing Industries, *Administrative Science Quarterly*, 13, No. 2 (1968), pp. 229–45

Ryle, G. (1949) *The Concept of Mind*, London: Hutchinson

Salaman, Graeme (1978) Towards a Sociology of Organizational Structure, *Sociological Review*, 26, No. 3 (August, 1978)

Sayles, Leonard R. (1958) *Behaviour of Industrial Work Groups; Prediction and Control*, New York: Wiley

Schein, E. (1970) *Organizational Psychology*, 2nd edn, Englewood Cliffs, New Jersey: Prentice-Hall

Schoonhoven, Claudia Bird (1981) Problems with Contingency Theory: Testing Assumptions Hidden within the Language of Contingency 'Theory', *Administrative Science Quarterly*, 26 (1981), pp. 349–77

Schreyogg, Georg (1980) Contingency and Choice in Organization Theory, *Organization Studies*, 1, No. 4 (1980), pp. 305–26

(1982) Some Comments About Comments: A Reply to Donaldson, *Organization Studies*, 3, No. 1 (1982), pp. 73–8

Scott, Bruce R. (1971) *Stages of Corporate Development*, Harvard Business School

(1973) The Industrial State: Old Myths and New Realities, *Harvard Business Review*, 51 (March & April, 1973), pp. 133–48

Siegel, S. (1956) *Nonparametric Statistics*, New York: McGraw-Hill

Silverman, David (1968) Formal Organizations or Industrial Sociology: Towards a Social Action Analysis of Organizations, *Sociology*, 2, No. 2 (1968), pp. 221–38

(1969) Correspondence: Organization: A Rejoinder, *Sociology*, 3, No. 3 (September, 1969), pp. 420–1

(1970) *The Theory of Organizations*, London: Heinemann

(1975) Accounts of Organizations – Organization 'Structures' and the Accounting Process, in John B. McKinlay (ed.), *Processing People: Cases in Organizational Behaviour*, London and New York: Holt, Rinehart and Winston

Silverman, David and Jones, J. (1973) Getting In: the Managed Accomplishment of 'Correct' Selection Outcomes, in J. Child (ed.), *Man and Organization*, London: George Allen and Unwin

Simon, H. A. (1965) *Administrative Behaviour: A Study of Decision-Making Processes in Administrative Organization*, 2nd edn, New York: Free Press
(1976) *Administrative Behaviour*, 3rd edn, new York: Free Press
Skinner, Burrhus F. (1948) *Walden Two*, New York: Macmillan
(1971) *Beyond Freedom and Dignity*, New York: Knopf
Smith, D. and Nichol, R. T. (1981) Change, Standardization and Contingency Theory, *Journal of Management Studies*, 18, No. 1 (1981), pp. 73–88
Starbuck, William H. (1965) Organization Growth and Development, in J. G. Marsh (ed.), *Handbook of Organizations*, Chicago: Rand McNally
(1981) A Trip to View the Elephants and Rattlesnakes in the Garden of Aston, in The Aston Program Perspective, Chapter 4 of A. Van de Ven and W. Joyce, *Perspectives on Organization Design and Behaviour*, New York: Wiley
Stinchcombe, Arthur L. (1965) Social Structure and Organizations, in James C. Marsh (ed.), *Handbook of Organizations*, Chicago: Rand McNally, pp. 142–93
Stopford, J. M. and Wells, L. T. Jr (1972) *Managing the Multinational Enterprise*, New York: Basic Books
Suzuki, Y. (1980) The Strategy and Structure of Top 100 Japanese Industrial Enterprises 1950–1970, *Strategic Management Journal*, 1 (1980), pp. 265–91
Tannenbaum, Arnold S. and Cooke, Robert A. (1979) Organizational Control: A Review of Studies Employing the Control Graph Method, in Cornelis J. Lammers and David J. Hickson (eds.), *Organizations Alike and Unlike: International and interinstitutional studies in the sociology of organizations*, London: Routledge and Kegan Paul
Taylor, Bernard (1976) Managing the Process of Corporate Development, *Long Range Planning*, 9, No. 3 (June, 1976), pp. 81–100
Thompson, James D. (1967) *Organizations in Action*, New York: McGraw-Hill
Toulmin, S. E. (1962) *The Philosophy of Science*, London: Arrow
Turner, Stephen D. (1977) Blau's Theory of Differentiation: Is it Explanatory?, in J. Kenneth Benson (ed.), *Organizational Analysis: Critique and Innovation*, Sage Contemporary Social Science Issues 37, Beverly Hills: Sage Publications, pp. 19–34
Udy, S. H. Jr (1959) *Organization of Work*, New Haven: Human Relations Area File Press
Urwick, L. F. (1973) Semantic Hay – The Word 'Organization', *Omega, The International Journal of Management Science*, 1, No. 1 (1973), pp. 97–105
Van de Ven, A. and Ferry, Diane L. (1980) *Measuring and Assessing Organizations*, New York, Wiley
Vroom, Victor H. and Yetton, Philip W. (1973) *Leadership and Decision-Making*, University of Pittsburgh Press
Walker, K. (1974) Workers Participation in Management: Problems, Practice and Prospect, *Bulletin of the International Institute of Labour Studies*, 12 (1974), pp. 3–35
Walton, Eric J. (1980) Formal Structure: A Review of the Empirical Relationships Between Task Differentiation, Role Prescription and Authority Dispersion, *Organization Studies*, 1, No. 3 (1980), pp. 229–51
Walton, Richard E. (1969) *Interpersonal Peace-making: Confrontation and Third Party Consultation*, Palo Alto, California: Addison-Wesley
Webb, B. and Webb, S. (1901) *Industrial Democracy*, London: Longmans

Weber, Max (1947) *The Theory of Social and Economic Organization*, translated by A. M. Henderson and Talcott Parsons, New York: Free Press
(1968) *Economy and Society: An Outline of Interpretive Sociology*, ed. Guenther Roth and Claus Wittich, New York: Bedminster Press
Weick, K. E. (1969) *The Social Psychology of Organizing*, Reading, Mass.: Addison-Wesley
Westhues, Kenneth (1980) Class and Organization as Paradigms in Social Science, in Amitai Etzioni and Edward E. Lehman (eds.), *A Sociological Reader on Complex Organizations*, 3rd edn, New York: Holt, Rinehart and Winston, pp. 74–84
Wheeler, Jo, Mansfield, Roger and Todd, Dave (1980) Structural Implications of Organizational Dependence upon Customers and Owners: Similarities and Differences, *Organization Studies*, 1, No. 4 (1980), pp. 327–48
Whisler, Thomas L. *et al.* (1967) Centralization of Organizational Control: An Empirical Study of Its Meaning and Measurement, *Journal of Business*, 40 (1967), pp. 10–26
White, J. Patrick (1979) *On a Clear Day You Can See General Motors: John Z. de Lorean's Look Inside the Automotive Giant*, New York: Avon Books
Whitley, R. D. (1977) Concepts of Organization and Power in the Study of Organizations, *Personnel Review*, 6, No. 1 (Winter, 1977), pp. 54–9
Willer, Judith (1971) *The Social Determination of Knowledge*, Englewood Cliffs, New Jersey: Prentice-Hall
Winch, P. (1958) *The Idea of Social Science and its Relation to Philosophy*, London: Routledge and Kegan Paul
Wittgenstein, L. (1963) *Philosophical Investigations*, Oxford: Blackwell
Woodward, Joan (1965) *Industrial Organization: Theory and Practice*, Oxford University Press
(1970) *Industrial Organization: Behaviour and Control*, Oxford University Press
Wrigley, Leonard (1970) Divisional Autonomy and Diversification, unpublished doctoral dissertation, Harvard Business School
Yoshino, M. Y. (1968) *Japan's Managerial System: Tradition and Innovation*, Cambridge, Mass.: MIT Press
(1976) *Japan's Multinational Enterprises*, Cambridge, Mass. and London: Harvard University Press
Zwerman, W. L. (1970) *New Perspectives on Organization Theory: an Empirical Reconsideration of the Marxian and Classical Analyses*, Westport, Conn.: Greenwood

Index

193